The Protestant Faith

The Protestant Faith

By

George W. Forell

1960
PRENTICE-HALL, INC.
Englewood Cliffs, N.J.

M S: Protestantism, Theology, Doctrinal, Creeds

To my former students

Protestant, Catholic, Jewish, Agnostic

at the State University of Iowa

Preface

For some years it was my privilege to teach a course on the Protestant Faith in one of our state universities. My students came from the most diverse backgrounds. Every shade of belief and unbelief was represented. But one characteristic was shared by almost all of them: they knew very little about the Protestant Faith. The effort to explain to them the common faith of this great Christian tradition eventually produced this book. While assuming very little previous knowledge, it tries to cover the basic teachings of the main stream of Protestantism. The emphasis is upon the great central Christian assertions and upon the essential unity of classical Protestantism. The apparent diversity of the multitude of denominations should not blind us to the common witness of Protestant Christianity. Denominational differences are real, and some are very important; yet it is apparent that the vital theological discussions of the day are not carried on along denominational lines. Today as in the past, classical Protestantism has found eloquent spokesmen in many of its different branches. That I am indebted to them all, the informed reader will easily perceive. The writing of this book is an effort to express my gratitude to all the Christian thinkers here and abroad whose work has made classical Protestantism a live option for modern America.

G. W. F.

Table of Contents

GOD'S WORLD (Continued):

x   Table of Contents

The Protestant Faith

1

Faith and Its Consequences

There are always people who would like
to divide mankind into two groups, the
believers and the unbelievers. But this is
an arbitrary division indeed, for strictly
speaking there are no "unbelievers." Faith
is universal. Everybody believes in something or somebody. This does not mean
that all people go to some church or syna-
gogue. That is obviously not the case. But
all people have some God, at least a god
with a small *g*. The question is not
whether to believe, but rather *what* to
believe.

There are the men who believe in
money. They are convinced that money
is the answer to all problems. Friends are
people you buy with money, happiness is
the result of having lots of money, and
the purpose of life is to accumulate as
much money as possible.

Then there are the believers in education, who hold that all the world's problems can be solved by education. If you are stupid, reading the right books will make you intelligent. If you are ugly, there is a book that can teach you how to become beautiful. If you are worried, there are many books that can teach you peace of mind or how to rearrange your whole life. Even if you weigh only 92 pounds and have trouble *lifting* a book, you can buy one (written by some muscular superman) which will teach you to be six feet six and weigh 250 pounds. Those who believe in the absolute power of education know of no obstacle that cannot be overcome by reading the right book. This widespread faith in education helps to explain the "do-it-yourself" craze. If you want to become an Albert Schweitzer, you can buy a book called *How to Play the Organ,* with a double-your-money-back guarantee. If you want to build your dream house or make money on the stock market, there is a book to teach you how.

There are those who believe in the innate goodness of man. Man is by nature good, they say. He does evil things because of the pressures of society, because of faulty training in childhood, because of private property or the lack of it, but hidden within every man is a saint. This would be the best of all possible worlds if we would only remove the outward circumstances that bring in the evil. This is the attitude that Voltaire ridiculed so violently in his book *Candide.* It is as popular today as in Voltaire's time and long before; there have always been people who believe with all their heart in the basic goodness of man.

Others, again, believe firmly in the basic goodness of only a few men, perhaps the Germans, or the Americans, or only the white Americans. I remember a man who was convinced of the innate and indestructible goodness of the Scotch. There are no criminals among the Scotch, he told me. And if ever a Scotchman is accused of a crime in the newspaper, he is either innocent or a member of some other nationality who has changed his name. The man was completely sincere in this assertion; he had absolute faith in the Scotch.

And some believe in the absolute goodness of their own motives and actions. Whatever others might say, these good people are convinced of their own infallibility. They have absolute faith in themselves. There is at least one person like this in every college class. He may have a D average, but he will explain that this is not a reliable indicator of his true worth. He is not trying just now. Or the faculty has joined in some black conspiracy to keep the world from knowing that such a superior intelligence exists among them. These examples may suffice to illustrate the assertion that everybody believes in something or somebody. The interesting question is not *whether* you believe, but *what* you believe.

"Belief" in the sense in which we have been using this word so far is not another expression for uncertainty, but rather the description of that certainty that undergirds life. This is the kind of belief that we call faith. There are certain data that seem absolutely reliable, the axioms from which you proceed. They are self-evident truths and not really debatable. They are verified in life, but you do not believe them because they are verified; you believed them before they were ever verified. We confront such basic faith, which represents the key to all sorts of human behavior, everyday. We have learned that we will have trouble understanding a person's actions unless we know the axiom from which he proceeds. Let us take a man who is in love with a certain girl, or a girl who is in love with a certain man. This is the basic fact. The basic fact may be verified by the observation that he travels three hundred miles every week end in order to see her for a few hours. Or by the fact that she isn't interested in having a date with anybody else and that other men bore her. But note—it isn't *because* he travels three hundred miles every week end that he is in love with her—rather, it is because he is in love with her that he is willing to travel three hundred miles. Or it isn't because she is bored with all other men that she is in love with him (this would be a serious maladjustment); rather, it is because she is in love with him that she is bored by the others.

This is what we mean when we say that faith is axiomatic;

it is the fundamental assertion that gives meaning to all other assertions. Belief, in the sense in which we are going to talk about what Protestants believe, is primarily of this axiomatic nature.

It is, of course, true that the word "believe" has many meanings. Generally, it denotes uncertainty. We say, "I believe it is going to rain tomorrow," or, "I believe he likes apple pie." This means that it may not rain tomorrow or that perhaps he likes cherry pie. But we are using "believe" in the way you would use it when you are talking not about the weather or pies but about another person.

Let us assume you have a good friend and his name is Paul. Now somebody comes to you and says, "Paul has stolen my watch." If you answer, "No—I believe in Paul!" you are saying a lot more than, "He didn't steal your watch," or, "He doesn't steal"; you are making a commitment to Paul, for you believe in him.

This is the way in which we are going to use "believe" and "faith" in this book. In describing the Protestant Faith we will deal with the statements Protestants make to explain all other statements, the axiomatic hidden or open assertions which are the key to the life of Protestant people. The great medieval theologian Anselm of Canterbury said, *"Credo ut intelligam,"* or, "I believe in order to understand." Actually all people believe in order to understand. The question is, what do they believe?

Let us look for a moment at some of the axioms from which we can choose. All these are possible alternatives to the basic axiom from which Protestants and Christians in general proceed. One might say, "I believe in nature." He can look around and try to discover the pattern of nature and conform to it. He can start with the axiom that man is merely a part of nature, a complicated part, to be sure, but in no way more than nature. He therefore should conform to the pattern that nature reveals. What is this pattern? People do not all agree, but the great German philosopher Friedrich Nietzsche suggested that the pattern of nature showed that man is merely a bridge to the superman of tomorrow. He is a bridge that has to be crossed. "Man," he said, "is a rope stretched between the animal and the Superman—a rope over an abyss." Man of today has to be sacrificed to the superman of tomorrow.

To apply this axiom to the life you have to live from day to day means the abolition of all those sentimental feelings which would slow up the coming of the superman. For example, we seem to think that it is kind to protect the sick, even those who will never get well. A consistent believer in the survival of the fittest as the axiom of life would say that this is bad. To care for the sick and the senile takes money and time which should be devoted to the development of the superman. Nature does not protect the weak and the sick. In nature the weak and the sick are destroyed by the strong and the healthy. The effort to protect the weak and the sick is therefore unnatural. It is foolish and dangerous. "The sick are the greatest danger for the healthy," Nietzsche claimed. How many millions do we spend to prolong life unnaturally, to preserve life which contributes nothing to the superman of tomorrow? We should quit all this nonsense. Nietzsche believed that Christianity was an invention of the weak to keep the strong from doing the natural thing, namely, destroying the weak.

And similarly, what nonsense it is, once we have adopted this axiom, to spend much money and effort to teach people who will never be very bright anyway. Let us use all our resources to do a great deal for those who will have the best chance to produce the superman of tomorrow. Nietzsche disdained the masses, the common man. Democracy seemed to him the unfortunate offspring of Christianity. He was logical and consistent in his belief that what is natural is good, that nature supplies us with the proper axioms for living. Survival of the fittest is the universal law.

This is a faith; it is an alternative by which we can pattern our lives. It may be somewhat shocking or even revolting to some of us, but at least it is logical. If you grant the axiom that nature supplies us with our standards of life, this attitude makes a great deal of sense. Most of us just do not admit this axiom.

There are, of course, many other equally possible axioms. For example, the pragmatic axiom: good is whatever works or whatever produces socially useful consequences. Or the existentialist axiom: to act is good, to vegetate is subhuman. The humanist axiom: man is the measure of all things. The Marxist axiom: the universe operates according to the laws of dialectical materialism as discovered by Karl Marx and his disciples.

Obviously, such basic faiths are all around us. Let us ask as we observe ourselves and the people around us, "What are the axioms by which we live?" This can be very interesting, because such axioms are like eyeglasses, which help you to see a certain way but have a tendency to make you forget that you are wearing them. You can see them on other people but it takes some effort to notice them on yourself. Some of the people who have the most fun with other people's faith-axioms are completely and amusingly oblivious to their own. For example, when somebody tells us, "I have no prejudices, I am absolutely objective," we can be pretty sure that what he really means is, "I haven't been able to discover my prejudices and you had better not call them to my attention or I'll get angry."

Often a man proclaims one set of axioms, and even thinks that he adheres to them, but really lives by another set of axioms altogether. What counts is not what he says he believes but what he really believes, not the axioms which he proclaims but the axioms by which he lives. Although they can be most evasive, they are always present. Every man has some faith.

So far we have claimed that every man has a faith which is descriptive of the axioms which undergird his life. Perhaps we are now ready to ask, "What is the Christian axiom that underlies the Protestant Faith?"

This Christian axiom can be put very simply in a sentence from the New Testament: *God was in Christ reconciling the world unto Himself. (II Corinthians 5:19)* Of course this sentence may seem quite obscure at this point, but so are the other axioms when we try to reduce them to one sentence. This would be as true of a naturalistic, a pragmatic, an existentialist, or a humanist axiom as of the Christian axiom. Therefore we must try to discover what this sentence means, if it is the clue to the faith upon which Christians are willing to build their lives. It is the assertion that the pattern for man and the world is not found in nature as we observe it all about us. It is not found in the agreement of the group, in the opinion of the majority, and it is not found in man, at the very center of his being. It is not existentialist and it is not materialist—though it says a great deal about existence and matter. Christians claim that the structure of life has been revealed in Jesus Christ. Not the superman of Nietzsche, not the successful man, the well-adjusted man, the proletarian, the capitalist, or the American—but Christ is the true man. He is the God-man, the translation of God into human language. This is the axiom, and what it means to Protestants is the subject of this book.

But let us make it very clear that we are discussing real alternatives. Some people think you can reconcile all these various faiths and come up with some sort of superfaith. But this cannot be done honestly. If you want Nietzsche's superman, you must be as honest as Nietzsche was and say, "God is dead!" You cannot say the supreme law of the universe is the survival of the fittest— and also say: *You shall love the Lord your God with all your heart, and with all your soul, and with all your strength and with all your mind; and your neighbor as yourself.* (*Luke 10:27*) You have to make a choice.

There are many people today who would like to have exchangeable faiths: one for Sunday morning, another for Monday to Friday, and a third for the early part of the week end. These are the people who have given substance to the statement of the American comedian, "What this country needs is a good five-cent psychiatrist."

It was said of the great Spanish-American philosopher George Santayana that his creed was: "There is no God—and Mary is his mother!" In other words, he wanted the aesthetic aspects of religion —he liked the music and the paintings, the stained-glass windows and the odor of incense—without the faith which produced them. Santayana is not alone in this position. But here we are not interested in the popular by-products of Christianity; we want to study the faith which produces the by-products.

Every faith involves a decision. To believe in man or in God, in money or in education—one must decide. And this brings us to the next question. Once a person has made a decision about these faith-axioms, this decision has consequences. The kind of pattern, the kind of axiom which undergirds your life makes a great deal of difference.

Again, there are many people who put faith into the same class as fox hunting and pinochle playing. These are interesting leisure-time activities which do not really matter. And so they say, "It doesn't really matter what a man believes—what really matters is how much money he has or how smart he is!"

Like most other notions which are generally accepted, this one is obviously false. Of course it makes a great deal of difference whether you believe, for example, in a moral law or whether you believe that right is whatever you can get away with.

This is not hard to prove. Let us say two people try to borrow money from you because they are temporarily caught short of cash. One of these borrowers is actually well-to-do, but he is the kind of person who says, "Right is whatever I can get away with." He does not say it openly, but this is one of the axioms by which he lives. The other person has no money at all, but he believes with all his being that a man is honor bound to pay his debts. Now, who is the better risk for your loan? The man with the principles is the better risk, for we know that having money has never yet by itself made a person pay his debts.

This is what is meant when we say that faith has ultimate significance. What a person believes will make a great deal of difference in his life. Please note, not what he *claims* to believe— that's fairly unimportant—but what he *really* believes. The same principle applies to nations. But let us emphasize once again that it is only the genuine faith, not the assumed faith, which is important.

An American nurse who had just returned from India stated

recently in a radio interview that one of the difficulties she encountered among the people in India with whom she and her health team worked was the relative nonchalance about life and death. People simply did not seem to be as much concerned about staying alive as Americans are.

Indeed, in order to go to the kind of trouble we are willing to go to in order to stay alive, one must really believe that life is meaningful, that it is worth while, that it is a gift that you have to protect, or that "you will be dead for a long time." Many Hindus don't believe this at all. For them this present life has no final meaning, and death is not a permanent condition. In fact, a rebirth takes place immediately, and the next life may be far better than the present one.

If you believe this, it will certainly make a great difference in your attitude toward life and death and in your behavior in general. This is what the American nurse discovered in India. But the fact that faith has consequences can be observed everywhere. It is an important clue to the history of individuals and nations. Without the understanding of the significance of faith for human behavior, behavior remains completely incomprehensible.

When Christians and Moslems were locked in battle in the Middle Ages, the Christian participants in these wars were astonished and shocked by the heroism of the Mohammedan soldiers. Finally they realized that the disdain for death which characterized these enemy soldiers was the direct result of the Moslem faith. These Moslems believed that their life was governed by a divine kismet. God had decided beforehand what would happen to them, and nothing they could do could change this divine design. If they were to die, they would die; if they were to survive, they would survive. Furthermore, they were convinced that death in battle would bring the faithful immediately into a paradise far more desirable than this life. While the Christians might not agree with these ideas, knowing them made it possible to understand the mentality of their enemies. Whether true or false, these were the axioms of their life, and these axioms had measurable consequences. Axioms always exercise a great amount of influence.

And who would not be reminded in this context of the behavior of the Japanese pilots during World War II who in suicide flights crashed their planes into American vessels. Here again faith, Shinto faith, had observable consequences. Nothing could be less scientific and more obscurantist than to ignore the fact that faith makes a difference. For good or ill, what people really believe is far more important than even their blood pressure, their basal metabolism, or their intelligence quotient.

It took the almost pathological fear of religion that has clouded the minds of so many otherwise highly intelligent people in our time to make the startling claim that religion is man's private affair, that one's faith does not matter, that religious convictions are in the same class as hobbies, such as playing cards, or as inconsequential as preferring baseball or football. Thus the serious study of faith as an aid to understanding man and his society was neglected, and many otherwise intelligent people pride themselves on their religious illiteracy. Wishing that faith were marginal in the life of man, they talked themselves into believing that this is so. Actually, this assertion is so far from the truth as to be almost ridiculous, and this neglect of the study of faith can only be understood as the result of an almost obsessive fear of religion, which has blinded many observers to the facts as they confront us everywhere.

The situation here is quite similar to the situation in regard to sex in the nineteenth century. Even then everybody knew that sex was a real force in human life, but until Sigmund Freud came along nobody wanted to admit it. Some piously hoped that, if the fact of sex were persistently ignored or loudly denied, it would quietly disappear. But the Victorian age was quite unsuccessful in its attempt to ignore the reality of sex. Indeed, the very effort to ignore and repress it became the basis for the obsession with sex of a later generation. And we can say the same about religion. All the efforts on the part of twentieth-century man to ignore religion and hope that it will disappear have proven completely ineffective.

A man's faith is one of the basic components of his life, and ignoring this obvious reality will not change the facts for a moment. One may not like the fact that faith is so important for human life. One may wish it to be otherwise. But what one likes does not really matter. The only important question is: Has faith ultimate significance? It is our claim that the evidence available shows that it has.

Compare the Jewish people with their pagan neighbors. They lived in an age in which God and the gods were only loosely related to the concepts of right and wrong. They lived in an age in which morality and piety were not at all identified. Then the Jews heard God speak to them—and reveal Himself to them as a moral God, a God who was concerned about right and wrong, a God who loved justice and hated injustice. This made a tremendous difference. The difference between the Jews and their Canaanite neighbors was not racial or linguistic, not cultural or economic, but rather a difference in faith, which had striking consequences. It is this unique faith which has maintained the Jewish people while the Assyrians and Babylonians, the Persians and Philistines have all passed away.

If we look at Christianity we find similarly striking results of faith. Nobody who has ever traveled from a Protestant section to a Roman Catholic section in Germany would deny the difference in the understanding of life which exists even among Christians who belong to different major forms of Christianity. The attitude toward work and leisure, the attitude toward church and home are deeply colored by this fact of faith.

One illustration, which comes from a sociologist rather than a theologian, should suffice. It was Max Weber who, in his famous book *The Protestant Ethic and the Spirit of Capitalism,* pointed out that Protestantism in general, and Calvinism in particular, had supplied the faith-axiom which made *modern* capitalism possible. This theory has been modified by R. H. Tawney and others, but it is interesting from our point of view that an observant sociologist or economist, who is not so emotionally wrapped up in his rejection of religion as to be unable to think clearly when the word occurs, will be struck by the sociological and economic fruits of faith.

It is simply not true, and frequent repetition is not able to make it true, that all religions are the same. It is no more true than that all cultures are the same, or all economic systems are the same, or all philosophical systems are the same. Religions differ vastly, creating vastly different attitudes toward life in their believers and vastly different patterns of life. Our axioms make a difference. We ought to know them and be aware of them and use them consciously as well as unconsciously or discard them.

This question is particularly important in our time when we are confronted not only by the various historical faiths which have dominated mankind for centuries but when an entirely new faith has come upon us. One of the reasons we are so dumbfounded by communism is that we are unable to see that it is a religion. It has its own faith-axioms, its dogma, and its high priests. It has most of the outward paraphernalia of a bona fide religion, lacking only a god.

The trouble with communism is not merely that it has an economic system with which we disagree or that it promotes a police state and slave-labor camps. These conditions certainly exist, but they are only the by-products of the Communist faith-axioms. The faith-axioms of communism, like all others, are bound to produce fruits in society. Our inability to understand communism has been caused by our unwillingness to take faith seriously, our own faith as well as the faith of our opponents. If we want to understand friend or enemy, or even ourselves, we must understand the faiths which undergird all lives.

It is the importance of faith as a key to the understanding of man and society which makes the study of religion so very important. And it is this fact that makes the Protestant Faith so interesting to us. We live in a culture whose character is largely determined by the Protestant Faith. Even those who do not share it are influenced by it, because it is "in the air." For this reason the study of the Protestant Faith may help us to a better understanding of our society and of ourselves.

THE NATURE OF PROTESTANTISM

A HISTORICAL AND STATISTICAL SURVEY. Historically, the name "Protestant" was first used in connection with the so-called II Diet of Speyer (1529). Speyer is a city in southern Germany, and the Diet was an assembly of the leading citizens, the princes, and the representatives of the free cities, for the discussion and solution of common problems. Unlike the Congress of the United States the German Diet did not meet regularly but only when some special political situation made a meeting desirable. It should be kept in mind that not all people were represented but only the princes, the nobility, the Church, and the wealthy burghers of the free cities. Since most of the political leaders of the Church, the archbishops, bishops, and abbots, belonged to the nobility, the common people were hardly represented at all.

The II Diet of Speyer had been called by the Emperor Charles V in order to get the support of the leaders of the German people for his plans to suppress what he considered the heresy of Luther and his followers, who would not recognize the supremacy of the Church of Rome and the Roman Pope. The Emperor had never been very friendly toward Luther and his supporters. After he had met the Reformer at the famous Diet of Worms in April 1521, he had charged the political leaders of Europe to do everything in their power to stamp out the Reformation movement. In 1521 he had said, "I regret having so long delayed to proceed against this Luther and his false doctrine."[1] However, his own political difficulties made it impossible for him to take firm action. Ironically, much of the opposition to Charles V came from the Pope. The very Pope whose religious power the Emperor was

[1] Roger A. Hornsby (trans.), "Luther at the Diet of Worms, 1521," in *Luther's Works,* ed. George W. Forell, Vol. XXXII (Philadelphia: Muhlenberg Press, 1958), p. 115.

trying to uphold conspired against him for political reasons. The result was that the Emperor was forced to defeat the Pope and his allies militarily before he had a free hand to try to re-establish the Pope's religious authority. In 1529 the Emperor was finally in a position to enforce his will against the supporters of Luther, for he had just defeated the Pope in the military campaign which had ended with the famous *sacco di Roma,* the sack of Rome (1527). Charles V had at the same time defeated his archenemy, the King of France, who had given him a good deal of trouble since he had become German Emperor.

With these enemies taken care of, the Emperor was in a position to deal with the heretics in general and Martin Luther in particular. The II Diet of Speyer was supposed to be the springboard for action looking forward to the complete suppression of the new heresy.

It may seem odd that the Emperor wanted to suppress this movement to overthrow the authority of the Pope after he had defeated the Pope. But this was an odd period of history. Charles V, the German Emperor and King of Spain, was a loyal subject of the Pope as the *spiritual leader* of Christendom. He only failed to get along with the Pope as the *political leader* of Italy. Charles V didn't mind that the same person held both positions. He was willing to use Lutheran soldiers to defeat the Pope militarily and politically and then turn right around and try to re-establish the power of the Pope as spiritual leader of the Western World.

In order to understand this reasoning one should compare it with the attitude of a good Democrat toward a Republican President of the United States. This Democrat will do everything in his power to defeat the President as leader of the Republican party, yet at the same time he will do his best to support him as chief executive of the government of the United States.

Although Charles V had defeated the Pope politically, at the II Diet of Speyer he was trying to support and strengthen him as spiritual leader of Western Christendom and thus prevent the breakup of the religious unity of his empire.

Of the four hundred estates represented at the Diet, only nineteen opposed the decision of the Emperor and the majority of the Diet to work toward the re-establishment of the teachings and practices of the Roman Catholic Church everywhere in Germany and to suppress what they considered "heresy" with all the power at their command. These nineteen estates protested against the use of force to re-establish the Roman Church and said:

> In matters which concern the honor of God and the salvation of our souls, every individual must stand alone before God and give his account. Therefore, nobody can excuse himself in these matters by relying on the decisions of others.[2]

In other words, at Speyer in 1529 these first Protestants (technically speaking) protested that matters of conscience could not be decided by government action. What Luther had said alone at Worms in 1521 was now repeated only eight years later by some of the mighty political leaders of Germany. At Worms Luther had said before Emperor Charles V:

> Unless I shall be convinced by the testimony of Scriptures or by clear reason, I must be bound by those Scriptures which have been brought forward by me. Yes, my conscience has been taken captive by these words of God. I cannot revoke anything, nor do I wish to; since to go against one's conscience is neither safe nor right: Here I stand, I cannot do otherwise. God help me. Amen.[3]

After the II Diet of Speyer this individual protest was now the position of thousands in Germany and all over Europe. And the people who took this position were called "Protestants."

In spite of all opposition the movement grew. It soon embraced two-thirds of Germany, all of Denmark, Sweden, Norway, and Finland, large sections of Poland, Bohemia, and Hungary. Soon other Reformers spread the Protestant understanding of the Christian Faith to Switzerland, France, the Netherlands, and

[2] Karl Brandi, *Deutsche Geschichte im Zeitalter der Reformation und Gegenreformation* (3d ed.; Leipzig: Koehler & Amelang, 1941), p. 183.
[3] *Luther's Works,* XXXII, 112 f.

the British Isles. And from the British Isles Protestantism spread to the New World, to America and Australia. Finally, through the great missionary movement, particularly of the nineteenth century, Protestantism in its various forms has spread also to Asia and Africa. Today entire peoples in Asia, as for example the Bataks in Indonesia, are Protestants.

Some statistics might be helpful in order to illustrate this tremendous growth of Protestantism from the sixteenth century to the present.

Of the total population of the world, approximately one-fourth are Christians. Of the Christians, about one-fourth are Protestants; the others are Roman Catholics or Eastern Orthodox. This means that approximately 6 per cent of the people in the world are Protestant.

But while a large proportion of these Protestants live in Europe and North America, there are 2.5 million Protestants in South America, approximately 10 million in Asia, about 9 million in Oceania, and almost 7 million in Africa. Thanks to the missionary movement, Protestantism has come a long way since the nineteen estates at the II Diet of Speyer made their protest on behalf of religious freedom.

What is the relative distribution of Protestants in the United States? Of those Americans who claim church membership about 60 million are Protestants, about 35 million are Roman Catholics, and about 6 million are Jews. Almost 3 million are Eastern Orthodox, and the rest belong to other groups.

The 60 million Protestants in the United States are members of many different church bodies. But if one looks a little more closely one discovers that most of them can be divided into some great denominational families.

Alphabetically and statistically first are the Baptists, who number approximately 20 million. Alphabetically next come the Episcopalians or Anglicans with about 3.5 million members. Next come the 8 million Lutherans and the 12 million Methodists. The Presbyterians, Reformed, and Congregationalists belong historically in the Calvinist Family with approximately 6 million together. Finally, there are the historic pacifist groups, such as the Quakers and the Mennonites, with about 120,000 each.

Of course this does not exhaust the hundreds of Protestant groups, but almost all of these groups belong closely or loosely to one of the following families: (1) Baptist Family, (2) Episcopal-Anglican Family, (3) Lutheran Family, (4) Methodist Family, (5) Presbyterian-Calvinist Family, (6) Quaker-Mennonite Family.

These families are by no means completely different from each other. Rather there are firm ties of relationship among them. For example, the Methodists are closely related to the Episcopal-Anglican Family. At the same time, the Episcopal-Anglican Family is related to Calvinists and Lutherans. But the significant fact is that the 250 or more Protestant denominations can easily be classified into 6 or at most 10 major denominational families. And we are here not so much concerned with their differences as with that which they have in common and which enables us to speak of "Protestantism" and "The Protestant Faith."

THE SPIRIT OF PROTESTANTISM. While the history and the statistics of a religious movement are important, a faith is more than its history and its statistics. The question arises: What are the particular identifying marks of Protestantism? If it is a spiritual entity, what are its characteristics? How can we best describe the spirit of Protestantism?

In a movement of the scope and diversity of Protestantism there are literally thousands of "marks" which may seem to some members or observers of the movement to express its very essence. However, there are five which recur with such regularity and consistency that they can be used as basic identifying marks. They are the emphasis upon

(1) Grace and the sovereignty of God
(2) Faith
(3) Scripture as the rule of faith
(4) The priesthood of all believers
(5) The fallibility of man and all human institutions

Protestants insist that the New Testament Church was Protestant, in the sense that the Protestant emphases can be clearly
discerned in the Apostolic Church. But what do these five emphases
mean?

The stress on God's grace and sovereignty means that Protestants assert that in the relationship between God and man it is
God who takes the initiative. In this respect Protestantism differs
from religion in general. Religion has often been defined as man's
way to God, the result of human aspirations and human hopes.
Religion is for many a way to reach God. Various methods of
finding God have been suggested by religious people through the
ages. There are those who say that we become religious, that we
come in touch with God, by obeying His law. This method of
reaching God is known as legalism. It asserts that God's will for
man can be defined as a legal code. If we obey these rules we are
true believers, and if we fail to obey them we are irreligious. The
rules are of various kinds. They regulate what the believer may
eat and when he may eat it, they tell him what to wear and where
to wear it. There are a thousand and one rules dealing with such
varied matters as the amount of hair on the chin and the type of
mechanism used to button one's coat. They deal with the alcohol
content of beverages and the literary content of books. But the
religiously significant fact about legalism in all its forms is that
legalists claim that our relationship to God is dependent upon our
obedience to these rules and regulations. Legalism asserts in some
manner or form that we reach God by way of this legal code.
Legalism tends to reduce God to a celestial bookkeeper. He merely
keeps books, or, perhaps better, he merely keeps score. He does not
intervene in the game of life. Whether we reach Him or not is
entirely up to us. He has given us the law; if we obey the law
we can reach Him, and if we do not obey the law we will not
reach Him. But, to use a theological term, *salvation* is up to us. We
are saving ourselves by obeying the law, or we are losing ourselves
by disobeying the law. The initiative is with man.

Against this view, so very common in the world's religions,

one of the Protestant emphases found in Luther and Calvin as well as in Arminius and Wesley, among Anglicans as well as Baptists, is the conviction that man's salvation is the result of what God has done and not the result of anything man can do. God is the sovereign Lord of all life. He is not a spectator in the drama of history but a director as well as the most active participant. And it is only through the participation of God that man can be saved. In other words, God saves man through *His* grace. Man is not saved through any of his works, be they ever so splendid, but entirely and solely because God is merciful. It appears that most people know that this is the view of Lutherans and Calvinists. But Wesley was as convinced of justification by faith as any Calvinist or Lutheran. In defending his position and the position of Jacobus Arminius, John Wesley wrote:

> No man that ever lived, not John Calvin himself, ever asserted either original sin or justification by faith in more strong, more clear and express terms, than Arminius has done. These two points, therefore, are to be set out of the question; in these both parties agree. In this respect, there is not a hair's breadth difference between Mr. Wesley and Mr. Whitefield.[4]

And in the Articles of Religion of the Anglican Communion, the Episcopal Church, we read in Article XI:

> We are accounted righteous before God, only for the merit of our Lord and Saviour Jesus Christ by Faith, and not for our own works or deservings. Wherefore, that we are justified by Faith only, is a most wholesome Doctrine, and very full of comfort, as more largely expressed in the Homily of Justification.[5]

Protestants who stand within the stream of classical Protestantism as expressed in the writings of the Reformers and their successors agree unanimously that salvation, that is, release from man's misery without God and communion with God in service

---

[4] Harry Emerson Fosdick, *Great Voices of the Reformation* (New York: Random House, Inc., 1952), p. 515.
[5] See Appendix p. 270.

to Him, is not the result of any merits or good works on the part of man. Man cannot save himself. It is God who through His sovereign grace saves man.

Of course, there are considerable differences of opinion among Protestants as to the manner in which God accomplishes this goal and as to the degree of human co-operation necessary, but all agree that the initiative is entirely with God, and nothing that man does has any saving value. God's sovereignty, that He is Lord and Savior, is the common faith of all Protestants. *Sola gratia,* through grace alone, is one of the watchwords of classical Protestantism.

The attitude expressed in this phrase rules out also all other religious efforts to attain salvation from God. Besides the legalism we have described, there have been other attempts on the part of man to reach God in his own way, the most popular of these being rationalism and mysticism.

There have always been people who have conceived of God as the supreme intelligence of the universe, and they have suggested that He can be reached by the exercise of our reason. Others have insisted that God can be reached through certain mystical experiences. This question will be discussed later in another context. Suffice it to say here that the Protestant emphasis on God's sovereign grace rules out all efforts on the part of man to reach God in his own way, be they legalistic, rationalistic, or mystical.

This brings us to the second Protestant emphasis, the stress on faith. In our discussion so far, considerable emphasis has been placed on faith-axioms, the life-sustaining basic affirmations that man must make and which undergird his life. The cardinal doctrine of Protestantism is known as "justification by faith." This means that according to classical Protestantism the character of the faith-axiom makes all the difference. A person is a Christian because he puts his entire trust in Jesus Christ. Justification by faith must be clearly distinguished from its most prevalent distortion, namely, faith in faith. Classical Protestantism asserts that God wants fellowship with man and that if we trust completely in Jesus Christ and His work we will have communion with God. This complete and utter trust in Jesus Christ is faith. It is making the life, death, and resurrection of Christ the foundation of life. It is trust in what God has done through the life of this unique and all-important person.

This point must be stressed because a number of obvious confusions immediately come to mind. For some people faith is the acceptance of propositions about God or the Church. For example, somebody might tell you that the average distance between the moon and the earth is 238,857 miles. You haven't either the time or the inclination to measure the distance yourself, but you "believe" that this is the average distance. This isn't faith in the sense in which we are using it; rather, it is the acceptance of a proposition. Now all of us accept lots of propositions, some that can be easily verified, others that cannot be verified at all. And there are some people who think that the Christian Faith consists of the acceptance of propositions about God, about Jesus, about the Church. If we accept certain propositions of this kind we are Christians.

But faith in the sense in which it is used in the phrase "justification by faith" means complete trust in Jesus Christ as the revelation of God and the key to the meaning of life. This is not just one proposition among others; justification by faith means that Christ has become the cornerstone of your life. This is a biblical phrase (Ephesians 2:20); another biblical phrase is that you have become a member of the body of which He is the head (Colossians 1:18); another that you are now His slave (Romans 1:1, Philippians 1:1, and so forth). If a man becomes the slave of another man, this is not one fact among others, like buying a new car or getting a new job; it is the fact which changes all other facts, which gives new meaning to all his relationships, which explains everything he does and everything he fails to do. The Apostle Paul described himself frequently as *doulos Iesou Christou*, that is, a slave of Jesus Christ; this is the picture that came to his mind to indicate the new relationship which faith in

Jesus Christ had created. The fact of faith had changed all other facts radically; it had given his life a completely new direction. Another New Testament word picture describing the new situation which faith creates is used by Jesus Himself when He says, *You must be born again.* (*John 3:3*) While this phrase has often been used merely as a theological platitude, it is actually a highly significant statement, for truly "being born again" would mean that all our other relationships would be changed, that what is new is not one new thing in addition to a lot of old things. The newness which faith creates is not like the newness which a new hat or even a new car or a new house bring into our life. Such new things add new facts, but they do not change all other facts. This is why this phrase "being born again" is such an accurate description of the ultimate meaning of justification by faith. It points to the fact that everything has changed. All things have become new.

And here we must guard against another misunderstanding. Justification by faith—or *sola fide,* only by faith—does not mean that faith as an emotional attitude is able to save. There are many people especially in our time who proclaim loudly that it doesn't matter *what* we believe as long as we are sincere. Faith is for them a helpful posture. It is a certain approach to life which is valid quite apart from its object. What matters is the strength of the emotion, the profundity of our feeling; *what* we believe doesn't really matter at all. Faith is here something like Emile Coué's "every day in every way I am getting better and better." It is a psychological technique to help you keep your chin up or to keep a stiff upper lip. From the point of view of psychology such autosuggestion may be very effective and at times very helpful. But in the context of our discussion it must be stated that this type of faith has nothing to do with the justification by faith of the Reformers and of classical Protestantism.

It is certainly true that any sincere conviction can help you do things that would otherwise be impossible, from winning a war to sleeping on a bed of nails. We have no right to underestimate the power of faith as a psychological source of strength. The "faith" of the Nazis helped them sweep all over Europe during the early part of World War II. The "faith" of the Communists has helped them conquer large sections of the world. It would be indeed foolish to deny that these people have faith or that their faith is effective. But at the same time the very success of these faith movements in our time helps to show clearly that the object of faith makes all the difference in the world. Faith in a Hitler can be a demonic force leading millions of men and women to destruction. Faith in a medical quack can lead to needless suffering and death. Faith is by no means always a positive force in human life. This must be said especially in view of the many books written in recent years which exalt faith as a psychological "gimmick." Here you find the tendency to claim that belief is in and of itself valuable. We grant that it is indeed necessary, but from within the context of the Protestant Faith we have to say that justification by faith does not mean justification by sincerity or justification by strength of feeling—but rather justification through God's invasion into history in Jesus Christ. According to classical Protestantism, Christ is the object of the faith which justifies, and no other faith but faith in Christ can save man.

The Protestant emphasis on *sola fide,* only through faith, denies the efficacy of other approaches to God, even as respectable an alternative as the way of reason. There are many people who believe that God can somehow be approached by means of almost mathematical demonstration. There are certain proofs of the existence of God which have been popular since the days of Plato and Aristotle. These proofs are supposed to demonstrate to every reasonable person that there is a God, and if one doesn't believe in God after having been subjected to them, it shows only that he cannot follow a logical argument. This use of reason to prove the existence of God actually roots unbelief in stupidity rather than in revolt against God and has therefore the tendency to make unbelief a less serious offense than the New Testament indicates. Furthermore, such proofs of the existence of God tend to place God in the same class with the objects of proof in the realm of mathematics and thus reduce Him to one object in the same class with others. And, finally, they do not seem to prove the existence of God to people however intelligent who do not want to believe in God. Thus, while many Christians have tried to use reason as one way of demonstrating at least the existence of God, Protestants have generally been reluctant to make use of these proofs. This, too, is a result of their emphasis on *sola fide*—by faith alone!

This brings us to a third emphasis which is typical of Protestantism as a whole, the emphasis on Scripture as the rule of faith. One of the common assertions of Protestantism is stated in the Articles of Religion of the Anglican Communion as follows:

> Holy Scripture containeth all things necessary to salvation: so that whatsoever is not read therein, nor may be proved thereby, is not to be required of any man, that it should be believed as an article of the Faith, or be thought requisite or necessary to salvation. In the name of the Holy Scripture we do understand those canonical books of the Old and New Testament, of whose authority was never any doubt in the Church.[6]

This statement is also part of the Methodist Discipline,[7] and similar statements can be found governing all Protestants. While this stress on the authority of Scripture identifies all those who are in the stream of classical Protestantism, church history shows that there have also been other sources of authority in Christendom. The most popular alternatives to the Bible as the "only rule and standard according to which at once all dogmas and teachers should be esteemed and judged"[8] are the addition or substitution of tradition, the inner light, and the decrees of the institutional church.

It is easy to understand the development of the authority of tradition, for Christianity has a long history. In two thousand

---

[6] See Appendix p. 268.

[7] *Doctrines and Discipline of the Methodist Church* (Nashville, Tenn.: Methodist Publishing House, 1952), p. 26.

[8] "Formula of Concord," *The Book of Concord,* ed. H. E. Jacobs (Philadelphia: United Lutheran Publication House, 1908), I, 491.

years much happens to any living community of men. For some Christians the beliefs which have evolved over the years have become of equal value with the teachings of the Scriptures. In any community a custom can become a law and be enforced long after the factors which gave it birth have disappeared. Thus also in the Christian Church practices have become hallowed by usage to the point that to change them would be unthinkable. It is only a short step from the development of such customs to their sanctification. Among some Christians there are regular methods by which such hallowed customs can become officially authoritative. Occasionally a church will actually pronounce a belief an official dogma which apparently up to this point was merely a possible opinion, hallowed by custom. The Immaculate Conception of the Virgin Mary, for example, was merely a possible opinion in the Middle Ages. It was not shared by such outstanding theologians as Anselm of Canterbury or Thomas Aquinas. However, when Pope Pius IX proclaimed the Dogma of the Immaculate Conception in 1854, it became binding on all Roman Catholics. Here tradition is obviously considered a valid source of Christian dogma, quite independent of the teachings of the Bible. Protestantism has consistently rejected all teachings which in its opinion could not be found in the Scriptures. There have been some basic disagreements among Protestants about what is in fact found in Scripture, but classical Protestantism has accepted the Scriptures, that is, the universally accepted books of the Old and New Testaments, as the standard by which Christian teaching is to be judged.

Other Christians, again, have emphasized the direct communication of God with the Christian believer through mystical raptures and inspirations. In Luther's time a number of people whom he called *Schwaermer,* or enthusiasts, claimed to have what one could call in twentieth-century terms a "direct wire to God." Men like Thomas Münzer were convinced that God was guiding them through special dreams and visions. They felt in no way bound by the teachings of Scripture. In the light of their special revelation they were willing to contradict the Bible. Martin Luther,

Huldreich Zwingli, and John Calvin wanted nothing to do with these people. Luther, whose language was nothing if not colorful, referred to them as people who sounded "as if they had swallowed the Holy Spirit, feathers and all." And he completely rejected the authority of such direct revelations. This has been the position of the overwhelming majority of Protestants.

Other Christians, again, believe that the institutional church, through its leaders, is infallible in matters of faith and morals. This position has been stated by the Vatican Council in 1870 in the following words:

> That the Roman Pontiff, when he speaks *ex cathedra* (that is, when fulfilling the office of Pastor and Teacher of all Christians— on his supreme Apostolical authority, he defines a doctrine concerning faith or morals to be held by the Universal Church), through the divine assistance promised him in blessed Peter, is endowed with that infallibility with which the Divine Redeemer has willed that His Church—in defining doctrine concerning faith or morals—should be equipped: And therefore, that such definitions of the Roman Pontiff of themselves—and not by virtue of the consent of the Church—are irreformable.[9]

This position is rejected by all Protestants without exception. For classical Protestantism Scripture is the only source of authority for the teaching of the Church.

The fourth emphasis which is part of the common Protestant heritage is the understanding of the Church as the fellowship of saints and the priesthood of all believers. In the Apostles' Creed, most Christians confess that they believe in the "holy universal church, the communion of saints." This phrase "communion of saints," though obscure in its original meaning, is for Protestants an explanation of the holy universal Church. The Christian Church is the Christian people brought together by the Word of God and the sacraments. We shall discuss these concepts in greater detail later. But this understanding of the Church as primarily a fellow-

[9] Henry S. Bettenson, *Documents of the Christian Church,* cap. 4, in Session IV (New York: Oxford University Press, 1954), p. 383.

ship rather than an institution or organization is a significant accent that almost all Protestants have in common. This involves also the universal priesthood of all believers. A priest is generally conceived to be a person who has direct access to God. In many non-Christian religions and in some branches of Christendom the priest is a mediator between God and man. Through the priest the individual believer can address himself to God, and through the priest God speaks to the individual believer. But, guided by the First Epistle of Peter in the New Testament, Protestants in general assert that all Christians are priests through their new birth in Baptism: through the work of Christ all alike are God's people called to serve Him and to proclaim His word to each other. In Christ they have direct access to God without the help of another man.

In the Old Testament priests were not elected but were born to their office. A man was a priest by virtue of the fact that he was a descendant of Levi. In the same manner, say the Protestants, Christians are priests through the new birth in Baptism. In the words of the New Testament:

But you are a chosen race, a royal priesthood, a holy nation, God's own people, that you may declare the wonderful deeds of him who called you out of darkness into his marvelous light. (I Peter 2:9)

And as the Apostle Paul writes in his letter to the Galatians:

For as many of you as were baptized into Christ have put on Christ. There is neither Jew nor Greek, there is neither slave nor free, there is neither male nor female; for you are all one in Christ Jesus. (Galatians 3:28)

This, of course, does not mean that Protestants do not have ministers or pastors or that they might not even call their ministers or pastors priests. But this ministry, which is maintained by the overwhelming majority of Protestants, is a functional office. Ministers are people called by God through the Church to serve the fellowship of believers by preaching, teaching, and administering the sacraments. For the Protestant the pastor is not a mediator between him and God. He is a leader and servant of the fellowship and a priest by virtue of the fact that he is a Christian like all other Christians.

This may at first sound rather theological and complicated. However, it has immensely practical results. The relatively decentralized character of Protestantism is a direct result of these beliefs. The Church is not so much a human organization as a divine organism, held together not by human laws and decrees but by the divine will. It is therefore not entirely surprising to see Protestantism organizationally divided; the very emphasis on the Church as the communion of saints would preclude an emphasis upon hierarchy and organization. Protestants generally do not claim that it is necessary for salvation to belong to any particular Christian organization, though most of them would assert that it is indeed necessary to belong to the Christian organism, to the body whose head is Christ.

It is customary for Protestants to accept other Christians as true Christians even though they might belong to other forms of organized Christianity. Although they may quarrel about organizational structure, they do not believe that the organizational structure has any particular saving significance.

While other Christians might say, "We declare, state, define and pronounce that it is altogether necessary to salvation for every human creature to be subject to" some ecclesiastical dignitary,[10] Protestants tend to define the Church with the Augsburg Confession of 1530:

> They teach that the one Holy Church will remain forever. Now this Church is the congregation of saints, in which the Gospel is rightly taught and the sacraments rightly administered. And for that true unity of the Church it is enough to have unity of belief

[10] Pope Boniface VIII in the Bull *Unam Sanctum*, November 18, 1302, in Bettenson, *Documents*, p. 161.

concerning the teaching of the Gospel and the administration of the sacraments. It is not necessary that there should everywhere be the same traditions of men, or the same rites and ceremonies devised by men.[11]

The fifth and final emphasis that characterizes classical Protestantism is the emphasis upon the fallibility of man and of all human institutions. For the Protestant even the empirical Church is an all too human institution. It is a common Protestant belief that human institutions are always in need of reformation, that human pride and sin pervert even our best efforts, and that the perversion of the best is the very worst. For that reason men must operate with a large margin for error. No man, even the finest Christian leader, is infallible, and no human institution is perfect. Methods must be built into the organizational structure of the Christian community that will tend to correct the errors that are certain to arise in every generation.

In other words, Protestants are well aware of the fact that the Reformation is not merely something that was necessary in the sixteenth century, but they realize and insist that the Reformation is a principle that must cleanse the Church again and again.

In the Old Testament we read how Prophets such as Amos would come down from the hills and try to reform the corrupted Church of the Old Testament. The Reformers are considered as following in these prophetic footsteps. Protestants generally believe the Reformation must continue. Thus the Reformation is not merely a historical date but a vital principle in the present life of the Church. Whenever the Church becomes self-satisfied and fat, relying on her own words rather than God's, the Reformation principle must stir her up.

Historically, this has been the function of Methodists and Pietists, of Oxford Movement and Social Gospel, of Neo-Orthodoxy and Christian Existentialism. This process has by no means ended, for the Reformation must continue. If Protestantism is to be true to its genius, it can never rest on its laurels. It must always interpret

[11] See Appendix p. 259.

the eternal message of the Gospel of Christ in a manner that makes it meaningful to every new age.

This does not mean that Protestants doubt the eternal truth of the Gospel which they proclaim. It means, rather, that this truth is so great that it again and again bursts the institutional and systematic chains in which it is bound. It is therefore dangerous to place too much emphasis on these temporal forms.

Perhaps a few illustrations will help. For some people the Christian Faith is so closely related to the local congregation where they first heard the Christian message that they are unable to transfer their faith when they leave their home community. There are innumerable people who were active Christians in one town and are completely estranged from the Church in a town five hundred miles away. The Church for them was a particular brick building on the courthouse square, with a particular picture in front, or with a particular minister; they had entombed the Gospel in this local institution. Others entomb the Christian Faith in a particular type of architecture, taking the attitude that unless the building is imitation Gothic it is not a church, regardless of what is being preached. There are people who have the Gospel chained to certain types of hymns; if they do not hear these hymns, and particularly these melodies, they do not feel that they can find the Church.

All these are chains which the Reformation principle must break. There is no type of architecture, no style of music, no systematic theology that is the absolute expression of the Christian Gospel for the Protestant. In fact, the Christian Gospel must find new expressions in every age in order to speak understandably to contemporary man.

Protestants insist that the language of the Church ought to be the language the people can understand. Just as Jesus spoke Aramaic to the people in Palestine whose mother tongue was Aramaic, so Paul spoke Greek to the Greeks. Protestants assume that they must have the Gospel in a language that they can understand, but they often forget that this means more than mere translation.

Anybody who has translated anything from one language into another knows that it involves more than finding the same words in the other language. If you go to Germany and get hungry on the train, you might want a hot dog. If you should translate the words directly and say that you would like to have *"einen heissen Hund,"* people would think that you had lost your mind; what you want is a *"Wiener Wuerstchen."* Even in such a simple transaction, translation involves reinterpretation.

This is far more profoundly true of the message of the Church; it has to be reinterpreted to every generation. The Protestant principle of Reformation emphasizes that one can never rest on his laurels, that the task of proclaiming the Christian message in a non-Christian world is never done. There is no final solution.

So far it has been asserted that there is such a movement as classical Protestantism. Furthermore, this movement has certain outstanding marks. They are (1) grace and the sovereignty of God, (2) faith, (3) Scripture as the rule of faith, (4) the Church as the fellowship of saints, (5) the fallibility of man and human institutions.

It is now of the utmost importance to remember that among the historical Protestant denominations there are great differences in emphasis. One group might emphasize one point almost exclusively. There are genuine Protestant traditions that are somewhat atypical; none is wholly typical. But the marks listed above have by and large characterized Protestantism, just as they were also marks of the New Testament Church. Protestants did not adopt these emphases because they considered them congenial, but because they considered them biblical. The beliefs of Protestantism are not, as some people seem to believe today, merely a matter of personal taste. On the contrary, they are circumscribed by the testimony of Holy Scripture. This emphasis is the particular genius of the Protestant Faith.

2

God's Revelation

It is impossible to speak about Christianity in general and the Protestant Faith in particular without using certain technical terms. We have, of course, used a number of them already, such as "grace" and "faith" and "salvation" and "church." Some of these terms we have tried to explain, others we hope to explain in the future. Some, we hope, will become clear as we use them in these pages. But the term we are going to discuss now will have to be explained with particular care because of the many misunderstandings that have accumulated about it. The term is "revelation." We cannot discuss Christianity without discussing revelation because it is a key word for the understanding of the Christian Faith.

The task of discussing revelation has not been made easier by the fact that most people have highly inaccurate notions about it. Professor Spurrier in a splendid little book called *Guide to the Christian Faith*[12] lists three prevalent misunderstandings of revelation. First of all, revelation as we use it in the study of the Christian religion is not some hallucination that an individual has as a result of great personal stress or some alleged special inspiration. Protestants by and large have been very suspicious of people who hear voices which nobody else can hear and which tell them to do extraordinary things. To be sure, visions are an important aspect of the psychology of religion. In many religions such visions establish one's claim to spiritual authority, and some will encourage the use of certain drugs to produce the desired hallucinations. But this kind of experience is not what is meant in classical Protestantism. One could say that classical Protestantism has been almost stodgy, or at least extremely conservative, in its attitude toward claims of "revelations." Hallucinations or visions are not what Protestants call revelation.

Furthermore, creedal statements and theological systems are not revelation. Most Christians accept certain creeds. Some Protestants say that they have no creeds, but that is a very debatable claim. In any case, Protestants do not claim that these creeds or the systems of theology based upon these creeds are revelation. For example, the Apostles' Creed and the Nicene Creed are not revelation, and the writings of Luther, of Calvin and of Wesley are not considered revelation by Lutherans, Calvinists, or Methodists. Even the most brilliant theological statements are not revelation. They may talk about revelation, but they are not themselves revelation.

Thirdly, revelation is not the easy way to information concerning areas of human knowledge where we are still in need of a great deal of information. Protestants do not claim that revelation is a short cut to the kind of knowledge that can be attained by careful research in the natural sciences or the social sciences or even the humanities. You cannot be slipshod in the laboratory and then hope that revelation will supply the information which you missed

[12] William A. Spurrier, *Guide to the Christian Faith* (New York: Charles Scribner's Sons, 1953), pp. 38 ff.

because you were inaccurate or lazy. There are tremendous unsolved problems in all areas of human knowledge, but revelation is not a short cut to their solution.

Furthermore, Protestants in general do not use the word "revelation" in connection with the kind of hunches that we sometimes have in regard to decisions we have to make. It is, of course, true that we all have to make many decisions in the course of a day, that people who are believing Christians will pray for guidance in these decisions and that they will often feel that they have received such guidance. But this guidance is not what we call revelation. Revelation does not tell you what kind of a job to take or what kind of a girl to marry or who might make a fine husband for you. It is indubitably true that we need help in all these decisions, but the term "revelation" is reserved for an entirely different experience.

Revelation, as this term is used by Protestant Christians, refers to the fact that God reveals Himself to men. Men could not know God unless God had chosen to make Himself known to them. Very simply, Christians believe that the God who is the "Father Almighty, Maker of Heaven and earth, and of all things visible and invisible" is vastly beyond the comprehension of all human minds. We could not know Him had He not chosen to reveal Himself, had He not chosen to remove the veil which hides divine power from human powerlessness, and divine wisdom from human ignorance.

Now the main assertion of all Christians is that the unfathomable God has revealed Himself to man in Jesus Christ. We shall discuss shortly the meaning of this special revelation, as the theologians call it. But first we should note that Christians distinguish between this special revelation in Jesus Christ and what they call general revelation. And we want to discuss general revelation first.

GENERAL REVELATION

For classical Protestantism general revelation is revelation which hides. What does this mean? In the Acts of the Apostles in the New Testament we have the report of a sermon which the Apostle Paul preached before the curious philosophers in Athens. In this sermon Paul asserts that in God we all—Christians and non-Christians alike—*live and move and have our being.* (*Acts 18:28*) This means that man is at all times and everywhere confronted by God. We could not breathe for an instant, we could not do anything we are doing, we could not even deny God, say the Christians, were it not for the fact that *God is.* He is the source of our being and of all being. He created us and all that exists and preserves us and all that exists. God is the most overwhelming reality and thus He confronts us everywhere and at all times.

There are some people who will ask you, "Have you found God?" This is a very odd question, viewed from within the context of the Christian Faith, for it seems to imply that God is lost, that it takes effort on our part to find Him or to discover Him in some out-of-the-way place. On the contrary, Christians assert that it takes a tremendous effort for man to ignore God, to deny Him. An angry small child may make the effort to ignore his mother, but it is a tremendous effort, because everything he does and sees reminds him of his mother. His good comes through the efforts of his mother; he is fed, washed, entertained, and put to bed by his mother—the most real fact in his life is his mother. He still might try to ignore her but it is a fairly hopeless cause. In a far more profound way all men, the Christians say, are at all times and everywhere confronted by God. In Him all men, good and evil, and all things, important and unimportant, big and small, live and move and have their being. This is the basic fact of general revelation: *God is!*

In the preaching of the early Christians we find frequent references to this conviction that God has revealed Himself and ought to be known by all men. Let us just look at a few of these instances. In his letter to the Romans the Apostle Paul writes:

For the wrath of God is revealed from heaven against all

ungodliness and wickedness of men who by their wicked-
ness suppress the truth. For what can be known about
God is plain to them, because God has shown it to them.
Ever since the creation of the world his invisible nature,
namely, his eternal power and deity, has been clearly
perceived in the things that have been made.

And then St. Paul continues:

So they are without excuse; for although they knew God
they did not honor him as God or give thanks to him, but
they became futile in their thinking and their senseless
minds were darkened. (Romans 1:18–21)

The claim of the Apostle Paul is that man could indeed know God, since He has revealed Himself in His creation, but that in fact man has chosen to ignore this revelation.

In other words, this revelation of God is very real but man has chosen to act as if it had not occurred. He is trying to ignore the God who everywhere surrounds him. There are other examples in Scripture of this idea of general revelation. A very strange thing happened to Paul and Barnabas in Lystra on their journey through Asia Minor. The Apostle Paul had healed a cripple and the people who had seen it were sure that this meant that some of their gods had come down to earth. They believed that Paul was Hermes and that his fellow missionary, Barnabas, was Zeus, the king of the gods. Since the people of Lystra had in their excitement reverted to their native dialect, Paul and Barnabas had no idea what was going on until a priest of Zeus came with oxen and garlands to begin his sacrifices to the presumptive deities. It was then that Paul spoke to them. He said:

Men, why are you doing this? We also are men, of like
nature with you, and bring you good news, that you should
turn from these vain things to a living God who made the

heaven and the earth and the sea and all that is in them. In past generations he allowed all the nations to walk in their own ways; yet he did not leave himself without witness, for he did good, and gave you from heaven rains and fruitful seasons, satisfying your hearts with food and gladness. (Acts 14:15-17)

This conviction permeates Christian thinking, that although God has indeed revealed Himself to all men, they have chosen to ignore and misinterpret the revelation. Though they could know God they do not know Him, and they worship idols rather than the Creator. The Christian claim that man is guilty before God, that he is a sinner, is based upon the assumption that he could have known what is right and wrong and that it is his fault that he does not do what is right but rather chooses to do what is wrong.

It is the Christian position that this general revelation is the root of all religion. Man is hopelessly religious. Everywhere man is trying to find an ultimate meaning in life. Everywhere man is trying to find an answer to such questions as: Where do I come from? Why am I here? Where am I going? As far as we know we are the only beings on this earth that ask these questions. And yet it is doubtful whether any person can live to be an adult without sometime asking one or all of these questions.

Because these questions are part of his nature, because he cannot help asking them, man is religious. Christians assert that man is hopelessly religious because he is in fact confronted by God all the time. And it is this confrontation which forces him to try to find answers. Religion is man's answer to the fact of God as He reveals Himself to man in general revelation. It is a thoroughly human undertaking and full of the weaknesses of human beings. Religion is an effort to give answers, but it is an unsuccessful effort because man cannot find these answers by himself. Christians do not say people in India or China cannot find these answers. Rather, they insist that nobody can find these answers, neither Americans nor Europeans nor Africans. While every man must ask these questions, no man can find the answers. If an answer is available, it must be an answer which God himself chooses to give us. General revelation is the incomprehensible fact of God all about us, and man's response to this revelation is religion. For Christians this human response is false and idolatrous, but it is a response nevertheless.

REVELATION OF LAW. A second fact about general revelation is that it is the revelation of law. The way God confronts man in the universe is through the words "thou shalt!" and "thou shalt not!" The Apostle Paul claims that men know that they must obey certain rules. He asserts in Romans 2:15 that those who do not have a written law have a law in their hearts. He claims that although all men know that there is right and wrong, they do that which is wrong and leave undone that which is right. For our purposes here let us just attempt to understand this one assertion: All men know that there is law.

This is indeed quite an assertion, since so many of us are convinced that there really is no absolute law, that we make up laws as we go along, and that these laws are completely arbitrary.

Christians assert that man, living in this world created and maintained by God, is confronted by a definite ready-made structure. He does not make up this world; he has to take it as it is. The rules he makes up are by and large his reaction to the structure as it confronts him. They are the codified good sense of the race.

For example, man does not make up the fact that fire burns. This is an experience he has on the basis of the way things are. Now, when a mother warns her little boy that he will be burned if he touches the hot stove, she is stating a rule which is not arbitrary but a description of the way things are. If the little boy does not heed his mother's warning—and he probably will not—he will of course be burned. He will probably cry bitterly, but he will stay away from the stove in the future. The mother's rule does not make the stove hot; rather, the fact that hot objects burn you is the structure, and the rule, "Don't touch the stove," is a human adaptation to the way things are.

Or we could say that a heavy object running over a small live object will kill the small live object. This is the way things are. We don't make up this situation. But we make up rules which take this situation into consideration. For example, parents make rules for their small children such as, "Don't run into the street without looking." But this rule is based upon the way things are and the mother is merely transmitting her information about the way things are to her little boy by means of this rule. In this instance, unfortunately, if the child does not obey the rule his mother lays down for him and he experiences these facts which have caused people to formulate the rule, it will be too late for him to change his mind and to admit that his mother was right. He will be run over by a car—killed—because he did not obey the rule his mother told him. The rule did not kill him, of course; the situation which produced the rule did.

It is obvious that wherever there are people there are rules. And these rules which we shall call law are the result of the experience of mankind that this world has a structure which is given, which we cannot change, and to which we must conform.

To put it quite simply—there are no noble savages who run around without clothing and without laws. Wherever there is man there is law. Every tribe has rules governing its conduct, rules which are the result of the experience of these people living in a world whose structure they have experienced as given. They try to adjust to this structure with the help of rules. Now, these rules are not identical. There are fantastic variations—but rules can be found everywhere. In the interesting book by Professors Ford and Beach called *Patterns of Sexual Behavior*[13] the most significant fact is that these researchers have not been able to find any tribe where sexual behavior is not subject to rules. The authors seem to approach the subject with considerable prejudice. Somehow they would like to show that human beings are merely very highly developed cousins of the higher apes. But what they do demonstrate

[31] Clellan S. Ford and Frank A. Beach, *Patterns of Sexual Behavior* (New York: Harper & Brothers, 1951).

is something entirely different—that, while sexual behavior among the apes is governed by instinct, sexual behavior among human beings is governed by law. To the everlasting disappointment of the admirers of the "noble savage" the laws restraining the sex impulse are frequently far more restrictive among the so-called "primitive people" than among the so-called "higher cultures."

Nowhere is man merely nature. He reacts to nature with the help of law. According to the Christians this law is part of general revelation. St. Paul says it is written in the hearts of men. Men everywhere know that there is a difference between right and wrong, between good and bad. The character of this law in some cultures may be summarized as the "Golden Rule." The Golden Rule was stated by Jesus in the Sermon on the Mount in the following words: *So whatever you wish that men would do to you, do so to them; for this is the law and the prophets.* (*Matthew 7:12*) This is the summary of the law, as Jesus points out. And the law is nothing particularly Christian. There is something like the Golden Rule in most so-called higher religions. Hindus, Confucians, and Buddhists all have some statements very similar to the Golden Rule. As the Apostle Paul pointed out, those people who do not have the Old Testament law have the law written in their hearts. It may seem that some have rather poor copies. The law written in the hearts of Ruth Benedict's notorious Dobus is not very impressive. It seems to be an illegible version.[14] But, by and large, rules govern the behavior of all men everywhere.

At this point the question arises, if the law is essentially universal, then what is the special contribution of Christianity? Why do Christians send missionaries if everybody has the law anyhow? And what becomes of Rudyard Kipling's famous phrase about "the lower breeds without the law"?

These questions can be answered at this point only in a preliminary manner. Classical Protestantism asserts that the Good News proclaimed by the Christian Church, the distinctively new

[14] Cf. Ruth Benedict, *Patterns of Culture* (New York: New American Library of World Literature, Inc., 1946), pp. 120 ff.

message, is not the law at all but the Gospel, the Good News of what God has done. In other words, most Christians, perhaps one could say all Christians, are Christians not because of the uniqueness of the Sermon on the Mount or the Golden Rule but because of the Good News that God has given men in Jesus Christ's birth, life, death, and resurrection. Not the Golden Rule but Christ is unique. What this actually means will be discussed in greater detail later.

When we observe the fact of law and structure as part of God's general revelation, we notice that this law confronts us essentially in six areas: (1) relation to God, (2) relation to the family, (3) relation to one's neighbor's life, (4) relation to sex, (5) relation to truth and integrity, and (6) relation to property. These are also the areas covered by the Ten Commandments.

Apparently these relations are nowhere instinctively established among human beings, but they are ordered and circumscribed by rules and regulations; they are governed by law. Many people who are not Protestants would agree with us. During the entire recorded history of mankind we find few people who deny the existence of law or that man is bound by these laws. The existence of a law that is binding for all men is one of the most universal human notions.

However, Protestants go one step further. They not only assert that such a law exists and that it is valid for man, they assert that man is unable to obey this law out of his own resources. In other words, the law condemns man. It is universal, it is obligatory— and because men always disobey it, it always accuses. This realization is most clearly expressed by St. Paul in his letter to the Romans. *For no human being will be justified in his sight by works of the law since through the law comes knowledge of sin. (Romans 3:20)*

According to the Protestant Faith the law is a wonderful gift. It is like a road map of the United States. If you want to drive from Chicago to New York a road map will be useful in finding your way. But the mere possession of a road map does not guarantee your arrival in New York. You must follow its direction. If the map indicates that your destination is in the east, you must go east. The road map is a most useful tool—but only if you follow it. Similarly, the law is good and useful. This is true of the law of the Old Testament and in a sense of the law written in the hearts of all men, including the laws of Confucius, Mohammed, Buddha, and Zoroaster insofar as they agree with the underlying structure which God has given. But it is the Apostle Paul's assertion and the assertion of classical Protestantism that man does not, in fact, obey the law. The road map says to go east and we go west. This is not the fault of the map but of the people who think they know better than the map how to get to New York.

The Apostle Paul says:

> *For I know that nothing good dwells within me, that is in my flesh. I can will what is right, but I cannot do it. For I do not do the good I want, but the evil I do not want is what I do.* (*Romans 7:18, 19*)

Note that here a great leader and apostle of Christendom is speaking. This is not the description of the predicament of a few bank robbers and murderers but, at least according to classical Protestantism, the condition of all men.

It is important to pause here for a moment because most of us have a number of preconceived ideas about Protestantism which are completely at odds with the claim which has just been made. Most of us associate Protestantism with the ideas of nice, middle-class, white Americans. In short, we identify Protestantism with the opinions of people belonging to a particular sociological stratum, who quite generally go to Protestant churches. It is indubitably true that all these good people tend to believe that a good Christian is a person who does not get into trouble with the law—except perhaps when it comes to parking or income-tax matters. A Protestant is a pillar of society.

Prevalent as this notion may be, and you must judge that for yourself, it is the unanimous witness of classical Protestantism that all men are law breakers, that the law accuses and condemns them. If God were only a judge who judges righteously according to the law, all men without exception would be found guilty. Man may have a glimmering of what is right because of God's general revelation, but he does what is wrong. He disobeys the law.

And here classical Protestantism makes a shockingly negative judgment about one of man's highest accomplishments, namely, religion. For the great Reformers religion is man's attempt to ignore the situation created by general revelation. Man knows that there is a structure, that he is in a world which runs according to rules man has not made. And now, in fear and trembling, he is trying to devise his own methods to get away from this awe-inspiring, terrible, and terrifying universe.

For Protestants *human religion* is an effort to domesticate Almighty God. In religion people give God the scraps and remnants of their life. They whistle in the dark in order to drive away their justified fears. Here we can look again at the most prevalent forms of religiosity.

There is legalism. The legalist says, "I won't do this, and I won't do that, and I'll give you so much money every month or every week, God, but the rest of the time and the rest of the money are my own. I can do with them as I please." Against this attempt to bargain with God Protestantism says that everything that man has is God's, that man himself belongs to God, and that it is blasphemy to act as if any part of a man's life does not belong to God.

The well-intentioned, middle-class attitude states, "I am a good Christian; I go to church once in a while, I contribute to my church occasionally, and I have never been in jail. I live a good life!" This attitude may be perfectly satisfactory to make a person conform to the social customs of twentieth-century American society, but it has precious little to do with the Protestant Faith.

A second kind of religiosity is mysticism. The mystic may have raptures, he may see visions, he may hear voices and speak in tongues—but these experiences, be they ever so powerful and impressive, do not make him into a Christian.

Similarly, there is rationalism. A person may know all the

arguments for the existence of God and be able to reason anybody into the acceptance of his theological position. But even the most reasonable philosophical system about God does not make a person a Christian.

This is, of course, the Protestant criticism of the non-Christian religions. The Reformers never denied the sincere religious zeal of other believers. Luther, for example, never tired of pointing out to his fellow Germans how much greater the religious zeal of the Moslem Turks was. He admired their zeal and devotion. But at the same time he asserted that nothing that man can do out of his own power can change the fact that before God's law all men are guilty—Germans and Turks, Americans and Chinese.

But this criticism of religion was not only directed against the non-Christian religions. The Reformers asserted that Christianity can become a mere religion, an escape from God, an effort to limit God's influence on our life by turning over to Him some of the least important matters and keeping the rest for ourselves.

Let us return to our illustration which pictures man as a person driving his car from Chicago to New York. Man's trouble is that he is going west. Human religion is his vain effort to correct this trouble by inflating the tires of the car, having the motor tuned up, and having the oil changed. These are good and useful measures, but they do not help you reach New York if you are driving west from Chicago. In fact, they may help you go faster in the wrong direction. They may give you a false feeling of security. With the beautifully running motor you may be less tempted to ask, "Am I going in the right direction?" General revelation turns out to be of little use in the solution of man's ultimate problem. Indeed through general revelation we know of law and we know of God, but what we know only confuses us and gives us a false sense of security, according to the Protestant Faith. General revelation is indeed the revelation which hides!

REVELATION ROOTED IN MAN'S EXPERIENCE. But even though it hides God from us, general revelation has its roots in very real experiences of man. As a living being, man encounters God. And the experiences which make all men so hopelessly religious are awe-inspiring and overwhelming.

The first of these experiences is that described by the phrase, *Man is impressed by the fact that there is something and not nothing!* It is, of course, quite possible that you have never thought of this fact in exactly these words. But, as we begin to reflect on things, we sooner or later are tempted to follow in the footsteps of the great French philosopher, René Descartes, and doubt all things. It is easy to doubt the reality of the world about us and even our own reality. But sooner or later, when we philosophize in this manner, we are struck by the fact that though nothing would have to be—although everything is contingent—there is this vast universe! There is something and not nothing! There is man—and what an odd creature he is! Blaise Pascal in his *Pensées* describes beautifully the human reaction to such reflection:

> What shall man do in this state? Shall he doubt everything? Shall he doubt whether he is awake, whether he is being pinched, or whether he is being burned? Shall he doubt whether he doubts? Shall he doubt whether he exists? We cannot go so far as that; and I lay it down as a fact that there never has been a real complete skeptic. Nature sustains our feeble reason, and prevents it raving to this extent. Shall he then say, on the contrary, that he certainly possesses truth—he who, when pressed ever so little, can show no title to it, and is forced to let go his hold? What a chimera then is man! What a novelty! What a monster, what a chaos, what a contradiction, what a prodigy! Judge of all things, imbecile worm of the earth; depository of truth, a sink of uncertainty and error; the pride and refuse of the universe! Who will unravel this tangle? Nature confutes the skeptics and reason confutes the dogmatists. What then will you become, O men! who try to find out by your natural reason what is your true condition? You cannot avoid one of these sects, nor adhere to one of them. Know then, proud man, what a paradox you are to yourself. Humble yourself, weak reason; be silent, foolish nature; learn that man infinitely transcends man, and learn from your Master your true condition, of which you are ignorant. HEAR GOD![15]

[15] Blaise Pascal, *Pensées* (New York: E. P. Dutton & Co., Inc., Dutton Everyman Paperbacks, 1948), pp. 120 ff. Part of Fragment No. 434.

This is the true meaning of the ontological argument for the existence of God, that is, that the idea of God implies His existence. It is not a mathematical proof but an experience which no one can escape. There is something and not nothing!

The second of these universal experiences which give us a sense of the reality of something far greater than we are is the *reality of law*—the standards of law that we have discussed above. We all know that there is truth and that there is falsehood, that there is justice and that there is injustice. And we all are frustrated by the fact that we would like to know so much more—and will always know so very little. A visit to a library makes one keenly aware of the reality of truth and of one's failure to grasp it. The countless books which give some insight into truth and which one will never find time to read make one aware of his limitation in regard to knowing the truth.

Some time ago an article appeared in a national magazine by a man who had just come to the realization that he would never become an ice skater. Watching the graceful figures at Rockefeller Plaza, he had suddenly admitted to himself that it was too late, that he would never have the time to learn to ice skate. This brought recognition of a long chain of other things that he would never do. In philosophical terms this man had come face to face with existential finitude, the very limitations involved in being a human. You may have had this experience already, the realization that for many things it is already too late—you will never become a great pianist or a great baseball player. This experience is related to the thoughtful person's experience in a library: all these books—most of them of some interest, many of them fascinating—and the great majority he can never read. Each would help him a little bit toward the truth, but he will never attain this goal.

This is in a sense a universal human experience. We all know that there is truth, and we know at the same time that we are very far away from it. What we know is partial and limited.

The same is true of justice. We all believe that there is right and wrong; even if we deny its existence with our mouth, we believe it with our total being. Some of the people who are most insistent that there is no right or wrong, who accuse the Christian of being a spokesman for medieval notions, and who shout loudly that right is only what everybody says is right are actually very sensitive to right and wrong. The very same people who have just denied the existence of justice become very emotional when a little Negro boy is lynched somewhere in the United States. They know very well that this is wrong. They know that somehow the structure of the universe as man knows it has been violated. There are standards of justice that we perceive with our very being. Antigone knew that she had to bury her brother! Electra knew that her father had to be avenged! Go through the myths of the ancients and the preliterate people of the present, and everywhere you will discover that man knows himself to be confronted by structures that are greater and more important than himself.

People are willing to die for the truth because they believe that this truth is more important than their lives. People are dying for the truth today. Perhaps it is a partial truth, a very confused truth, but the mere fact that these people are willing to die for it indicates that man knows that there are standards that are more important than life itself. Truth and justice simply are, even if we cannot demonstrate them to everybody's satisfaction. We know that they exist and we try to live by them.

This is the validity of the so-called "ethical" or "moral" proof of the existence of God. It is not a proof in the sense that it is conclusive to the person who does not want to believe, but it is an argument which describes the situation as it confronts us in life.

Thirdly, there is the *reality of beauty and art.* Some of the earliest men of whom we have any records scratched pictures of the animals of their environment into the walls of the caves in which they lived. We are not merely mammals who eat and sleep and reproduce. We want beauty and despise ugliness; we want to create beautiful things and are frustrated by our failures. Have you ever watched a child trying to put on paper what he sees in his mind's eye and being disappointed because he cannot create the beauty he would like to create? What is true of children is more true of grownups. One of the most sensitive authors of our century was Franz Kafka. He left all his novels unfinished because they never were what he wanted them to be. It was his last will and testament that all his novels, such as *The Castle* and *The Trial,* were to be destroyed. They were published posthumously by a friend who felt that they expressed this insight into man's confrontation with a beauty that he cannot attain better than most other works which are proudly completed by less sensitive men than Kafka.

Man has always been an artist. He has used art to come to terms with a universe he could not understand. In Greek tragedy and in William Shakespeare, in Johann Sebastian Bach and in Pablo Picasso, we see the results of general revelation. Man's coming to terms with the universe makes some become artists and gives all of us a sense of beauty and artistic appreciation.

Fourthly, there is the *reality of love.* The Christian Bible is full of allusions to the reality of love as it confronts us everywhere. And this love gives us some inkling of a structure which includes love. Parental love, the love of parents for children, is one of the most basic facts of our life. Nobody can quite understand it unless he has experienced it, and no amount of cynicism touches the reality of the experience.

Further, we observe and experience the overwhelming reality of marital love. The Old and the New Testaments describe the relationship of God to man through the image of marital love as well as parental love. God is our heavenly Father; we are His children. The Church is the bride of Christ. For the Prophet Hosea the relationship between himself and his unfaithful wife became a symbol of the relationship between God and His people.

Love is a fact of general revelation. Obviously, not only Christians but all human beings are capable of love. Just as people often talk about love but never perform the works of love, so many people also ridicule love and then show love, to their own surprise and to the surprise of everybody else. Love is a reality. Human beings are capable of showing human love. It is often clearly selfish and always at least affected by selfishness and pride, but it is nevertheless real. The experience of love becomes a basic experience for man's realization that he does not stand alone.

A fifth area in which general revelation confronts us is *history*. This does not mean that in history the good people always come out on top and the evil people are always defeated. This is not at all the witness of biblical Christianity. But there are certain facts in history which point us toward the realization that this is an orderly universe and not chaotic.

This insight is in no way particularly Christian. In fact, it was Plato who pointed out that a minimum of order and honesty is necessary to have any kind of society. Even robbers cannot rob effectively unless there is some "honor among thieves." A gang of robbers who desire to hold up a bank must trust each other to a certain extent in order to achieve their goal. If they do not trust each other at all, they will fail in their attempt. The lookout must look out, the driver of the getaway car must stay in the car, and the man who is getting the money must bring it out to the others. This minimal amount of mutual trust is necessary even for a band of robbers. A society cannot be built on chaos; it needs order and mutual trust.

Furthermore, individuals in a community must have some sense of vocation in order to build a successful society. If everybody is concerned only with his own interests, the society will not flourish. There has to be a service motive besides the profit motive for great cultural achievement. To use Arnold Toynbee's phrase, men must answer the challenge of their historical situation with an adequate response. If they fail to do so, the culture fails.

Another aspect of this confrontation by God in history is the peculiar way in which we experience time. As usual, the Greeks had a word for it; in fact, they had two words for it. In the Greek language, the language in which the New Testament is written, we find two different words that we translate as "time," namely, *chronos* and *kairos*.

Chronos time is the time that we can measure with the help of a watch or a calendar. It is the time that can be divided into seconds and minutes or days and years and centuries. Chronological time is measurable time, divisible into equal parts which are all somewhat alike.

But when the Greeks use the word *kairos* they mean another kind of time altogether. The New Testament translations usually render the word *kairos* by "the accepted time" or "when the time was fulfilled." This means that time, besides being this divisible, measurable, even stream on which we are carried along, has another quality which is quite disturbing. It becomes *kairos,* the accepted time, the time for decision.

This can be illustrated with some examples from everyday life. A young man and a young woman are going steady. They have been good friends for a long time and now they have decided to give up all other girl friends and boy friends and go steady. All this takes place in *chronos.* But there comes a moment when this *chronos* becomes *kairos,* when this time becomes the accepted time. The crucial moment arrives in which this particular boy asks this particular girl to marry him—and if he delays too long the relationship will surely deteriorate until it finally breaks, and she will marry somebody else. There will still be lots of *chronos,* but when she is married to somebody else and has half a dozen children the *kairos* is gone. There is still time, but the accepted time is past.

Or a student is taking a course at the university. He gets up early every morning to make it to class, where the instructor drones along for fifty minutes. All this is *chronos.* And then one day, after all this *chronos,* the instructor announces a test for the following Thursday. Suddenly *chronos* has become *kairos;* time has become the accepted time. And in this Thursday's fifty minutes the fate of the student is decided as far as this course is concerned. He either knows the answers to the questions he is asked *at this particular time* or he fails in this course. This particular time block has also minutes and seconds but somehow these minutes and seconds are different. They are *kairos,* not merely *chronos.* If the student knows the answers at this time, he passes; otherwise, he fails. It does not help for him to go to the instructor afterward and say, "I knew all this material backward and forward; I just couldn't remember it during the test." This is a heartbreaking story and it may even be true, but it won't do him any good. It is what you do when *chronos* becomes *kairos* that really counts.

Or two people work on a flying trapeze, a man and his wife. The woman flies through the air from one side and the man, holding on with his feet, flies through the air from the other side. And then for a split second *chronos* becomes *kairos,* time becomes the accepted time: the man catches his wife and she is safe or he fails and she will fall. It is not enough for this man to say, "My muscles are generally in wonderful shape," or "My coordination is usually extraordinary." That's all very interesting, but what counts is the split second when *chronos* becomes *kairos* and he can grab his wife.

What has been illustrated here is a general aspect of time as it involves human beings. For all of us, as individuals and as members of groups, time has this double aspect. There comes a time for decision. Indeed, without knowing the technical terminology, without knowing a word of Greek, people know about the significance of decision. They know about this double aspect of time. They know that they must act and that they are held responsible for their actions. Their actions have ultimate significance, for time is not reversible. This reaction to time is the result of man's confrontation with God. It is part of general revelation. It does not prove the existence of God to the unbeliever. It is not "scientific evidence," but it is a very real experience shared by all men.

And this brings us to the final aspect of this confrontation with God in history. The German poet and historian Friedrich Schiller said, *"Die Weltgeschichte ist das Weltgerichte,"* "World history is the judgment over the world." Schiller was an idealist, and, as it stands, this statement is far too optimistic. But looked at from the negative side it describes a human experience which results from man's confrontation with God. "Lo, how the mighty are fallen!" All human power is powerlessness in the long run. Think of the founders of the so-called "Thousand-year Reich," the Nazi leaders

in Germany whose empire collapsed after only twelve of the thousand years. "O where are kings and empires now, of old that went
and came?" This is a universal human experience. And it is
pathetic when people attempt to fight this reality by trying to build
a structure that will last forever, trying somehow to perpetuate
themselves through buildings or institutions, and fail miserably.
Confronted by this fact of judgment, we try to have at least a
vault in which our bones will rest unharmed forever. We are com-
forted by the double-your-money-back, unconditional guarantee that
the vault will last forever. But all these frantic efforts only point
up the reality of the judgment, which is one of the most basic
experiences of man. This is the reality that Greek tragedy and
American tragedy speak about.

Man also experiences general revelation, the confrontation with
God, when he realizes that this universe is an orderly universe, a
kosmos and not a *chaos*. When the biologist describes the development of greater and greater complexity in nature, and when the
physicist describes the orderly way in which the universe runs down
according to the second law of thermodynamics, they are both
describing the order of the universe. Almost intuitively we discover
pattern and design everywhere, and in this pattern and design we
feel ourselves confronted by God. This is the basis for the teleological proof of the existence of God, which proves the existence of
God by the purposefulness of the universe. And here most people,
even if they are not convinced by the proofs as logical proofs, admit
that they stand in awe before "Nature and Nature's God," as our
deistic predecessors liked to say.

And so, again, man experiences in many ways this confrontation
with God as the wholly other. He experiences it through (1) the
realization of his own contingence and the contingency of all that
exists, the fact that there is something and not nothing, (2) the
existence of standards that confront us from the outside and that we
cannot change, (3) the reality of beauty and of art, (4) the reality of
love, (5) history, and (6) nature.

But here classical Protestantism takes what may seem to be an odd position. General revelation, it says, is real, and all these things that we have described are real experiences of man, but general revelation fails to reveal God. Instead of giving us a way to God, it is, on the contrary, at the root of our unwillingness to listen to God, and it causes us to devise our own methods of reaching Him. Because man is in revolt against God, general revelation gives him just enough knowledge to befuddle him, confuse him, and lead him astray. This is not God's fault, for He wants to reveal Himself. It is man's fault, says Protestantism. We use even the very revelation of God to deny Him. Again we can see how the Apostle Paul expresses this experience of man:

Although they knew God they did not honor him as God or give thanks to him, but they became futile in their thinking and their senseless minds were darkened. Claiming to be wise, they became fools, and exchanged the glory of the immortal God for images resembling mortal man or birds or animals or reptiles. (Romans 1:21–23)

This is the human experience, according to the Christian Faith; even God's general revelation is perverted by man to hide God. God reveals life and man sees only death; God reveals law and man sees only punishment; God reveals love and man sees wrath; God reveals beauty and man sees ugliness. Nature shows not the true God but the *Deus absconditus,* the hidden God. Man's perversion of general revelation creates the situation which makes necessary the special revelation of God in Jesus Christ.

According to classical Protestantism there is no continuity between the religion of man and the revelation of God. Human religion is in a sense man's effort to escape God. It is the religious man who is particularly stubborn in his refusal to admit his need for revelation. In the New Testament we read a good deal about Pharisees and publicans. It appears that the Pharisees were very religious people—but their very religiosity was their great trouble. As the New Testament describes it, these Pharisees knew so much about religion that they were unwilling to listen to God when He confronted them in the person of Jesus Christ. The publicans, in spite of their religious ignorance and their moral imperfection, were better off than the Pharisees because they at least admitted their shortcomings. It is man *with his religion* who is in need of the special revelation in Jesus Christ.

REVELATION IN JESUS CHRIST

THE REALITY OF REVELATION. The Christian Church confesses on the basis of the Apostolic Witness as recorded in Scripture that God has revealed Himself to man—who is guilty before the law and driven to despair by general revelation—as Lord and Savior. Protestantism insists that this is God's act. Revelation is not something that man has; it is something that God does. It is an act of His sovereign grace. In other words, we have no right to revelation, we have no claim upon God. It is not something to which we are entitled. But, like creation, it is an act of God's sovereign grace. If you ask why God revealed Himself you cannot find the answer in man. It is not because man is so good or so valuable, but because God is what He is that He reveals Himself in Jesus Christ.

Holy Scripture is the record of this revelation. It tells us what God has done in history through Jesus Christ. And through the witness of the Church based on Scripture each generation can hear this message.

General revelation hides the true being of God and, because of man's attitude of disobedience, tends to confuse man and fails to save him. Special revelation is entirely different. In Jesus Christ God confronts man as Savior (II Timothy 1:10). In Him God speaks to us. This is expressed in the Epistle to the Hebrews in the following words: *In many and various ways God spoke of old to our fathers by the prophets; but in these last days he has spoken to us by a Son.* (*Hebrews 1:1, 2*) In Christ the eternal Word (*Logos*) has become flesh (John 1:1 ff.). God as God, apart from His revelation in Christ, would be eternally hidden from us. The Christians, unlike adherents of some other religions, do not have a patronizing attitude toward God. In some primitive religions, especially in all those religions in which magic is used, the gods can be dominated, they can be controlled. It is possible to punish them by punishing the fetish that contains divine power. And there are certain attitudes in contemporary religion which would indicate a sub-Christian approach to God. The God of the Old and New Testaments is not "the Man upstairs." It is hard to imagine any of the great theologians who have been the spokesmen of classical Protestantism addressing God in the patronizing manner which is part and parcel of so much contemporary religiosity.

Classical Protestantism knows God as the sovereign Lord. Statements which emphasize the absolute sovereignty of God abound in the works of Luther and Calvin. John Wesley said about God, the Creator:

> He has acted in all things according to his own sovereign will. Justice has not, cannot have any place here; for nothing is due to what has no being! Here, therefore, he may, in the most absolute sense, do what he will with his own. Accordingly, he created the heavens and the earth, and all things that are therein, in every conceivable respect, "according to his own good pleasure."[16]

This is hardly the God of contemporary juke-box religion. This is the God of the electrons and the spiral nebulae and He is hidden from human eyes.

It is because God is so utterly different from us, because of His sovereign majesty, that we can never reach him out of our own power. According to classical Protestantism, man simply cannot reach God. Every effort to do so is doomed from the start and must lead to despair.

But while man cannot reach God, God can reach man. The gulf between God and man can be bridged only by God. Special revelation is the assertion of the Church that God has in fact bridged the gulf in Jesus Christ.

[16] Fosdick, *Great Voices*, p. 518.

Perhaps the simplest illustration of what Protestant Christians believe here is one taken from the realm of language. If a person visits a foreign country and wants to make himself understood he will learn the language of that country. It is then possible for him to translate his sentiments and ideas into the language of the people he has gone to visit. In a far more profound sense, asserts Protestant Christianity, God has translated Himself into human language in Jesus Christ. He speaks to us in language that we can understand, and He lives with us in a human life, the kind of life that is meaningful to us. In I John we read:

> *That which was from the beginning, which we have heard, which we have seen with our eyes, which we have looked upon and touched with our hands, concerning the word of life—the life was made manifest, and we saw it, and testify to it, and proclaim to you the eternal life which was with the Father and was made manifest to us. (I John 1:1, 2)*

The eternal life entered into time, the Christians say. God became man. The Immortal took upon Himself mortality. The infinite entered into space, in order that men might know God.

This is the assertion which Christianity makes and upon which all other assertions depend. In other words, the key to the Christian Faith in general and the Protestant Faith in particular is the statement which was quoted in the beginning: "God was in Christ reconciling the world unto Himself." People who believe this are called Christians. But this is certainly *not* something which is obvious or self-evident. The possibility of this assertion depends upon the reality of revelation.

The first assertion which the Protestant Faith makes concerning special revelation, the revelation in Jesus Christ, is that it is real. The second assertion deals with the form of revelation. And here the Protestant Faith asserts that the revelation in Christ is historical revelation. It took place in time and history. It is not the revelation of abstract truths that are accepted but revelation through events.

Here Christianity is quite different from most of the other great religions. What Confucianism or Buddhism or Hinduism insist upon is the truth of their ideas. The historical events are of no significance. They have only a symbolic meaning. If there had never been a man like Confucius, and if historical scholarship should establish that such a man never lived, it would make little difference to Confucianism. The message of Confucianism is based upon the truth of the ideas which Confucius expressed. These ideas are valid quite apart from any events in Confucius' life. They are valid even if Confucius never existed. The events in Confucius' life are accidental and have at best a symbolic significance.

We could say almost the same thing about Buddha; the teachings of Buddha rather than the events in Buddha's life are the clue to Buddhism. Hinduism offers perhaps the clearest contrast in this regard, since Hinduism also speaks about God coming to man in incarnations. But note that there are many incarnations of which no one is of absolute significance. These incarnations, to continue through all eternity, are opportunities for God to teach men the truth, the proper ideas and the proper way of life. For the Hindus incarnations are a pedagogical device which the supreme God uses to communicate ideas. What matters are these true ideas. The events in the life of the various incarnations have merely symbolic significance. Neither history nor time has any significance in Hindu thought. Everything is myth and symbol. To go back to the idea which we mentioned before—there is no *kairos* in Hinduism. There is no accepted time, a time for decision, when man's destiny hangs in the balance. The Hindu doctrine of the transmigration of souls offers man infinite time and infinite opportunities to achieve the goal of identification with God.

It is therefore of considerable significance to note the insistence upon time and history in Christian revelation. Man is a historical being; only that which occurs in time is real to him. This does not necessarily mean that time is real for God, but it does mean that time is real for man and that events must take place in time in order to be real and meaningful to him. Here the Christian Church asserts that God entered into time and history in order to save man. This is why Pontius Pilate is in the Apostles' Creed. The Apostles' Creed is really a very short statement of the Christian Faith. There is not a word about Jesus' ministry on earth or about Peter or John— yet Pontius Pilate is in the Creed. It says that "He suffered under Pontius Pilate." This is an expression of the typical Christian emphasis upon the historical character of revelation. The incarnation, the translation of God into human terms, is for the Christians not a general principle, not a symbol, but an event! Something that happened! As St. John puts it: *And the Word became flesh and dwelt among us! (John 1:14)*

And time matters. Christians do not believe that they have infinite incarnations in which to attain God. The challenge of Christianity, the challenge of the Christian Gospel is that now is the accepted time—the *kairos*—now is the day of salvation. History is not an eternal circle, a wheel that keeps turning for ever and ever. No! History is a line, with its beginning in God. This is the doctrine of creation. It has a center, the incarnation of God in Jesus Christ. And it has an end. But the significant insight is that history is a line rather than a circle. And what we do on this little piece of the line which is ours has ultimate meaning for us.

When we say that the revelation in Christ is historical revelation, we say that Christ entered into this line—intersected this line, if you please. The revelation in Jesus Christ from the time when Quirinius was governor of Syria, recounted in the Christmas story, to the time when Pilate was Rome's representative in Jerusalem, as we read in the Passion story, is revelation in time. It is not repeatable, it is not a parable, it is event!

And if the first thing that we can say about the form of revelation according to the Protestant Faith is that it is revelation in time and history, then we must say simultaneously that the Protestant Faith insists that the historical once-and-for-all character of God's revelation in Jesus Christ is history, but it is not *mere* history. We become Christians when revelation is no longer "mere history" to us and when Christ becomes our own eternal contemporary.

This means that it is certainly not enough to believe in Christ as you may believe in Caesar. You may believe that there was a man like Caesar who crossed the Rubicon and was eventually assassinated in Rome. You may believe these as events in history. There are some people who believe in Jesus Christ in the same manner. They believe that there was a certain Jesus Christ who was the son of a Virgin and who lived a life of preaching and healing. They believe that He did all the miracles which the Bible reports, and then He was killed and on the third day He was raised from the dead. There are people who believe that in the same manner in which they believe that Caesar crossed the Rubicon or that Socrates was a sculptor and the son of a midwife and was executed by the Athenians because he asked too many embarrassing questions.

The Protestant Faith asserts that it isn't enough to believe facts about Christ. Jesus Christ isn't another Caesar or another Socrates. You have to believe *in* Him; it is not enough to believe things *about* Him. One must in a sense become a disciple, just as Peter and John became disciples. There were many people in Jesus' time who saw all the things Jesus did and who did not believe Him. A few people believed and became His disciples. Revelation is revelation *for you* only if it makes you into a disciple. Here we are again dealing with the subject of faith which was discussed at the beginning. Faith is complete and utter trust. It isn't mere information about things that happened or didn't happen.

Revelation is not revelation for us until we accept it in faith. And here we must mention a word which will come up again and again in the course of our discussion. The all-important emphasis upon the historical character of revelation and the emphasis upon experiencing personal fellowship with Christ, the eternal contemporary, are *complementary* to each other. This means that in the Protestant Faith there are a number of basic convictions which cannot be expressed by saying one thing only. We have to make two assertions simultaneously. Often two such statements will appear contradictory on the surface. But only if both are made do we express the Protestant Faith adequately at this point. We borrow this concept of complementarity from physics. There it means that various pictures used to describe atomic systems are adequate to certain experiments, yet mutually exclusive. For example, an atom can be described as a planetary system or as a nucleus surrounded by waves, whose frequency is decisive. These different pictures are complementary to each other. While they seem to contradict each other, they are both correct if used properly. Similarly, in theology we often get at the truth by saying two things that seem on the surface to be contradictory. We will notice this again and again in our discussion of the Protestant Faith. It is in the letters of the Apostle Paul *and* the letter of the Apostle James that we receive the total message. It is through the Gospel of Mark *and* the Gospel of John that the living Christ is presented to us. The emphasis may seem different, but this very difference helps us to get a deeper insight into the Christian message.

This necessity of using seeming contradictions in order to describe our experience of God's revelation has been very admirably expressed in Professor D. M. Baillie's book, *God Was in Christ.* He says:

> The attempt to put our experience of God into theological statements is something like the attempt to draw a map of the world on a flat surface, the page of an atlas. It is impossible to do this without a certain degree of falsification, because the surface of the earth is a spherical surface whose pattern cannot be produced accurately upon a plane. And yet the map must be drawn for convenience's sake. Therefore an atlas meets the problem by giving us two different maps of the world which can be compared with each other. The one is contained in two circles representing two hemispheres. The other is contained in an oblong (Mercator's projection). Each is a map of the whole world, and they contradict each other to some extent at every point. Yet they are both needed, and taken together they correct each other. They would be either misleading or mystifying to anyone who did not know that they represent the surface of a sphere. But they can serve their useful purpose for anyone who understands that they are intended simply

to represent in handy portable form the pattern covering the surface of this round earth which he knows in actual experience. So it is with the paradoxes of faith. They are inevitable, not because the divine reality is self-contradictory, but because when we "objectify" it all our judgments are in some measure falsified, and the higher truth which reconciles them cannot be fully expressed in words, though it is experienced and lived in the I-Thou relationship of faith towards God.[17]

This is true of the tension between the eventful-historical character of revelation and the subjective eternal acceptance of these events as governing and transforming the Christian life. For it is not merely history that revelation deals with but the meaning of these events to men and women today.

Of course, this raises quite a number of very significant problems which we can only touch upon in this context. For example, how are we to depict these events artistically in painting and sculpture? At times people have insisted on the imitation of the historical situation in the artistic reproductions which are supposed to illustrate the life of Christ. This means the artist has tried to depict Jesus and his disciples as Palestinian natives of two thousand years ago. He has tried to be as faithful as possible to the archeological and historical data that tell us about the dress and customs of the people of Palestine in the first century A.D. The result of this approach has often been that Jesus and the disciples have become people from a faraway land, wearing odd costumes. They have become museum pieces, archeological exhibits, as interesting to our life as the dinosaur or the Neanderthal man. Much of the Sunday school art that is distributed to the children in Protestant churches all over the country has this tendency to attempt historical accuracy in a very superficial sense and to remove Christ from our experience as the eternal contemporary. In an effort to be faithful to history, it becomes unfaithful to the core of the Gospel message.

Often the greatest artistic masterpieces dealing with the preaching of the Christian Church have been efforts to depict Christ and

[17] D. M. Baillie, *God Was in Christ* (New York: Charles Scribner's Sons, 1948), pp. 109 f.

the events of his life as if they had occurred in the time of the artist. If one looks at the art of the Middle Ages, one finds that the great medieval painters depicted Christ as a contemporary, as a medieval man, a man of their time. No effort was made to be historically accurate or to depict Jesus as a man from a faraway world. Rather, the effort was to make Him and His life understandable to the contemporary world. While in a sense historically inaccurate, these great artists were able to communicate the message of the New Testament and of the Old Testament amazingly well. And this is not only true of the great painters. It is equally true of the great anonymous sculptors who contributed their artistic masterpieces to the medieval cathedrals. Here, too, we find an effort to make these statues speak to contemporary man of the great deeds that God has done in history.

And the great music of the Christian Church is not an effort to go back to the Palestinian music of Jesus' day but to sing of the wonderful deeds of God in such a manner that contemporary man can feel their terrible significance. Here lies the importance of men like Palestrina and Bach. Listening to the *Passion According to St. Matthew* by Johann Sebastian Bach, one discovers that the great musician uses his inspired genius to proclaim the eternal message concerning God's deeds by means of the baroque music of the eighteenth century.

Interestingly enough, there are contemporary Chinese Christian artists who depict Christ as a Chinese. Their paintings show an Oriental Virgin Mary and Christ child in Chinese surroundings against the background of a Chinese landscape. Again we see the artistic effort to make the historical relevant and meaningful to contemporary man.

Yet this tendency can also go too far. The very effort to make Christ speak to modern man can also lead to a denial of the Christ it is supposed to proclaim. Much of contemporary religious art prettifies Jesus to the extent that we forget what the Scripture teaches concerning Him. Looking at some of the popular pictures found in Christian churches today, the question arises: Is this the

Man of Sorrows? Is this the Suffering Servant? Is this the crucified Christ, or some American movie star with long hair? The pretty Christ is hardly the Christ of the New Testament. Here an effort to be relevant, to make Jesus appeal to the teen-age set may have gone so far that the message is utterly obscured by the very effort to make it meaningful.

Perhaps one of the most striking examples is a famous book about Jesus that was popular about a generation ago, *The Man Nobody Knows*. The author tried to depict Jesus as the big business executive. The motto of the book, "Wist ye not that I must be about my Father's *business!*" was printed on the dedication page with the word *business* in italics! The Table of Contents read as follows: I. The Executive; II. The Outdoor Man; III. The Sociable Man; IV. His Methods; V. His Advertisements; VI. The Founder of Modern Business; VII. The Master.

Here we see how important it is to maintain the tension between history and contemporaneity. Revelation is never merely history, never merely something that occurred in the distant past. Yet at the same time it is never merely the proclamation of ideas which happen to be popular today. Its contemporary importance is based upon the historical event. Revelation is all-important today *because* it took place in history; it is significant for the world of present ideas *because* it is based upon the fact that God entered time. Whenever Protestantism lets go of one or the other assertion it falsifies the form of revelation.

We must admit that both have happened all too often. Some Protestants have at times become so concerned with the events of the past as to forget their meaning for today, while others have become so concerned with meanings for today that these meanings became dissociated from the event of the past. But classical Protestantism has tried to maintain both assertions at the same time.

And now we are ready to turn to the next question: What is the content of revelation? As we have indicated a number of times in passing, for the Protestant Faith the content of revelation is Jesus Christ. For Protestants Jesus Christ is not primarily the teacher of a revelation. It is not His message which is the object of our faith but rather His person. Classical Protestantism does not call you to faith in Christ's teachings as much as to faith in Christ as God's revelation. Here we should remember again that the ecumenical creeds of Christendom, the Apostles' Creed and the Nicene Creed, as well as most other creedal statements deal with the person of Christ and not with His teachings. This does not mean that His teachings are insignificant or unimportant, but it does mean that His person validates His teachings and not vice versa. Protestants will try to follow the teachings of Christ because they believe Christ to be revelation; they do not say that they know Him to be revelation because of His teachings. Thus the content of revelation is Jesus Christ. But what is it that is revealed through this revelation in Jesus Christ?

In Jesus Christ we learn that God is Creator and Lord. General revelation gives us a vague sense of God the Creator, but special revelation in Christ purifies, clarifies, explains, and focuses these vague notions.

All major religions have some notion of creation and a creator. In much religious thought the creator of the earth is evil. Creation, although always an act of power, is not always an act of goodness. For the Buddhist, for example, this world is a prison to be escaped. To be a living creature is to be imprisoned in a body and estranged from the divine soul. Even the great Greek philosopher Plato held the body to be the prison of the soul. The attitude toward the world is quite different if we take seriously the revelation in Jesus Christ that the Father of our Lord is the Creator. Christians know that this is God's world.

Secondly, in Jesus Christ we learn that God is absolute love. The New Testament word for it is *agape*. This is a love that overcomes hate and revolt and bridges continually the abyss of separation that we have established and continue to maintain by our revolt against God. Christians assert that the very character of God is revealed in Jesus Christ. They admit that the evidence we have before us in nature is in some ways inconclusive. God's power may be seen, as well as His wisdom and justice. But the study of nature will not tell us anything of God's love, for cruelty and hate are at least as obvious in nature as mercy and love. A fair case could be made, indeed, that they are more obvious. As we read the literature of the ages we find that while many wise and sensitive men have been overwhelmed by the existence of radical evil in the world, few have caught a glimpse of love as undergirding creation.

A look at some of our contemporary literature shows that the love of God is not obvious on the basis of the data which this world supplies. We cannot know God as love unless He reveals Himself to us as love. To the Christian it is not nature or history or the human personality but Jesus Christ who shows us the ultimate character and purpose of God. The Protestant Faith asserts that only through Christ can we know that God is absolute, self-giving love—love that is not dependent on our goodness and our worth but love that has its sources entirely in His own goodness and worth.

These statements may appear to some to be the most obvious platitude that could possibly be proclaimed. Everybody knows that God is love. But while we are indeed very familiar with the phrase, this does not mean that we are at all familiar with the reality. There is nothing obvious and self-evident about the assertion that God *is* love; it is far from being a universal assertion. Other people besides the Christians have said that God loves, but that He loves His friends and hates His enemies. Others again have said that God loves the good. Their logic leads them to say that since He Himself is the best He will love only Himself with a perfect love and that He loves man only insofar as he is perfect.

Against all these very reasonable and intelligible views the Protestant Faith asserts that God is love because He has revealed Himself as love in Jesus Christ. It is not through an analysis of nature—the observation of flowers or trees or butterflies—that we learn that God is love. Nor is it through an analysis of man. The analysis of man reveals libido, will to power, interesting drives and responses of many sorts, but no God of love. The Protestant assertion that God is love is based only upon the revelation of love in Jesus Christ.

HOLY SCRIPTURE AS THE BEARER OF REVELATION

This raises the next question: How do we know about Jesus Christ? Protestantism's answer is that we know about Him through God's Word. The peculiar authority which Holy Scripture holds among Protestants is based upon the fact that it is considered the bearer of revelation. Here we come to a subject which has been quite controversial among Protestants for a long time, the question of the authority of Scripture.

The Protestant Faith considers Holy Scripture, that is, the canonical books of the Old and New Testaments, the record of the original witness concerning the revelation of God in history. This means that for Protestants in general it is not the Bible which saves men, but the deeds of God which are described and interpreted in the Bible. This may seem obvious, but there are, especially among Protestants, some magical concepts concerning the Bible which have nothing to do with classical Protestantism. There are people who believe that carrying a Bible or a New Testament on your body keeps you from having accidents and prospers you in your business affairs. This is a magical concept. It is not the Bible in your coat pocket but the Christ on the Cross who saves men according to the Protestant Faith.

Protestants do not claim that the Bible fell from heaven. Rather they hold that it is a library of books written over a long period of time and by many different people. For most Protestants, what makes the Bible unique is not its grammar, its spelling, or the scientific world view expressed in it. Its uniqueness rests in the fact that God inspired the writers of these many books in such a manner that what this book says about man in his relationship to God, God in His relationship to man, and men in their relationship to each other, under God, is true. Protestants claim that God speaks to them authoritatively in the Bible. The Bible tells the story of God's dealings with men; it contains holy history, or the history of salvation.

This means of course that each passage of Scripture must be understood in the light of all other passages and that it is a very dangerous practice indeed to take passages out of context. Most Protestants reject an approach to the Bible which advocates opening it at random, putting a finger on some passage, and then claiming that this is God's word for you. Although there have always been people who have used the Bible in this manner, this is not the way in which the Bible is used as authority by the great spokesmen of the Reformation.

For Protestants, Holy Scripture is the means through which the contemporary Word of God reaches each generation in the preaching of the Church. The Bible is history, in some cases very ancient history. It is poetry, in some cases very beautiful poetry. But for the Protestant Faith these ancient writings are vehicles through which God speaks to men today. It is the task of the preaching of the Protestant churches to proclaim the message for today on the basis of the Holy History recorded in the Scriptures.

An illustration of such a relevant use of Scripture can be found in an editorial which appeared in *Life* magazine some years ago. A Negro boy had been lynched. The murderers were not found. *Life* commented as follows:

> In Mississippi the murder of 14 year-old Emmett Till still goes unpunished. It will be punished, nevertheless, for there is a higher law than Mississippi's. Emmett Till was a child. One of the South's traditions is the religion of Jesus, who said: "But whoso shall offend one of these little ones which believe in me, it were better for him that a millstone were hanged about his neck, and that he were drowned in the depth of the sea." Men can be forgiven for prejudice, as a sign of ignorance or an imperfect understanding of their religion; no righteous man can condone a brutal murder. Those in Sumner, and elsewhere, who do condone it, are in far worse danger than Emmett Till ever was. He had only his life to lose, and many others have done that, including his soldier-father

who was killed in France fighting for the American proposition that all men are equal. Those who condone a deed so foul as this are in danger of losing their souls. The soul of Emmett Till was known but to few but it was a thing of value. It was fashioned on July 25, 1941, by the Lord God Almighty who placed on it this distinctive seal: This is My son, akin to all others, but unlike any one of them. Like each of my children he is unique, irreplaceable, immortal. I hereby send him among other men, who are his brothers. He went and was slain. In the dark night of this deed his childish cries for mercy fell on deaf ears. But they were heard, nonetheless, and the Hearer made an entry, that night, beneath certain names, writing once more: "It must needs be that offenses come, but woe to that man by whom the offense cometh." Sleep well, Emmett Till; you will be avenged. You will also be remembered, as long as men have tongues to cry against evil. It is true now as it was when Christ said it almost 2000 years ago: "For there is nothing covered that shall not be revealed; neither hid that shall not be known. . . . Whatsoever ye have spoken in darkness shall be heard in the light. . . . Be not afraid of them that kill the body. . . . Fear him, which after he hath killed hath power to cast into hell. . . . Are not five sparrows sold for two farthings, and not one of them is forgotten before God? . . . Fear not, therefore, ye are of more value than many sparrows."[18]

This is good preaching. Its frequent references to Scripture do not make its message irrelevant. On the contrary, Scripture used as authority is the very source of its relevance. Here we become aware of the tension between history and contemporaneity. The Bible is history, an account of events in the past, but at the same time it is God's Word for today. Protestants assert that God speaks to all men today by means of this Holy History.

The authority of Scripture, then, derives from the fact that it confronts us with the Living God through the library of books and through the Holy History which they record. For most Protestants its infallibility is the infallibility of Christ, whose "cradle" it is. Luther put it thus:

Think of the Scriptures as the loftiest and noblest of holy things,

[18] *Life,* October 10, 1955. Copyright, Time Inc.

as the richest of mines, which can never be worked out, so that you may find the wisdom of God that He lays before you in such foolish and simple guise, in order that He may quench all pride. Here you find the swaddling-clothes and the manger in which Christ lies, and to which the angel points the shepherds. Simple and little are the swaddling-clothes, but dear is the treasure, Christ, that lies in them.[19]

The book itself is not the object of Protestant worship, but the Christ who meets us in the Bible. The Bible teaches us that God confronts man as a person. He does not reveal Himself to us as a logical proposition or an unconscious power—but person to person.

According to classical Protestantism, all Scripture must be understood in the light of the revelation in Christ, and Christ must be seen in the light of all Scripture. You may have had the experience of joining a circle of people engaged in a spirited conversation which makes absolutely no sense to you as a late-comer until someone mentions a key word. This key word suddenly makes the subject of the conversation clear, and the remarks which seemed contradictory and nonsensical fall into a sensible pattern. Similarly, Christ is the key to all of Scripture.

The story of the deciphering of the hieroglyphics also illustrates the significance of Christ for the understanding of Scripture. These hieroglyphics made sense for many centuries—but not to us. We could not make any sense out of them until the Rosetta stone was discovered, which contained an inscription in both Greek and hieroglyphics. What had been utterly incomprehensible suddenly became clear with the help of this key.

This is the sense in which Christ is the key to the Scriptures. Without Him this Holy History and the literature which reports it is merely history and poetry. With Him this same history gives sense to all life and all history.

At the same time, Christ must be seen in the light of all Scripture. Just as a conversation becomes clearer to the listener when

[19] Martin Luther, "Introduction to the Old Testament, 1545," *Works of Martin Luther,* Philadelphia ed., VI, 368.

he knows what subject is being discussed, so the subject becomes clearer as the conversation throws light upon it. Similarly, the other hieroglyphic inscriptions that have been solved through the Rosetta stone, in turn, throw some light upon the particular inscription which became the key to solving the mystery of the hieroglyphics. In the same way, while all Scripture must be understood in the light of the revelation in Christ, so must Christ be seen at the same time in the light of all Scripture. Preserving this double relationship is one of the concerns of the Protestant Faith.

One problem in regard to Scripture which separates Protestants from other Christians is the canon of Scriptures. Canon is a Greek word meaning literally "rule" or "measuring rod." Which books constitute the Holy Scriptures? Protestants assert with the Articles of Religion of the Anglican Communion, "In the name of Holy Scripture we do understand those canonical books of the Old and New Testament, *of whose authority was never any doubt in the Church."* These are the twenty-seven books of the New Testament, on which all Christians agree, and the thirty-nine books of the Old Testament, which are also accepted as the Bible of the Jewish religion. The Roman Catholic Church accepts in addition certain other Hebrew writings as "canonical" although they are not so accepted by the Jews nor were they accepted as canonical by the ancient church. For Protestants these books are not acceptable because by definition canonical books are those "of whose authority was never any doubt in the Church." These Hebrew writings were not included in the Jewish canon, and they are not quoted in the New Testament. In the famous passage where Jesus refers to the witness of the Old Testament, these noncanonical books are conspicuous by their absence:

> *Then he said to them, "These are my words which I spoke to you, while I was still with you, that everything written about me in the law of Moses and the prophets and the psalms must be fulfilled." (Luke 24:44)*

The early church apparently did not accept these noncanonical books. One of the greatest scholars of this period, Jerome, who was the author of the Vulgate, a translation of the Bible into Latin, writes of the apocryphal books of the Old Testament:

> As, then, the Church reads Judith, Tobit, and the books of Maccabees, but does not admit them among the canonical Scriptures, so let it read these two volumes [Wisdom of Solomon and Ecclesiasticus] for the edification of the people, not to give authority to the doctrines of the Church.[20]

This canon of Scripture, that is, these sixty-six books, is normative for the proclamation of the Protestant Faith. All Protestant teaching and preaching are supposed to be in conformity with the witness of these books. The famous *Westminster Confession of Faith* of 1647 puts it thus:

> The authority of the Holy Scripture . . . dependeth not on the testimony of any man or Church; but wholly upon God (who is truth itself) the author thereof. . . . Our full persuasion and assurance of the infallible truth and divine authority thereof is from the inward work of the Holy Spirit, bearing witness, by and with the Word, in our hearts. . . . Nothing is at any time to be added—whether by new revelation of the Spirit or traditions of men. . . . The Church is finally to appeal to them. . . . The infallible rule of interpretation of Scripture is Scripture itself.[21]

Though this is a Presbyterian statement, it expresses the consent of classical Protestantism concerning the normative character of the canonical writings of the Old and New Testament.

The reason for this authority of Holy Scripture is that these books contain the record of the original witness to the Christ event. They tell what God did to reveal Himself to men. They are the record of revelation.

At this point these questions arise: Was there any disagreement

[20] *Nicene and Post-Nicene Fathers,* ed. Philip Schaff and Others, Second Series (Grand Rapids, Mich.: William B. Eerdmans Publishing Co., 1954), VI, 492.

[21] Bettenson, *Documents,* p. 347.

about the canon in the early church? Did Christianity know immediately which books were definitive and which were not? If they, in fact, eliminated some books as unfit for Scripture, were not, then, these church authorities who decided on the canon superior to Scripture? To these questions Protestantism, with common consent, answers *no!*

A study of the discussion of the canon will show that the leaders of the Church never claimed to have the power to declare something Scripture. All they tried to do was to select the apostolic writings. The early church very clearly placed itself beneath the authority of the teaching of the Apostles. The books which they rejected were rejected because they were clearly not apostolic. The early church recognized the standard of the apostolic witness: that which was apostolic witness was retained, and that which was not apostolic witness was rejected. They used no personal or subjective criteria. Such arbitrary selection was the procedure of heretics such as Marcion who selected certain books he liked and dropped from his Bible others he did not like. This procedure forced the Christian Church to define the canon. Marcion, a gifted amateur theologian, did exactly what the early church did not do; he acted as if his church had the right to pick and choose from Scripture and to accept certain books and reject others. The Gnostic heretics were willing to produce spurious gospels and epistles to spread their particular religious convictions. The early church rejected these "pseudepigrapha" not because the Gnostics liked them but rather because they were sure that these documents were in fact not written by the apostles to whom they had been attributed. There were other parts of the New Testament which notorious heretics like Marcion liked very much—but the Church retained them because they were considered clearly apostolic.

For the early church and for the Protestant Faith the testimony of Scriptures was authoritative and decisive. The teaching of the Church had to be substantiated from the witness of the Apostles to the Christ event. Other doctrines might seem attractive and useful but if they were not scriptural they were rejected. This is the authority of Scripture for classical Protestantism and for those Protestants today who remain in the stream of classical Protestantism. It is this position on the normative authority of Scripture which makes it impossible for Protestants to accept doctrines concerning the Bishop of Rome or the Virgin Mary which other Christians accept on the basis of the proclamation of church officials.

THE OLD AND NEW TESTAMENTS. As we have indicated, the Bible is divided into two parts, the Old Testament and the New Testament. A question arises as to the relationship of the two parts: Can both be called "the Bible" in the same sense, or is the New Testament more truly the Bible than the Old?

For classical Protestantism, the Old and the New Testaments have equal status; both are God's word to Christians, and both bear witness to Christ. They are part of the same Holy History, both telling of the events through which God has entered history in order to save man. The difference is that the Old Testament testifies to a Messiah who is to come, while the New Testament tells of the Jesus Christ who came. For the Christian Church and for classical Protestantism they are equally Christian books. Of course, it is quite possible to read the Old Testament as Jewish history or as Near Eastern literature—and if one does this it is not likely that one will come to the conclusion that it is a Christian book. But this is not the way the people of the New Testament read the Bible or the way in which the Christian Church, in all its branches, has read the Bible through the last two thousand years. For Christians in general and for Protestants in particular, the Old Testament is a book which points to Jesus Christ. It is read because it testifies of Christ and it explains the life and work of Christ.

An illustration may help to show what this means. If a young man receives a letter from his girl friend telling him that she is very much in love with him and agrees to marry him, this is a document which will change his life, because he is the person about whom it speaks. Now, it is quite possible that an English professor might find this document and discover many grammatical errors, poor spelling, and ambiguous expressions. This is a perfectly valid way to look at the letter, for it is a document in the English language besides being the document that will change the young man's life. But everybody will forgive him if he tells the good professor that he cares little about the spelling—the letter tells him that she loves him and that is all he is interested in. Or if this letter is written from Europe during a political crisis, it may contain interesting political and historical information which might make it a worth-while subject for the study of a historian. But, again, this is not the way the young man is going to read the letter.

Protestants will readily admit that the Bible is Hebrew and Greek literature and that it contains important historical and political data. They have no objection to people who study it from this or that point of view. But it is the Bible for them because God speaks to them person-to-person about those things that matter ultimately. It tells them the source, the purpose, and the goal of human existence. It is God's Word for them. And this is true of both the Old and the New Testaments. When the New Testament and Jesus speak of the Bible they always refer to the Old Testament. It is the Old Testament which is the Bible of apostolic times. The Reformers quoted and interpreted the Old Testament as often as the New. Luther, for example, considered Genesis, the first book in the Old Testament, and the Book of Psalms among his personal favorites in the entire Bible. For classical Protestantism the Old Testament and the New Testament are equally the Word of God. They both tell the Holy History, the story of God's intervention in history for the salvation of mankind.

A second question which might arise in regard to the relationship of the Old and the New Testaments deals with the specific content of these two main parts of the Bible. If part of the message of God to man is what man should do (often called the Law), and another part is what God has done for men (often called the Gospel), some might think that the Old Testament contains only Law and the New Testament only Gospel. As far as classical Protestantism is concerned, both the Old and New Testaments contain Law *and* Gospel. It is not only the Old Testament which tells us what God wants from man. The New Testament too reveals God's demands. The Ten Commandments in the Old Testament find their counterpart in the catalogues of vices to be avoided which we find in the epistles of the Apostle Paul. Both Old and New Testaments proclaim God's Law.

Similarly it is not only the New Testament which tells us the Gospel. Nowhere in the entire Bible is what God has done for men stated more beautifully than in the passage concerning the Suffering Servant in the fifty-third chapter of the Prophet Isaiah. And the twenty-third Psalm describes movingly what God has done, is doing, and will do for men.

Thus, as far as classical Protestantism is concerned, the Old Testament is not merely the history of some ancient Near Eastern tribe. It is not merely beautiful and primitive poetry. It is the revelation of God's will for men. It tells men what they should do— and at the same time tells them what God has done and is willing to do for them.

The contemporary neglect of the Old Testament in the preaching and the worship of so many Protestants only illustrates how far much of twentieth-century Protestantism has deviated from the classical Protestant Faith. If modern Protestants say that they cannot do anything with the Old Testament, that it does not mean anything to them, it only shows that they are really no longer within the main stream of Protestantism. It cannot be overemphasized that for classical Protestantism, *Old and New* Testaments are God's Word.

Thirdly, the center of the Old as well as of the New Testament is the Cross of Christ. To understand anything properly in the Old Testament or in the New Testament, it must be seen in its relationship to the Cross of Christ. A certain balance exists between the message of the Old and of the New Testaments. In the phrase of St. Augustine: "In the Old Testament the New lies hid; in the New Testament the meaning of the Old becomes clear." The method used to connect the two "testaments" is commonly called "typology." It has been defined "as the establishment of historical connexions between certain events, persons or things in the Old Testament and similar events, persons or things in the New Testament."[22]

The story of the Tower of Babel may serve as an illustration (Genesis 11:1-9). The parallel to this story in the New Testament is the story of Pentecost (Acts 2:1-13). For the Protestant Faith, these two stories complement and interpret each other and the Cross is the center of both. The story of the Tower of Babel tells how man's disobedience and alienation from God ended in the disruption of human society and the inability of men to understand each other. It told that if man is separated from God, in revolt against God, he is also separated from his neighbor and at odds with his neighbor. Peace among men and understanding among men depends upon their relationship to God. But while the Old Testament tells this story negatively, describing the misunderstanding and disruption caused by disobedience and revolt against God, the New Testament tells of the other side of the same problem. In the story of Pentecost we learn that people who came from different nationalities, people whose languages differed so that they could not understand each other, learned to understand each other through the power of the Holy Spirit. Once they were united with God, the disruption of the Tower of Babel was reversed. Languages no longer separated the crowd that was present at Pentecost. They could all understand the Apostle's preaching. They each felt themselves addressed in their own tongues, in their own languages.

The eternal message which Protestants gain from the Old and the New Testaments states that human understanding and peace among men depend upon peace with God. It states that men in revolt against God will also be at war with each other. It asserts that the tension and the strife that embitter the life of men on this earth, the misunderstanding and the hatred that disrupt all human

---

[22] G. W. H. Lampe and W. J. Woolcombe, *Essays on Typology* (Naperville, Ill.: Alec. R. Allenson, Inc., 1957), p. 39.

community, are the result of man's estrangement from God. Old Testament and New Testament looked at from the Cross proclaim that at the root of man's difficulty lies the fact that man is at odds with God. All his other difficulties are the result of this main and basic difficulty.

Similar illustrations could be multiplied. One of the most profound investigations of the nature of faith was written by the Danish philosopher Søren Kierkegaard. The story he uses to interpret the meaning of the Christian Faith is the Old Testament story of Abraham and Isaac. He retells the tale of the father who has one son upon whom all his hope for the future rests. And he tells about the decision that this father makes to kill the son, to sacrifice him upon the commandment of God. Kierkegaard does not gloss over this part of the story; he does not try to destroy its seriousness by jumping immediately to the happy end. Rather, he takes the Old Testament absolutely seriously. In doing so he tells us more about the meaning of the Christian Faith than most other writers in the last hundred years.[23]

What every Christian interpretation of the relationship of the Old and the New Testaments has in common is the effort to understand both through their center and key, the Cross of Christ. To the Protestant Faith, Christ is the clue to the Bible.

It is important to add here that the Old and the New Testaments cannot be understood apart from each other as far as the Christian Faith is concerned; they are complementary to each other. Disregarding either will falsify both. Protestants would say that much of the misrepresentation of Christianity in our time and in times past is the result of the neglect of some part of the biblical message. Whenever the Church has ignored social justice and acted as if the plight of the downtrodden were none of its business, the Old Testament prophets have reminded Christians that zeal for justice is part of the Christian life. Rationalism and Puritanism, Pietism and Orthodoxy—every theological movement and every

[23] Soren Kierkegaard, *Fear and Trembling,* trans. Walter Lowrie (Princeton, N.J.: Princeton University Press, 1954).

religious fad has been subjected to close investigation with the help of the Old and New Testaments. It is the message of the Old and New Testaments which has upheld the Protestant Faith through the ages, in spite of the deviations and conflicts which are freedom's price.

We are now ready to look a little more closely at the content of the Christian Faith as proclaimed by Protestantism. The first subject which comes up for discussion is the reality of God.

3

The Reality of God

As has been shown previously, the reality of God is not a proposition deduced by our reason, but rather an experience which confronts us everywhere. We experience ourselves as creatures in a universe which we share with other creatures and which is not of our making. We have a beginning—we all know and can even give the exact date of our birth—and we will have an end at a certain day in a certain year. But neither the beginning nor the end is in our power. Our whole life is not in our power at all; it is created and it is dependent. We are dependent upon many factors, from a very small temperature range to the make-up of the atmosphere. If the earth were only a hundred degrees hotter, no human life could exist. Take away the oxygen in our air and our fate is sealed. There are innumerable factors over which we have no control but upon which we depend. And the generation before us who knew little about the factors knew nevertheless that they depended upon the sun and the rain, upon the seasons following each other and upon innumerable other "facts" completely outside their sphere of influence. Man is also limited in many ways. We are limited in space, for we can be only in one place at one time; we are limited in time, and the older we get, the more obvious this fact becomes. But all these limitations only accentuate the assertion of the Christian Faith that *God is power*.

GOD'S NATURE

The theologians of the Christian Church have frequently discussed this assertion in very technical ways. They have discussed the power of God abstractly, apart from His revelation. This seems to be fruitless and can only lead to all sorts of self-contradictions. One of the great arguments of the Middle Ages revolved around the nature of this divine power—is it in any way limited, even by His goodness? If it is limited by His goodness, is it still absolute? In other words, if God cannot do that which is evil, is He still absolute power? Sometimes these discussions degenerated into pure speculation. In how far is God dependent upon the laws of logic? Can He make a four-cornered triangle? Can He make a rock so heavy that He cannot lift it?

All this abstract speculation about the power of God is meaningless and irrelevant to the Protestant Faith, for God is not abstract power, nor theoretical power, but power in relation to our weakness, infinity in relation to our limitations, freedom in relation to our bondage. God is holy and personal power as He confronts us in His creation.

This means that in classical Protestantism there is no room for the assertion of a limited God as He is sometimes posited by modern philosophers, a god who is limited by evil or matter or whatever else it might be. The Protestant Faith asserts: *With God all things are possible (Matthew 19:26)*; and *The things which are impossible with men are possible with God (Luke 18:27)*. The God who confronts the Christian in revelation is a God of power.

Furthermore, the reality of God confronts us in all our intellectual efforts. We are confronted by truth and meaning. And we make often-desperate efforts to be coherent, to be meaningful, and to be truthful. We want to convey what we believe, and the more profoundly we believe it, the more difficult it becomes to convey it. With the help of a meaningful statement it is fairly easy to convey the fact that a dog has four legs. This kind of statement is easily understood. But when we talk about justice and beauty, about the things that really matter to us and to all men, and when we talk about peace and democracy, it becomes very difficult to convey meaning. This is the lesson which political orators teach us in their drab routines. This is also the lesson which our own efforts to search for truth teach us; truth is elusive, and just when we think we have it captured, it has escaped us. It is in this very experience of the limitations of our own spirituality that we are confronted by the *God who is spirit*.

As the Bible teaches in many places: *No one hath seen God at any time. (John 1:18) Dwelling in the light which no man can approach unto; whom no man hath seen or can see. (I Timothy 6:16)* God is spirit, and all efforts on the part of man to reach ultimate truth shatter before this fact. This is the end of all religious rationalism which believes that God can be contained in some clever theological formula. The God who is Spirit cannot become a specimen in our collection of solved problems. His very spirituality sheds light upon our lack of it. And the assertion of the Protestant Faith that God is spirit should guard Protestants against vain efforts to identify their own puny accomplishments with ultimate and absolute truth.

The reality of God confronts us further in our experience of a given structure to which we must conform. Our will is never entirely free; we are confronted and surrounded by another will. This shows the reality of *God who is will*. To many non-Christian philosophers, absolute power and will appeared self-contradictory. Christians believe that God has a purpose which He is carrying out. What happens is not the result of some immutable law but rather of the personal will of God. Again, one can easily become involved in extended and sophistic argumentation about this divine will in the abstract. But the Protestant Faith asserts that we do not confront God's will in the abstract, but rather as the will to create, the will to preserve, and the will to redeem man.

This will is holy. This is the only attribute which does it justice. The holiness of God is more than moral perfection; it describes the fact that God is God and man is man. It expresses the essential difference between God and man. Man can be more or less clever, he can be more or less good, he can be more or less religious—but only God is holy. And when the Protestant Faith speaks of God as power and God as spirit and God as will, we must always keep in mind that all these assertions are made against the background of the holiness of God. As Gustaf Aulén has put it:

> Holiness stands as a sentinel against all eudaimonistic and anthropocentric interpretations of religion. Holiness meets us as unconditional majesty. . . . To meet God as the Holy One is to be placed under a supreme compulsion, and to be confronted by a power advancing in sovereign majesty. If God is the Holy One, He is also the One on whom we are absolutely dependent. We are in His power, not He in ours.[24]

It is against this background that the Protestant Faith asserts God as power, God as spirit, God as will!

The question arises: How can man be related to this holy God? Does God's holiness remove Him completely from the reach of our experience? Or do we have access to this holy God when we contemplate quietly the very source of our being? Theologians have stated this problem by asking whether God is transcendent or immanent. The dictionary defines transcendent in this way: "Of God, being prior to and exalted above the universe, and having

24 Gustaf Aulén, *The Faith of the Christian Church* (Philadelphia: Muhlenberg Press, 1948), pp. 123-24.

being apart from it." The Protestant Faith asserts that the God who confronts us as reality is indeed *transcendent*. The attributes with which He is described are expressions of this transcendence. When He is called *omnipotent*, or almighty, this is an expression for His transcendent power. He can do everything He wants to do. He is called *omnipresent*, or present everywhere at once, because there is no place where God is not present; there is no escape from Him in space. He is called *eternal*, or everlasting. There was no time when God was not and there will never be a time when God will not be. And He is called *omniscient*, or infinitely wise, knowing all things. All these are, of course, mere human attempts to describe, however inadequately, the vastness of God. These words must not be thought of as adjectives which describe God as an "object." They are the language of worship and adoration, rather than the detailed attributes of somebody we can understand and comprehend. As Calvin has put it:

> The majesty of God in itself goes beyond the capacity of human understanding and cannot be comprehended by it, *we must adore its loftiness rather than investigate it*, so that we do not remain overwhelmed by so great a splendor.[25]

The Protestant Faith is suspicious of all efforts to reduce God to the major premise in a syllogism. The Reformers' criticism of the grandiose theological systems that were taught by the Church in the Middle Ages was based upon their suspicion that in these systems God had been reduced to a mere object in the theological enterprise. Protestant Christians do not deny the validity of these theological descriptions which scrutinize the "attributes" of God. They do feel that this approach is presumptuous. They prefer to approach the description of God in the context of worship and adoration. Protestant hymnody is the best expression of this approach. For classical Protestantism the following hymn speaks

[25] From *Instruction in Faith* by John Calvin, translated by Paul T. Fuhrmann, 1949. Copyright, 1949, by W. L. Jenkins, The Westminster Press. Used by permission.

more adequately of God's almighty power than any logical analysis:

> Praise to the Lord, the Almighty, the King of creation!
> O my soul, praise Him, for He is thy health and salvation!
> All ye who hear, Now to His temple draw near;
> Praise Him in glad adoration.
> Praise to the Lord! Who o'er all things so wondrously reigneth,
> Shelters thee under His wings, yea, so gently sustaineth;
> Hast thou not seen How thy desires e'er have been
> Granted in what He ordaineth?
> Praise to the Lord! O let all that is in me adore Him!
> All that hath life and breath, come now with praises before Him!
> Let the Amen sound from His people again;
> Gladly for aye we adore Him.   (Joachim Neander, 1650–1680)

This difference is further illustrated if we examine the brilliant analysis of God's power in Thomas Aquinas' *Summa Theologica* in the discussion "Whether God can make the past not to have been?" He proceeds by stating the reasons for holding this view. Then he states his own view as follows:

> I answer that, as was said above, nothing that implies a contradiction falls under the scope of God's omnipotence. Now that the past should not have been implies a contradiction. For just as it implies a contradiction to say that Socrates is sitting and not sitting, so does it to say that he sat and did not sit. But to say that he did sit is to say that it happened in the past. To say that he did not sit is to say that it did not happen. Whence, that the past should not have been, does not come under the scope of divine power. This is what Augustine means when he says: Whosoever says if God is almighty, let Him make what is done as if it were not done, does not see that this is to say: If God is almighty let Him effect that what is true, by the very fact that it is true, be false. And the Philosopher says: Of this one thing alone is God deprived—namely, to make undone the things that have been done.[26]

This is certainly a very logical argument. Indeed, it is committed to the absolute validity of the logical law of Aristotle:

[26] From *Basic Writings of Saint Thomas Aquinas,* edited and annotated by Anton C. Pegis. Copyright 1945 by Random House, Inc. Reprinted by permission.

Whatever is, is; nothing can both be and not be; and everything must either be or not be. These laws are known respectively as the Law of Identity, the Law of Contradiction, and the Law of the Excluded Middle. In scholastic theology's approach to God these laws play a most important part.

Now let us look at a typical Protestant reaction to this entire philosophical approach to God. Luther says:

> We must speak in one way concerning God, as the will of God insofar as that will is proclaimed to us, revealed, offered to our acceptance, made the ground of worship; and in another wise, concerning God, insofar as he is unproclaimed, unrevealed, unoffered, and unworshipped. So far as God hides himself and chooses to be unknown by us, we have nothing to do with him. Here is the true application of that saying, "What is above us, is nothing to us." And lest anyone should suppose this to be my distinction, let him know that I follow Paul, who writes to the Thessalonians concerning Antichrist (II Thess. 2:4) "That he would exalt himself above all that is proclaimed of God, and that is worshipped," plainly indicating that a man may exalt himself above God so far as he is proclaimed, and worshipped; that is, above that word and worship by which God is made known to us, and maintains intercourse with us. But the God who is not worshipped nor proclaimed, but as he is in his own nature and majesty, nothing can exalt itself above him, but everything is under his powerful hand.
>
> Thus God must be left unexplored as far as his majesty and nature is concerned. In this regard, he has not willed to be dealt with by us. But only so far as he is clothed with his word and displayed to us thereby. This is the word, by which he has offered himself to our acceptance; the word, which is his glory and beauty, and with which the Psalmist celebrates him as clothed. Here only do we deal with him.[27]

These two quotations, the one abounding in philosophical reflection and references to the logic of Aristotle, the other stressing the sovereign grace with which God has revealed Himself in His Word, illustrate the peculiar difference between the Protestant

[27] *Weimar Ausgabe,* XVIII, 684 f.

Faith and other Christian positions in regard to the mystery of God's power. If we want to understand the transcendence of God as this notion occurs in the Protestant Faith, it will be well for us to understand it as an expression of adoration and prayer rather than logical analysis or objective description. As the great Calvinist hymn writer Gerhard Tersteegen said, "A God comprehended is no God." But the Protestant Faith does assert that God is transcendent, that is, prior to and exalted above the universe!

However—and here again the complementary character of all human assertions about God must be stressed—the God who confronts us as transcendent reality is at the same time *immanent*. The omnipotence of God is not merely an experiment in abstract thought. Rather, the God who is our Father in Jesus Christ is the Almighty. Protestant Christians do not only assert that there is an Almighty God—as one might assert that there is a Pacific Ocean —they assert that they have an Almighty Savior. The Almighty, Omnipresent, Eternal, Omniscient God is closer to the Christian than the Christian is to himself. Perhaps Luther's explanation of the First Article of the Apostles' Creed will help to illustrate the Protestant concept of God's immanence, the fact that He is closer to us than we are to ourselves.

The Creed says: "I believe in God the Father Almighty, Maker of heaven and earth." Luther explains this statement in the following words:

> I believe that God has created me and all that exists; that He has given and still preserves to me my body and soul, my eyes and ears, and all my members, my reason and all the powers of my soul, together with food and raiment, home and family, and all my property; that He daily provides abundantly for all the needs of my life, protects me from all danger, and guards and keeps me from all evil; and that He does this purely out of fatherly and divine goodness and mercy, without any merit or worthiness in me; for all which I am in duty bound to thank, praise, serve and obey Him. This is most certainly true.[28]

[28] *Book of Concord*, I, 366.

Here we see how a statement which could be understood as a fairly abstract statement about God becomes a profoundly personal expression of God's deeds for *me,* not only for man in the abstract but for the specific man who is making this confession. For the Protestant Faith even those terms which express God's majesty and power in the most overwhelming manner are related person to person. It is this overwhelming God who is always close to me. It is this Almighty God without whose knowledge not one hair falls from my head.

This simultaneous emphasis upon God's transcendence and immanence makes it unnecessary for the Protestant Faith to interpose mediators between God and man. There is no need for the Protestant to implore the intercession of other human beings living or dead in order to approach God. He believes that each believer can personally and at all times approach God directly. He will say, "The Almighty God is closer to me than I am to my best friend, my mother or my father; He is closer to me than I am to myself."

This brings us immediately to another significant assertion of the Protestant Faith, namely, the assertion that *God is person.* In the theological discussion of the last one hundred years a great deal has been said about this "personality" of God. The term is dangerous, if we assume that it means that God's personality is the same as any human personality. The great nineteenth-century theologian Friedrich Schleiermacher objected to the use of the term "person" because it seemed to him that it idolized and deified human self-consciousness. If Protestants by and large nevertheless retain the definition of God as person, the reason is that it explains many things which otherwise would be beyond comprehension. Though the word "person" as applied to God does not occur in the New Testament, many personal terms are applied to Him. In the Old Testament He is always addressed as Lord; the New Testament speaks of Him as Father. And when we think of the Twenty-third Psalm, we realize immediately that the word "person" is the most adequate expression of the fact that God is an

"I" who has become a "Thou" for us, that He is a "Thou" to our "I," in other words, that our relationship is an "interpersonal" relationship.

The assertion that God is a person guards us against a pantheistic understanding of God. A pantheist believes that God is the universal substance, that He is everything that is, that He is Nature or the underlying "stuff" that makes up everything that is. This position asserts that man as well as the universe is only one of God's expressions, one of God's appearances. This mystical pantheism is rejected by the assertion of the Protestant Faith that God is person who confronts us as a person.

At the same time this assertion guards us against all polytheistic notions that there are many gods. There is not one god in charge of the ocean, another in charge of fire, and other gods and goddesses, who fill the heavens. The assertion that God is person excludes all forms of polytheism, which denies that there is a Supreme Being.

God is person, He is Thou, He addresses us with His Word. We encounter Him person to person.

However, this does not mean that the word "person" is adequate to define the "form" of God. It does tell how He meets us, but it does not describe His appearance nor does it enable us to analyze His consciousness. The use of the term "person" must at all times be guarded against an attempt to confine God in some anthropomorphic shell. There is no room in a mature Protestant Faith for a God who looks and acts like a super–Santa Claus. The picture of God as a bearded sage sitting on a golden throne only confuses our understanding of the meaning of the assertion that God is the Absolute Person who meets us personally.

Here again we must pause to remind ourselves that the truth about God as the Protestant Faith sees it is expressed in complementary statements. The Protestant Faith asserts that God is the absolute ground of all being. Everything that is has its source in God. Yet at the same time He is the Lord of History, the personal spirit who is executing His plan.

This means that the Protestant Faith attempts to avoid a one-sided emphasis upon the omnipotence of God, which takes away the meaning of history and human decision and ends in fatalism. This possibility confronts us in the moment when we concentrate exclusively on God's power. History then becomes merely a performance that is played with prearranged parts. We are not even actors but puppets, who are pulled by invisible strings and whose lines are spoken by the director, who is a master ventriloquist and puts the words he wants us to say into our mouths.

The neglect of the complementarity of our speech about God may lead to an undue stress upon the omnipotence of God and thus to a complete neglect of the significance of human decision. This would deny the meaning of time as the accepted time and as the time for decision. Such fatalism is not entirely uncommon in our age. There are many people today who feel that whatever must happen will happen and who fatalistically and passively suffer their life rather than live it and "redeem the times" (Colossians 4:5). One is reminded of the two soldiers who were discussing their chances of survival in the coming battle. The one said quite fatalistically, "Well, I don't worry except for that one bullet that has my name on it." His buddy replied, "I don't worry about the bullet with my name on it, but I do worry about the bullet that says: 'To whom it may concern.'"

At the same time it is equally important to avoid one-sided emphasis upon the importance of historical decisions to the exclusion of the absoluteness of God. There are many Christians who have reduced God to a spectator or at best a referee in the game of life. In modern Protestantism the importance of human action has been so exclusively emphasized that the future of mankind—indeed, the future of the universe—is conceived to be in the hands of men. What we do today, our historical decisions, are alleged to determine the outcome of God's plan. This idea has frequently been expressed in terms of "bringing in the kingdom of God," as if man had it in his power to bring in God's kingdom or to prevent the arrival of God's realm. Here God is at best the coach on the "good" side. He can send in some plays, but their execution is up to men. And the game will be lost for the coach unless we play better.

This position assumes a very limited God, a God who is no longer the Lord of Lords and the King of Kings. Forgotten is the New Testament assertion that God can raise up children to Abraham out of stones (Matthew 3:9). He can accomplish His ends with us or against us, but His ends will be accomplished.

It is highly questionable that such sentiments as "God has no other hands but mine," or words to that effect, are in tune with the complete trust in the power of God which has characterized the classical Protestant Faith. It may be a good way to raise money for churches and other worthy causes to claim tearfully that God is lost unless we step in to act as His hands. However, it is dubious Protestant theology. According to the Protestant Faith *we* may very well be lost unless we step in and serve God and the neighbor —but God is not lost without us. The Protestant Faith asserts that while man is lost without God, God is not lost without man. His eternal counsels will ultimately prevail, with us or without us.

Here again it is of the utmost importance to maintain both sides of the dialectic. The Protestant Faith rejects at the same time a fatalism which reduces men to puppets and a concept of a limited God which reduces God to a spectator.

LAW AND GOSPEL

The God whose reality we have attempted to describe within the frame of reference of the Protestant Faith confronts man through two basic means. They are the Law and the Gospel. A clear distinction between these two basic means which God uses to deal with men is essential for an understanding of the Protestant Faith. Yet there are few Protestants who can actually tell the difference between these two terms. What do these words mean?

The Law is God's "thou shalt!" or "thou shalt not!" It represents God's justified demands upon man. The Ten Commandments are Law. We are confronted by Law when we read:

I am the Lord your God, who brought you out of the land of Egypt, out of the house of bondage.

You shall have no other gods before me.

You shall not make for yourself a graven image, or any likeness of anything that is in heaven above, or that is on the earth beneath, or that is in the water under the earth; you shall not bow down to them or serve them; for I the Lord your God am a jealous God, visiting the iniquity of the fathers upon the children to the third and fourth generation of those who hate me, but showing steadfast love to thousands of those who love me and keep my commandments.

You shall not take the name of the Lord your God in vain: for the Lord will not hold him guiltless who takes his name in vain.

Observe the sabbath day, to keep it holy, as the Lord your God commanded you. Six days you shall labor, and do all your work; but the seventh day is a sabbath to the Lord your God; in it you shall not do any work, you, or your son, or your daughter, or your manservant, or your maidservant, or your ox, or your ass, or any of your cattle, or the sojourner who is within your gates, that your manservant and your maidservant may rest as well as you. You shall remember that you were a servant in the land of Egypt, and the Lord your God brought you out thence with a mighty hand and an outstretched arm; therefore the Lord your God commanded you to keep the sabbath day.

Honor your father and your mother, as the Lord your God commanded you; that your days may be prolonged, and that it may go well with you, in the land which the Lord your God gives you.

You shall not kill.

Neither shall you commit adultery.

Neither shall you steal.

Neither shall you bear false witness against your neighbor.

Neither shall you covet your neighbor's wife; and you shall not desire your neighbor's house, his field, or his manservant, or his maidservant, his ox, or his ass, or anything that is your neighbor's.

These words the Lord spoke to all your assembly at the mountain out of the midst of the fire, the cloud, and the deep gloom, with a loud voice; and he added no more. (Deuteronomy 5:6 ff.)

Most people would agree that this is Law. Now let us look at another quotation from the Bible; is this also Law?

You have heard that it was said to the men of old, "You shall not kill; and whoever kills shall be liable to judgment." But I say to you that every one who is angry with his brother shall be liable to judgment; whoever insults his brother shall be liable to the council, and whoever says, "You fool!" shall be liable to the hell of fire. So if you are offering your gift at the altar, and there remember that your brother has something against you, leave your gift there before the altar and go; first be reconciled to your brother, and then come and offer your gift. Make friends quickly with your accuser, while you are going with him to court, lest your accuser hand you over to the judge, and the judge to the guard, and you be put in prison; truly, I say to you, you will never get out till you have paid the last penny. You have heard that it was said, "You shall not commit adultery." But I say to you that every one who looks at a woman lustfully has already committed adultery with her in his heart. (Matthew 5:21–27)

These verses are part of the famous Sermon on the Mount. They are clearly Law, for they too tell us of God's demands upon us.

The Old Testament and the New Testament abound in such

passages of Law. According to the Protestant Faith these passages tell man what the righteous demands of God are. But the same God who confronts man in the Law confronts him also in the Gospel. The word Gospel is a literal translation of the Greek word *euaggelion* which means "good news." The nature of this Good News is probably best summarized in the famous passage which most Protestant children memorize in Sunday school: *For God so loved the world, that he gave his only Son, that whoever believes in him should not perish, but have eternal life (John 3:16).* The Gospel is the Good News of what God has done for man and is willing to do for every individual. This Gospel is found already in the Old Testament. For classical Protestantism, Isaiah 53, for example, describes what God will do for all men in Jesus Christ:

Who has believed what we have heard? And to whom has the arm of the Lord been revealed? For he grew up before him like a young plant, and like a root out of dry ground; he had no form or comeliness that we should look at him, and no beauty that we should desire him. He was despised and rejected by men; a man of sorrows, and acquainted with grief; and as one from whom men hide their faces he was despised, and we esteemed him not. Surely he has borne our griefs and carried our sorrows; yet we esteemed him stricken, smitten by God, and afflicted. But he was wounded for our transgressions, he was bruised for our iniquities; upon him was the chastisement that made us whole, and with his stripes we are healed. All we like sheep have gone astray; we have turned every one to his own way; and the Lord has laid on him the iniquity of us all. He was oppressed, and he was afflicted, yet he opened not his mouth; like a lamb that is led to the slaughter, and like a sheep that before its shearers is dumb, so he opened not his mouth. By oppression and judgment he was taken away; and as for his generation, who considered that he was cut off out of the land of the

living, stricken for the transgression of my people?
(Isaiah 53:1–8)

Whatever this passage may mean to others, to classical Protestantism it represents the Gospel, that is, the Good News of what God has done for men in Jesus Christ, in its absolute purity—even though it is found in the Old Testament.

But granted that God confronts man in Law and Gospel, what is the specific purpose of the Law? Essentially the Law has two functions which theologians have sometimes called the political use of the Law and the theological use of the Law.

The *political use of the Law* describes that function of the Law which contributes to civil righteousness. Because there is law and order people act a great deal better than they would otherwise act. This is the same sort of reasoning that we find in many political philosophers, for example, in Thomas Hobbes. He asserted that without authority and law there would be a universal war of all against all. Hobbes described this situation very colorfully in the following words:

> In such condition there is no place for Industry; because the fruit therof is uncertain: and consequently no Culture of the Earth, no Navigation, nor use of the commodities that may be imported by Sea; no commodious Building; no Instruments of moving, and removing such things as require much force; no Knowledge of the face of the Earth; no account of Time; no Arts; no Letters; no Society; and which is worst of all, continual fear, and danger of violent death; And the life of man, solitary, poor, nasty, brutish, and short.[29]

Though the Protestant Faith does not claim that there ever was a time like this, but rather asserts that mankind has always been confronted by the Law, this Law in its political use prevents the collapse of culture. The relative justice which obtains in this world,

[29] From Thomas Hobbes, *Leviathan* (New York: E. P. Dutton & Co., Inc., Everyman's Library).

fragmentary and imperfect as it may be, is the result of the political use of the Law.

The Law in this political use affects all men. One does not have to be a Christian in order to use or benefit from the Law in its political use. All men are subject to it, all men do in fact benefit by it, and all men are to some degree aware of it. It may be regrettable, but it is unfortunately true that for many persons the only reason for socially acceptable behavior is the fear of punishment. This does not mean necessarily that they are afraid to go to jail—but they are afraid to lose face. The Law in its political use is designed to prevent the complete collapse of justice and equity among men by subjecting them to quite obvious pressures in the direction of order.

In this form the Law is extremely useful not only in order to maintain some sort of national civilization. It is of the greatest importance also for all international understanding. It is because there is law among all people that the terms good and bad make sense across national and religious boundaries. Organizations such as the United Nations depend for their success very largely on what Protestant theologians would call the political use of the Law.

It is also interesting and noteworthy that people who are estranged from Christianity or have never even heard of it may be expert in the political use of the Law. Luther, for example, never tired of pointing out the political superiority of the Turkish Empire, which was, of course, a Moslem empire. In many ways, he asserted, the Turkish Empire was governed far better than the German Empire. He also cited with approval the civil righteousness of Roman statesmen who had lived in pre-Christian times and who were pagans, but nevertheless men of justice.

It is not too difficult to see this political use of the Law in operation, for example, on the campus of a great modern university. All kinds of religious and irreligious, philosophical and antiphilosophical ideas may be current. The subjects on which universal agreement could be achieved in such a community would be fairly small. But because of the fact of the Law and its political use it would be easier to achieve some sort of common consent on propositions like "honesty is desirable" or "racial justice is good" or "respect for the rights of other people is necessary" than on almost any other propositions that might be offered. Here we see the political use of the Law in action. The Law suggests and establishes minimal justice and for this reason alone it is good and ought to be proclaimed.

Some of the approval for religious groups in our culture comes from people who have no use for religion personally but who notice that religion in the Hebrew-Christian tradition, at least, tends to contribute to civil righteousness. It was for this reason presumably that Voltaire said, "If there were no God He would have to be invented!" And it was for this reason that Plutarch asserted, "It is easier to erect a city in the clouds than a state without religion." Much of the pro-religious propaganda of our age is based upon this sentiment. It was because of the religious contribution to civil righteousness that the United States Congress inserted "under God" into the pledge of allegiance to the flag, which school children repeat so often. And the same reason probably motivated the legislators to insist that "In God We Trust" be added to coins and postage stamps.

However, from the point of view of the Protestant Faith, the contribution to civil righteousness of the Law is distinctly secondary in importance to the *theological use of the Law*.

The function of the Law in its theological use is to drive men to Christ. It is because of the Law and its demands that men become aware of their alienation and separation from God. It is the Law which reveals to men how different they are from what they ought to be. The Law shows them that the good deeds which they should do they do not do, and the evil deeds which they should avoid, these they commit. This is what the Apostle Paul meant when he said, *Through the law comes knowledge of sin. (Romans 3:20)* It is because of the fact of the Law that men are willing to listen to the Gospel. The Christian message that in Christ God bridges the gap which man has established by his revolt against

God makes very little sense to people who are not aware that such a gap exists.

It is through the Law that most men become aware of the abyss that separates them from God, for the Law describes the rightful demands that God can make. This is shown clearly in the New Testament summary recorded in Matthew:

> *And one of them, a lawyer, asked him a question, to test him. "Teacher, which is the great commandment in the law?" And he said to him, "You shall love the Lord your God with all your heart, and with all your soul, and with all your mind. This is the great and first commandment. And a second is like it, You shall love your neighbor as yourself. On these two commandments depend all the law and the prophets." (Matthew 22:35 ff.)*

This shows that the Christian Faith states the Law in all its sharpness. It doesn't weaken the Law nor does it change its demands. On the contrary, it accentuates the demands, as in the statement in Matthew 5:48: *You, therefore, must be perfect, as your heavenly Father is perfect.* This is the ultimate demand; no higher requirement can even be imagined. Yet the Protestant Faith insists that this mandate must be taken absolutely seriously. It does not permit glossing over. Neither must it be explained away. We might be tempted to say, "This doesn't really mean 'perfect'; it merely means try to do the best you can!" But such modification of the Bible goes counter to the very spirit of Protestantism. On this point the theologians of classical Protestantism are in basic agreement. God's demands are serious demands, and they must be taken seriously. Only if we take the Law seriously will it fulfill its theological function and drive us to Christ.

The Law when taken seriously shows man his true condition. He is supposed to be perfect—as God is perfect. But he is in fact most imperfect. And the more seriously the Christian compares himself with the revelation of God in Jesus Christ, the more aware he becomes of his own imperfection. This is the reason why people do not like to measure themselves by the standard of Jesus Christ. They prefer to compare themselves to other people who are just as imperfect as they are. And, indeed, there is no one who cannot find somebody whom he considers even worse than himself. Even in a prison there are caste distinctions; a burglar or a murderer, for example, feels himself vastly superior to a political criminal, a traitor to his country. It is fairly easy for a person of normal intelligence to use the process we call "rationalizing" in order to make a fairly good case for his own superiority over most of his neighbors. The Protestant Faith points out that the Law does not say, "Be perfect as the Jones family or the Smith family is perfect"; it says clearly, "as your heavenly Father is perfect!"

This closes all exits through which a man could flee and makes such an escape utterly impossible. The Protestant Faith asserts that under the judgment of the Law nobody can say, "I'll stand on my record"; for in comparison with the demand for God-like perfection every human record looks shabby indeed. Thus, in the light of the Law all must realize that they are utterly dependent upon the mercy of God as revealed in Jesus Christ.

However, only when the Law is taken absolutely seriously does it have the effect indicated. What is commonly called "legalism" tends to obscure man's understanding of the seriousness of the Law. If the Law is understood as little moral rules of legalism, rather than the demand to be as perfect as God, it becomes possible, even easy, to obey the Law. For example, if "do not smoke" becomes the Law, a person may become a paragon of virtue merely because he doesn't like to smoke. Or if "do not dance" becomes the Law, a person who cannot dance because he gets dizzy when he turns around more than once achieves a moral distinction which has its roots in his inadequate sense of balance rather than in his superior sense of God. The great classical Protestant thinkers took the Law seriously—and in doing so they asserted that no one can be justified by his own goodness, by his own moral accomplishments, by his own moral perfection. The Law accuses man and drives him to Christ.

Furthermore, only if the Law is taken seriously is the Gospel what the word implies, "good-spell," the "good news." The Protestant Faith asserts that the "divine love cannot be contained within the framework of the law or a legal system."[30] The "good news" is simply that God has decided out of His sovereign power to deal with us according to His love. To the people who are condemned by the Law the Apostle Paul says:

> *While we were yet helpless, at the right time Christ died for the ungodly. Why, one will hardly die for a righteous man—though perhaps for a good man one will dare even to die. But God shows his love for us in that while we were yet sinners Christ died for us. . . . For if while we were enemies we were reconciled to God by the death of his Son, much more, now that we are reconciled, shall we be saved by his life. (Romans 5:6 ff.)*

The Gospel announces that God is willing to base His relationship to man not on justice but on His spontaneous and unmerited love. What this means has been stated in far less theological terms in the stories of the lost sheep, the lost coin, and the prodigal son (Luke 15). In all these stories it is the housewife, the shepherd, the father, the symbols for God, who find what is lost and who forgive the prodigal. It is not the coin that finds itself. It is not the sheep that returns to the shepherd. The prodigal son has wasted his entire inheritance. He comes to the father penniless. He deserves only punishment—and this is what he would receive were it not for the fact that the Father is love.

It is in Jesus Christ that this love has been revealed. It is in Jesus Christ that God has identified Himself completely with man

[30] Aulén, *The Faith of the Christian Church,* p. 40.

in his lostness and the meaninglessness of his life and death. Christ is the reality of God overcoming for us the undeniable reality of God in the Law. Indeed, says the Protestant Faith, the Law is of God—but so is Christ. And in Christ God fulfills the Law and cancels it. Here we must state again what we pointed out as the clue to any understanding of the Protestant Faith: "God was in Christ, reconciling the world unto Himself!"

Lest we misunderstand this distinction between the Law and the Gospel as implying the existence of two gods, let us remind ourselves again that, as far as the Protestant Faith is concerned, the Law *and* the Gospel are valid expressions of God's will. Protestants do not believe in two gods, a god of law and a god of love. This was the heresy of the Gnostics and of Marcion and it is rejected by all Protestant theologians. The Gospel is God's expression of love overcoming the barrier of God's Law which would eternally separate man from God. The Gospel is God's miracle of love that makes it possible for man to live with and in spite of God's Law.

God as Law is not a lower form of God than the God of the Gospel. It is the same God who meets man in Law and Gospel. For the Protestant Christian Law and Gospel are not contradictory but complementary. This is the only way in which man can speak about God. If God as He speaks to us in Law is neglected—as He has been at various periods in the history of the Christian Church —Christianity degenerates into sentimentality. God becomes a super–Santa Claus or an overindulgent grandfather. The result is the understanding of the Christian Faith as symbolized by Heinrich Heine. On his deathbed he is alleged to have said: "God will forgive me—it is His business." The neglect of the proclamation of the Law makes the Gospel a meaningless platitude. Unless man sees that his separation and alienation from God are a serious matter, the healing of this breach seems irrelevant and immaterial. To the extent to which the proclamation of the Law has disappeared from Protestant preaching the Protestant proclamation of the Gospel has lost its meaning. If the message of Protestantism consists of stale jokes and superficial travelogues, it is not surprising that many people prefer the sharper jokes of the professional comedians and the more penetrating political analyses of the professional news analysts. The Christian message is betrayed if the Law is not proclaimed as an essential element of the Christian witness.

But once this has been stated it must be added that without the proclamation of the Gospel, the proclamation of the Law soon degenerates into mere scolding. Again we can say that the history of Protestantism shows many periods in which the Protestant Faith has been obscured because of a one-sided emphasis upon the proclamation of the Law, to the exclusion of the proclamation of the Gospel.

Many Protestants associate their own religious experiences with constant scolding about the fact that they are all miserable sinners. The scolding may be well deserved, but it is not particularly helpful unless it is delivered in the context of the Gospel—the Good News of what God has done, is doing, and will do with such shabby raw material.

It is significant that most people, if asked concerning the meaning of religion, define it almost exclusively in terms of Law. Religion is for them the obedience to certain rules, mostly quite marginal to life. They are often rules that have been inherited from the past and that make little or no sense in the present. Few would define religion as being a proclamation of God's deeds for us. Yet even as stern a Protestant as John Calvin knew perfectly well that the Law without the Gospel is not Christian proclamation. He says:

> The testimony of the Law, which convinces us of iniquity and transgression is not made in order that we should fall into despair, and having lost courage, stumble into ruin. Certainly the apostle (Rom. 3:19,20) testifies that by the judgment of the Law we are condemned, in order that every mouth be closed and the entire world be found guilty before God. Yet that very apostle elsewhere (Rom. 11:32) teaches that God has enclosed all under unbelief,

not in order to ruin them or let them perish, but on the contrary, in order that he may exercise mercy on all. The Lord therefore, after reminding us (by means of the Law) of our weakness and impurity, comforts us with the assurance of his power and his mercy. And it is in Christ his son that God shows himself to us benevolent and propitious. For, in the Law he appeared only as remunerator of perfect righteousness (of which we are completely destitute) and, on the other hand, as upright and severe judge of sins. But in Christ his face shines full of grace and kindliness even toward miserable and unworthy sinners; for, he gave this admirable example of his infinite love, when he exposed his own son for us, and in him opened to us all the treasure of his clemency and goodness.[31]

We repeat: for the Christian, Law and Gospel are not contradictory but complementary. Protestant Christians experience God as the source of Law and the source of the Gospel. If either aspect of God's revelation is neglected, the Christian message is falsified and obscured.

RIGHTEOUSNESS AND LOVE

This leads the Protestant Faith to assert that God is *both* righteousness and love. When the Protestant Faith speaks of God's righteousness, it speaks about it not as an abstraction, logically deduced from the nature of God, but as the righteousness of the God who is revealed in His dealings with His people recorded in Scripture and experienced in the life of His church and of every individual Christian.

It is impossible to read the Bible with any degree of attentiveness and still hold to the Santa Claus or "man upstairs" notion of God. The fact that strikes the reader is that God is a righteous God. This is stated again and again in the Old Testament. The Psalmist sings: *The righteous Lord loveth righteousness.* (*Psalm 11:7*) And Jesus prays in the famous high priestly prayer of the Gospel according to St. John: *O righteous Father, the world has*

[31] Fosdick, *Great Voices*, p. 222.

not known Thee, but I have known Thee; . . . (John 17:25)

It is because of God's righteousness that His own chosen people must suffer for their disobedience and betrayal. It is because of God's righteousness that the Church and the Christian are punished for unrighteousness. The righteous God reveals His Law, and punishes evildoers. But this is not all that the Protestant Faith has to say at this point. Though His righteousness is revealed in His wrath—and this word "wrath" as applied to God occurs innumerable times in the Old and the New Testaments—this is again not all that can be said about the righteousness of God. According to the Protestant Faith God reveals His righteousness also by carrying out His plan of salvation. In other words, His grace is also part of His righteousness. It is because God is righteous and faithful that He keeps His word even to the unrighteous. Even though men are not trustworthy, God is! For the Protestant Faith "In God We Trust" is not merely a numismatic platitude but a *faithful* assertion based upon the righteousness of God. The Christian can trust God, even though he cannot necessarily trust his best friend, his wife or parents or children—even though he cannot trust himself! He can trust God because God is righteous altogether! Thus, if the righteousness of God is frightening, it is at the same time comforting. For it is this righteous God who has established His covenant with His Old and New Testament people.

Here again the Protestant position is best stated by saying that God's righteousness is part of His Holiness. It contains both His wrath and His grace without abolishing either.

At the same time God is love. Again the Protestant Faith asserts that this statement rests upon God's self-disclosure in His dealings with His people as recorded in Scripture and demonstrated again and again in the life of the Church and the individual believer. "God is love" is for the Protestant Faith not an abstract philosophical proposition which is deduced from the nature of God. As Plato, Aristotle and, later, Spinoza have shown, in this philosophical manner one can construct very impressive deities—but any similarity between these philosophical constructs and the God who has revealed Himself to His people and in the life of His church, is quite coincidental.

God's love is revealed in His relationship with man. It is God's desire to have communion and fellowship with man—to meet man person to person. God is therefore far more than goodness; He is love. Goodness gives things, while love gives itself. Of course, God's goodness gives us many things. Religious people have always praised God for all the things they have received. There is a thanksgiving holiday among all people who have some sense of the eternal. Protestants will gladly join in the chorus of praise that sings hymns of gratitude for the gifts of God's goodness. We experience the goodness of God as creatures. And therefore our fellow creatures are just as much objects of His goodness as we are. As Jesus says in the Sermon on the Mount:

> *Look at the birds of the air; they neither sow nor reap nor gather into barns, and yet your heavenly Father feeds them.* Are you not of more value than they? . . . *And why are you anxious about clothing? Consider the lilies of the field, how they grow; they neither toil nor spin; yet I tell you, even Solomon in all his glory was not arrayed like one of these. (Matthew 6:26 ff.)*

All creatures are beneficiaries of this divine goodness. It is an impressive, in fact, an overwhelming, part of our experience. We are able to make long catalogues of the gifts of God's goodness which we and all other creatures receive.

But the love of God is something different. We experience the love of God not as creatures but as children! The Protestant Faith asserts that God's love is personal, involving a personal relationship which makes certain personal demands upon us.

The love of a parent for a child does something to the child. It transforms him. Psychologists tell us that it makes a better person out of the child. Children need the love of their parents, and there is no adequate substitute for this love. Modern child psychology has shown again and again that children who have the best of care, technically speaking—who have all the food they need, all the clothing they need, all the shelter they need—but who are not loved are likely to show in their personalities this lack of love. It seems easier for a child to put up with a deficiency in shelter or food or clothing if he is supplied with an abundance of love. There is no substitute for love. And the Protestant Faith asserts that God loves us—not in general, as one might love the British or the Irish, the Germans or the Swedes, or some other group of people— but He loves us personally. The Twenty-third Psalm says: *The Lord is* my *shepherd,* I *shall not want.* It is for that one sheep that is lost that the shepherd in Jesus' parable goes out into the night and leaves the entire flock of sheep. God's love is a personal love, a parental love.

If this is taken seriously it must have certain consequences. If a parent loves me it creates fear in me—the fear of hurting my father or my mother. It is because my mother loves me that I do not want to do anything that will hurt her. I am afraid to hurt her. This is a fear that is the result of love. The theologians have called it "filial fear," in contrast to the slavish fear of a person who is afraid to do something because he thinks he will be caught and punished. The love of God creates this filial fear. Personal love makes me fear to hurt the person who loves me. I do not want to disappoint such love. God's love, according to the Protestant Faith, is personal, individual, and fatherly.

There is another strange thing about this divine love. It is, as we said before, *agape.* This means that it has its source in God, the loving subject, rather than in man, the object of divine love. God's love is the result of the fact that God is love. It does not depend on the attractiveness of the object but only on the *agape* of God.

The Protestant Faith asserts that God's love is something entirely different from all forms of human love. We love somebody because the object we love does something for us. Perhaps we love it for its beauty or for its goodness. It may even be that we love it because of its helplessness, which gives us an opportunity to show our power. Human love is always acquisitive. It always wants something from the object of its love. In most cases this is quite obvious, while in some cases it takes some training in psychology to discover what we want for ourselves in loving something or somebody. This love we call *eros*. This does not mean that it is purely sensual love or that it is lust. *Eros,* as described so beautifully by the Greek philosophers, deals with the love of the True, the Good, the Beautiful. It purifies man by directing his attention toward these objects that will make him better. *Eros* is, in fact, man's way to all that is worth while, and ultimately man's way to God. For the Greek philosopher Aristotle, God is the unmoved mover, the goal of the universe to which all creation is moving. It is God's complete perfection which makes Him so desirable. It is because of His perfection that everything loves Him. It is through His perfection that He draws all love toward Himself. God Himself does not love anything except that which is absolutely perfect. This means that He loves only Himself. To love anything but Himself would be to love that which is imperfect and thus would detract from God's absolute perfection.

Aristotle's God loves only Himself, but He is loved by everybody and everything, and through this love for God everybody and everything is moving toward its goal. It is *eros* that makes the world go around, the love for the absolute perfection of God.

It is important to keep this *eros* concept of love in mind in order to understand the complete reversal which is involved in the Christian faith in God as *agape*. The God who has revealed Himself in Jesus Christ loves imperfect, sinful, miserable man. He loves sinners. Not because they are imperfect and miserable and sinful, but because *He is love*. According to the Protestant Faith God is overflowing, self-giving, radiating love. The love is in Him, not the result of the object. In fact this divine love does not find but creates its lovable object. God does not love us because we are lovable; we are lovable because God loves us. Nowhere has this been stated more clearly than in the First Epistle of John. Here we read: *In this is love, not that we loved God but that he loved us and sent his Son to be the expiation for our sins.* And a little later: *We love, because he first loved us.* (*I John 4:10 ff.*) As Bishop Aulén puts it:

> Every attempt to demonstrate something in man, some incorruptible essence or some quality pleasing to God, which would explain rationally why God meets man in love, is in principle foreign to Christian faith. Such attempts prove only that divine love is again incarcerated within the walls of rationalism and legalism.[32]

According to the Protestant Faith the most accurate description of God is that He is love. He is self-giving, self-sacrificing, overflowing love. He is *agape.*

Again, for the Christian the righteousness and the love of God are not contradictory but complementary. God's righteousness ultimately reveals His love, and it is God's love which ultimately reveals His righteousness. This assertion may seem almost completely self-contradictory at this point of our discussion of the Protestant Faith. It can only be said here that the meaning of such a paradoxical statement becomes clear only in the doctrine of Christ and His atoning death. In Him that which is here merely a paradoxical assertion becomes a saving event.

[32] Aulén, *The Faith of the Christian Church,* pp. 133 ff.

4

God's World

It is an important part of the Protestant Faith that the world in which we live and of which our little earth is such a very small part is God's world. This is what the doctrine of creation means. This world is not a cosmic accident but rather the expression of the divine will. "I believe that God has created me and all that exists."

CREATION

The Christian faith in creation is the result of our confrontation with God in Jesus Christ and His word. It is the result of revelation. It is an axiom of the Christian Faith. It is important to emphasize this against the well-intentioned efforts to deduce creation logically from the evidence that surrounds us.

There are, indeed, many theories about the origin of the world. Some, neither more nor less logical than others, arrive at a "god" as the ultimate cause of the universe. These theories may argue from the design observable in the world to the necessity of the existence of a designer. They may argue from the causal chain that everything must have a cause and conclude that God is the first cause. They may in many other interesting ways deduce the existence of a creator and therefore of the universe as creation.

The Protestant Faith is not particularly concerned with any of these theories about the origin of the universe or of this earth. The doctrine of creation is an article of faith, describing man's situation in this world. The Christian Faith does not furnish a theory about the origin of the world. Such theories are more or less interesting scientific abstractions and hypotheses which do not need to clash with the Christian assertion that this is God's world, unless they become articles of faith for the "believer in science."

The Protestant Faith believes that "God has created me and all that exists" because the Christian has met the living God in revelation. He knows this universe to be creation because he has encountered the Creator. Genesis tells us: *In the beginning God created the heavens and the earth*. Through faith this becomes a personal experience. As the great Quaker George Fox put it:

> One morning, as I was sitting by the fire, a great cloud came over me, and a temptation beset me; but I sate still. And it was said, "All things come by nature"; and the elements and stars came over me, so that I was in a manner quite clouded with it. But inasmuch as I sate still and silent the people of the house perceived nothing. And as I sate still under it, and let it alone, a living hope arose in me, and a true voice, which said, "There is a living God who made all things." And immediately the cloud and temptation vanished away, and life rose over it all; my heart was glad and I praised the living God. After some time, I met with some people who had such a notion that there was no God, but that all things came by nature. I had a great dispute with them and overturned them and made some of them confess that there is a living God. Then I saw that it was good that I had gone through that exercise.[33]

[33] *The Journal of George Fox*, revised by Penney (New York: E. P. Dutton & Co., Everyman's Library).

As Bishop Aulén puts it:

> It is, therefore, of fundamental importance to emphasize that faith's affirmations about creation do not imply a theoretical proposition about the origin of the universe, but rather a religious statement about the nature of the relation between God and man.[34]

In this regard we ought to distinguish clearly between the Christian faith in the almighty Creator of heaven and earth and the alternative positions of deism, pantheism, and dualism.

There are many people who believe in creation, but according to the ideas of deism. Deism's belief in the Creator reduces the relationship between God and the world to a causal connection that took place in the distant past. Once upon a time in a faraway age God created the machinery of the world, set the clock, wound it up and started it, and it has been running ever since. God is the watchmaker, and the universe is the giant clock which he built and set in motion. This reduces God to the distant, dim cause of the world. Instead of creation we have in deism the past event of the construction of the marvelous mechanism. Against these views the Christian Faith asserts that God indeed created the world but that He also creates and maintains it continuously. This creative relationship of God to the universe has never stopped. God is still the Creator today. That is why we can sing with the Psalmist, *Create in me a clean heart, O God, and renew a right spirit within me. (Psalm 51:10)* Creation continues! In every moment all the universe is upheld by God's creative power. The deistic view must be categorically rejected by the Protestant Faith because it reduces faith in the Creator to a theoretical proposition about something that happened a very, very long time ago. Whenever Christians think of creation merely as a past event they are in danger of the deistic perversion of the doctrine of creation.

But there is an equally dangerous pantheistic perversion. The Protestant Faith distinguishes carefully between faith in the

[34] Aulén, *The Faith of the Christian Church*, p. 182.

Creator who is clearly above His creation and the divine process of creation of pantheism. In pantheism everything that is real *is God*. God and the universe are conceived as being identical; God is the world and the world is God. Every tree, every flower, every rock, every star, every person is part of God. There is nothing that is not God. Sometimes the relationship between the world as we see it and the God who is underneath all this visible world is defined as one of reality (God) and appearance (world), but not in the sense that there is any conflict between the two. They are essentially identical. Looked at from the limited point of view of a small part of divine reality, looked at from your point of view or my point of view, it might appear as if there were a difference between God and the world. However, the pantheists say that *sub specie aeternitatis,* that is, from the point of view of eternity, there is no difference whatsoever. God and the world are identical.

This view makes God into the soul of the world, or the innermost essence of the world. Any distinction between God and nature becomes meaningless. God is nature and nature is God. Man is a part of God, his limitations being the result of the fact that he is such a small part. Good and evil disappear also, for an evil action appears evil only because of the limitation of our insight; if we had full knowledge, if we had a comprehensive rather than a partial view of reality, all evil would disappear. There is, of course, no creation in the sense that something came into being that was not. There is only eternal being, which may change superficially but which does not change essentially. This eternal being has always been and will always be. There is no creation and there is no end.

Against these views of pantheism the Protestant Faith asserts that God created and creates through His sovereign Word. Creation is the result of God's freedom. He created the world—which He did not have to create. Though creation is real, it is not necessary. The world is not the automatic emanation of God's Being but rather the result of a free act. This free act is not merely an event of the past but rather an eternal act. It is a result of God's will that the world continues to exist. Though God is creatively present in the universe He also transcends it. It does not contain Him, and He is not identical with it. Whenever Christians speak of nature as divine they are in danger of the pantheistic perversion of the Christian doctrine of creation.

There is a third interpretation of the relation of God to the world which in the light of the revelation in Christ must be rejected by the Protestant Faith. This is dualism. Dualism is the view that asserts that the universe must be explained as the result of the conflict of two eternal principles. These two principles are sometimes called light and darkness, good and evil, mind and matter, or soul and body. Whatever terms are used, this view implies *two* absolute and coequal principles which are engaged in an eternal struggle. The key to the understanding of life is the understanding of the nature of this conflict. In this view one aspect of nature is generally favored over its opposite—usually mind over matter or light over darkness, form over formlessness or soul over body. Here we find the theories which assert that matter and body are the result of the evil principle and that only mind and soul are the creation of the good principle. Actually, dualism operates with gods who are engaged in an eternal struggle in which man is in the middle.

In this world view the body becomes the prison of the soul, and nature as it appears to our senses, the bait of the evil one. God himself is here the fighter against darkness and chaos, and instead of creation we find the eternal struggle of form to overcome formlessness, of light to overcome darkness, of mind to subdue matter, and of the soul to subject the body.

Against this view the Protestant Faith asserts that God created the universe *ex nihilo,* out of nothing. All of it is ultimately the product of His creative power. This is true of darkness as well as light and of the body as well as the soul. While Plato could say that the body is the prison of the soul, the Apostle Paul says that the body is the temple of the Holy Spirit. Even those powers which oppose God have their source in God's creative will. They are not eternal or independent from God but are dependent upon God's creative power. Whenever Christians depreciate matter and the body in a false spiritualism, dualism has obtained a hold on them. The Christian doctrine of creation is categorically opposed to the dualistic conflict between good spirit and evil matter, good soul and evil body. The one God is creator of all that is. We repeat: According to the Protestant Faith the world is the product of God's sovereign power and in its totality in every instant completely dependent upon Him. However, this is not a reversible dependence. Though the universe is dependent upon God, God himself is not dependent upon the universe.

It is of some importance that the difference between the Protestant Faith and deism, pantheism and dualism be clearly defined because these very ideas have frequently penetrated deeply into Protestant thought. It would not be too difficult to produce numerous people who consider themselves "good" Protestants who hold a deistic view of the relationship of God to the universe. They do believe that God set the whole process in motion a long time ago. Now the universe runs, so to speak, by itself. God must be busy somewhere else. Such deism is far more prevalent than the doctrinal statements of Protestantism would lead one to believe.

Furthermore, there is a good deal of pantheism among people who consider themselves Protestants. It usually appears in the form of various kinds of nature worship. The most common form is probably to be found in the worship of the green grass of the golf course on Sunday morning. But there are many Christians who tend to think that God is nature and nature is God. The Psalmist sings: *The heavens declare the glory of God and the firmament showeth His handiwork. (Psalm 19:1)* However, many people are willing to accept the heavens and the firmament and nature as God without regard for the God which they declare.

Like pantheism and deism, dualism is not unknown in Christian garb. In the very earliest time of the history of the Christian Church, certain Christian sects claimed that the creator God and the savior God were two different Gods, that there was a difference between the Old Testament God who had created matter and the New Testament God who had saved men. This view was resolutely rejected by the main stream of Christian thought. Nevertheless, a certain depreciation of the body and of the world accessible to our senses seems to have been a lasting result of the dualistic approach, which can still be discovered among Protestant Christians. Such dualistic deviations from the main stream of Christianity are not uncommon in our own time.

It would therefore be wise if in our study of the Protestant Faith we would not ignore these alternatives which we have discussed briefly, namely, deism, pantheism and dualism. They may throw a great deal of light on some of the contemporary pressures upon Protestantism by new religious and antireligious movements. The Christian Faith in God, the Creator of heaven and earth, has always had to be stated in contradiction to very lively views which considered God merely the first cause, or which identified Him with the universe, or which had two gods fighting an eternal war for the souls of men.

For the Christian Faith creation means that the universe had a beginning and will have an end. This, of course, does not say anything about space and time or that the world is limited in space and time. For the Christian, space and time, whatever they are, are in themselves part of God's creation. The Protestant Faith does not take sides for a Newtonian or an Einsteinian universe; whatever the universe is, whatever space is, whatever time is, the Christian sees them as God's creation.

Before we leave the subject of creation it may be advisable to describe briefly the attitude with which the Protestant Christian accepts the world as God's creation. This doctrine of creation prevents two attitudes which could easily arise and which have, in fact, arisen in the past as far as man's understanding of the universe is concerned.

On the one hand, creation means that this is God's world, that all of it is God's world. The insistence upon matter as well as spirit as God's creation is in opposition to all those beliefs which tend to depreciate matter. The material world is not inferior and it is not in itself evil or demonic. The Protestant Christian has every right to enjoy the world of matter, to love the stars and admire the majesty of the universe, to love the flowers and the trees which beautify our world. There is nothing in the Protestant Faith which says that the material world is to be ignored or depreciated. As God's creation we may love it. The manner in which Jesus preached seems to indicate that He loved it. There is nothing in the Protestant Faith that would command us to desire ugliness instead of beauty and to run down the material world. The doctrine of creation is a constant reminder that it is God's material world. Man has the right, even the duty, to love and admire it because of its Creator.

On the other hand the doctrine of creation means we must make a clear distinction between creation and the Creator. While we may enjoy creation, we must never worship it, says the Protestant Faith. This is, of course, not an idle warning. Much pagan religion is, indeed, the worship of the creature and creation instead of the Creator. The stringent prohibitions against the manufacture of graven images, or idols, which we find in the Old Testament are an attempt to safeguard the Jewish people against the worship of creation, which was so common among the neighbors of the Israelites and which was such a serious temptation to the Hebrew people. The worship of creation in all its forms is always idolatry. The Protestant Faith insists that you cannot worship beauty, or nature, without being guilty of idolatry. Creation always points beyond itself to the Creator. That is what the Psalmist means when he sings: *The heavens declare the glory of God; and the firmament showeth His handiwork. (Psalm 19:1)* Here the doctrine of creation protects the Protestant Faith against what is commonly called "secularism," which is essentially the deification of all those things which are not God, the deification of God's handiwork. This is as much a temptation in our age as it was a temptation when Israel confronted the Canaanites. There are many people today who worship the creature instead of the Creator. There are those, for example, who worship the family. To have a family is a wonderful thing; to love and cherish a wife or a husband and children is a glorious experience. However, the man who worships his family is idolatrously worshiping the creature instead of the Creator. This is equally true whether the object of our worship is our work or money or even our country. All these parts of creation, if made absolute and worshiped, lead man to idolatry. The Protestant Faith rejects this kind of secularism.

PROVIDENCE

This brings us to another assertion of the Protestant Faith which grows out of the faith in God's power and love. Faith in God as Creator includes faith in God's providence. This means that everything that happens in the universe happens as the result of God's will and in order to accomplish His purpose. Again it must be stressed that this is not an effort to explain logically the events which in fact occur. The Protestant Christian does not pretend to have an explanation for everything. Indeed, he is quite suspicious of those who always have a ready explanation. Perhaps this is best illustrated by the story that was told about Count von Zinzendorf, the famous leader of German Pietism and of the Moravian Brethren. He was once asked by an inquiring lady to explain such theological conundrums as, "What did God do before He created the world?" and, "If God is Love and Almighty, why is there evil in the world?" Instead of answering these questions, Count von Zinzendorf replied, "Madam, I am trying to be God's servant—not His brain trust!"

This answer throws some light upon the Protestant understanding of providence. If the Protestant Faith asserts that all events are subject to God's power, this does not mean that Christians claim to have explanations for all events. Faith in providence does not supply pat and glib answers to man's perplexing questions. It rather proclaims that all events in nature and in history, however bewildering, are ultimately subject to God's purpose.

In the New Testament we read a story in which Jesus is asked to give the reason why a certain man was born blind. His questioners had a ready explanation. They gave Him two alternatives, that the man was born blind either because of his own sin or because of the sin of his ancestors. Jesus rejected both these answers and said: *It was not that this man sinned,* or *his parents, but that the works of God might be made manifest in him.* (*John 9:3*) This shows that faith in the providence of God is not intended to be a simple explanation of all that occurs. Christianity does not only not supply simple answers to complicated questions, but, as this story shows, it occasionally raises complicated questions where people are satisfied with simple answers. Again, it is impossible to understand the Protestant Faith if we remove the assertions of faith from their proper context. It is within the context of worship and adoration that the Protestant Faith asserts that all events in nature and history are ultimately subject to the divine purpose. This is not supposed to be a substitute for scientific explanations. Protestants are prepared to accept these gladly—as far as they go. They only claim that they do not go far enough. The Protestant Faith deals with man's ultimate questions. To the individual believer, this means what the Apostle Paul states in Romans in the following words: *We know that in everything God works for good with those who love him, who are called according to his purpose.* (*Romans 8:28*) If we trust God, if we lay hold on Him in faith, we will understand all the events in our life in the context of this faith. This is perhaps one of the most exasperating aspects of the Christian Faith for those who do not share it. People who do not trust God but trust their bank account, or their health, or their luck are utterly confounded when they meet with Christians who are willing to take whatever comes as an expression of the divine will. And since these Christians know that this will is good, they are firmly convinced that *ultimately* no harm can come to them.

Here we cannot be careful enough to separate this faith in God, which expresses itself in the conviction that ultimately no harm can come to those who trust in God, from its popular counterfeit. There are many people who claim that Christianity will make you rich, or healthy, or lucky. Their slogan goes somewhat like this: "Become a Christian and God will give you wealth." Or, "Become a Christian and God will give you health." And unfortunately they have innumerable tedious case histories to fortify their position. They'll tell you about some impoverished traveling salesman who hadn't sold a vacuum cleaner in weeks. Wherever he went people would slam the door in his face saying, "We don't want any!" The poor vacuum-cleaner salesman trudged through the ice and snow and nobody wanted to buy any vacuum cleaners. And then he met some minister, or perhaps he found his grandfather's Bible in the attic. It doesn't really matter what the "gimmick" is. In any case, we are told he became a Christian. And now everything was changed. Customers greeted him with, "I have been waiting for you; would you please sell me your vacuum cleaner?" To make a long story short: After he became a Christian, the man sold thousands of vacuum cleaners; his salesmanship brought him to the attention of the boss, whose beautiful daughter he subsequently married, and now this poor unsuccessful traveling salesman owns the biggest vacuum-cleaner concern in the world—all because he became a Christian. This may be a somewhat exaggerated version of this popular manner of establishing the truth of Christianity, but basically this is the form in which the Christian Faith is perverted and peddled like a patent medicine which will cure everything from falling hair to athlete's foot. "Become a Christian," they say, "and you will have everything you want. Try Jesus; He satisfies!"

It would be a waste of time to give much attention to this perverted view of what the providence of God means to the Protestant Faith were it not for the fact that so many people, especially in our time, are led to believe that this *is* the Protestant Faith. It is for this reason that we should point out a few facts: In the Bible we find no such materialistic perversion of the effects of the Christian Faith. It is common knowledge that Jesus Christ was not elected president of the Chamber of Commerce of Jerusalem, but rather that He was executed as a common criminal. And so, it appears, was every one of his disciples, with the possible exception of St. John. None of them became rich. Paul was a sick man all his life. His Christian faith did not take away his illness, but it made it possible for him to live with it. He tells us: *Three times I besought the Lord about this, that it should leave me; but he said to me "My grace is sufficient for you, for my power is made perfect in weakness."* (*II Corinthians 12:8,9.*) And Paul, too, was eventually executed for his Christian faith. Trust in God's providence does not mean that all events are understandable to the Christian. It does not mean that he does not have to suffer, that he will have a trouble-free life. It means that nothing can separate him from God, that he personally knows God, because God has made Himself known to him, and that therefore in all events, good, bad or indifferent, the works of God are made manifest to him.

This has, perhaps, been put most succinctly by the French-Jewish writer Simone Weil. In her book *Gravity and Grace,* she says: "The extreme greatness of Christianity lies in the fact that it does not seek a supernatural remedy for suffering, but a supernatural use for it."[35] The Protestant Faith does not deny suffering, anxiety, despair, and death. It asserts rather that God can use all of it for His purpose of love. This He has demonstrated most profoundly when He himself suffered and experienced anxiety, despair, and death in Jesus Christ. This is the point of reference, the perspective from which the Protestant Faith makes its assertions concerning the providence of God. It is never a theoretical proposition to be debated, but always a personal confession which must be lived.

Here we must add that as far as the Protestant Faith is concerned, there is a vast difference between faith in providence and

[35] Simone Weil, *Gravity and Grace.* Copyright 1952. Published by G. P. Putnam's Sons. Used by permission.

fatalism. Fatalism is the assertion that man "can't win," that there is a cold, immutable fate which rules gods and men and nature. For the Greeks, for example, gods and men are equally caught in the net of this inexorable fate. Whatever you do, you will finally be strangled by your fate; in fact, the harder you try to escape it, the more obvious it becomes that neither you nor anybody else can ever escape his fate. This philosophy is best illustrated in Greek tragedy, for example in the story of Oedipus. Oedipus has been told that he would kill his father and marry his mother. When he tries to escape his fate by leaving the people whom he believes to be his father and mother, he immediately fulfills the very fate he is trying to escape. For the Greeks, fate was cold, unchangeable, and impersonal.

By contrast, the Protestant Faith speaks of providence as a personal trust in a personal God, a living faith in a living God who confronts living men. The Christian faith in providence is the absolute opposite of the Greek surrender to fate. There is likewise no place in Protestantism for modern American fatalism which expresses itself in such slogans as, "You can't win, the dice are loaded," and all the other expressions of despair which are part of our everyday life. The Protestant Faith guards the Christian simultaneously against the superficial optimism of the men and women who think that trouble will go away if you ignore it and the profound despair of the people who insist that this life is the "tale told by an idiot, full of sound and fury, signifying nothing." Providence is personal trust in a personal God. As Luther sings: "Take they then our life, goods, fame, child and wife, When their worst is done, They yet have nothing won: The Kingdom ours remaineth."

PRAYER

At this point it would appear to be in order to say a few words about the relationship of prayer to the Protestant faith in the providence of God. What does it mean that Christians pray?

Do they actually believe that they know better what should happen than God in His providence? Are they trying to give unsolicited advice to the Creator and Ruler of the universe?

Again, it is utterly impossible to discuss the Christian meaning of prayer in an abstract, philosophical manner. The right and duty of the Christian to pray to God are not something that we can deduce logically from the nature of God as creator and preserver of the universe and of men. For the Protestant Faith prayer is not like sending an order to a mail-order house or, worse, giving orders to somebody who has to obey. This is magic, and there are religions where prayer is a form of magical incantation which can be used to make God do something that He apparently does not want to do. While prayer is central to most religions, it has often been sacrilegiously distorted by the religions. It has been perverted into routine and magic, even among Christians. Here again Jesus' words are abundantly clear:

> *When you pray, you must not be like the hypocrites; for they love to stand and pray in the synagogues and at the street corners, that they may be seen by men. Truly, I say to you, they have their reward. But when you pray, go into your room and shut the door and pray to your father who is in secret; and your father who sees in secret will reward you. And in praying do not heap up empty phrases as the Gentiles do; for they think that they will be heard for their many words. Do not be like them, for your father knows what you need before you ask him. Pray like this: . . . (Matthew 6:5 ff.)*

And here follows the Lord's Prayer. Note that Jesus says, . . . *your father knows what you need before you ask him.* Yet He wants us to pray. This can only be understood if we remember that, for the Christian, prayer is not informing God about things He might otherwise not know, although admittedly many prayers sound as if they were trying to fill God in on something He might have missed. The clue to prayer is the fact that here a child is speaking to his father. It is an expression of the father-child relationship, in which the child knows the father and the father knows the child. Thus prayer is an expression of confidence and faith. Once this has been established it becomes clear why there is nothing, absolutely nothing, that cannot be brought to God in prayer, according to the Protestant Faith.

The Protestant Faith does not say that man must only pray for high and exalted ends, such as world peace and brotherhood. Prayer is personal communication in the context of the God-man relationship which undergirds it. If world peace and brotherhood personally concern and move you, you may and should pray for it. But if your inability to get along with other people or your inability to make ends meet troubles you, you may pray about these matters just as readily as about world peace.

The essential ingredients in prayer are faith and sincerity. Since human beings are most sincere when their own interests are involved, our most sincere prayers are often those prayed when we are in trouble. There is nothing wrong with such prayers, for they may be, in fact, a real expression of our dependence upon God. In such prayer, we may earnestly feel that we are children and God is our heavenly Father. If this is the case, this is true prayer!

Perhaps an illustration will help. A father who loves his children wants his children to have confidence in him. This confidence may sometimes express itself in very odd ways. If you have a small boy, he may ask you, "Daddy, I want a gun which shoots real bullets." Of course, this is the kind of request that you will not fulfill as long as the child is too young to handle a gun. But you are glad he asked you. This is an opportunity for you to explain something about guns and about shooting, and even this unreasonable request is an expression of confidence.

According to the Protestant Faith, we can and should speak to God about everything. This does not mean that God will grant all our requests, but He will hear all our prayers. Though He knows what we need, He wants us to ask Him. This personal God desires to have personal fellowship with His children. Prayer is the most profound expression of this fellowship.

Prayer as a problem in metaphysics is unsolvable. (Once we become involved in the controversy of freedom versus determinism we will drown in the philosophical difficulties which this problem raises.) But in the Protestant Faith prayer is not presented as a philosophical problem. On the contrary, whenever the Bible speaks about prayer, it speaks about the father-child relationship which God has established with man. Prayer is the action which gives expression to the reality of this relationship. Thus, there has never been a Christian leader, a prophet, an apostle, or a saint who did not pray! For it is through prayer that the Christian shows that his theological assertions are not merely intellectual games.

The Protestant Faith must reject firmly the contemporary efforts to reduce prayer to some sort of psychological self-hypnosis. Nothing could be more misleading and dangerous than to say that although God is in His heaven, running the universe without regard to your prayer, go ahead and pray if it makes you feel better. Either prayer is communication between the child and the father— or it is not Christian prayer. It is certain that much can be said for the psychological value of a quiet hour and even of some routine prayers. But in the moment the quiet hour and these words are used as a psychological device to make me feel better, to help me in business, or to soothe my ulcers—I am not praying to God. All these devices may be indeed very helpful. This is a question for a competent psychologist to decide. All that the theologians can say is that self-hypnosis is not prayer. Prayer is the supreme human expression of the father-child relationship.

MIRACLE

This brings us to another subject deeply involved with the creative power of God, the subject of miracle. The word "miracle" has suffered a great deal from the inflationary tendencies of our language. We use it loosely for all sorts of events that we consider astonishing from the catch of a forward pass in football to the description of the effects of some detergent by the advertising fraternity. "Joe Doaks made an absolutely miraculous catch," we will say; or we will hear, "Glutch's Soap is truly a Miracle Soap."

The dictionary defines a miracle as "an event or effect in the physical world deviating from the known laws of nature, or transcending our knowledge of these laws." However, this definition implies that if no laws of nature were known, then there would be nothing that could be considered miraculous, in other words, that the breach of the laws of nature makes the event miraculous.

If we want to look at miracle from the point of view of the Protestant Faith, we might as well ignore the event's relationship to the laws of nature. For the believer, any event that opens his eyes to God is a "miracle." God can make any event translucent, so that it leads to faith and thus becomes miracle for the person who meets God in this event. Strangely enough, the same event may not be miracle to the unbeliever; he will have some other explanation, some device which enables him to remain an unbeliever though he has observed the very same event.

An example from the New Testament may help explain what this means. In the Acts of the Apostles, we read the story of Pentecost as follows:

> *When the day of Pentecost had come, they were all together in one place. And suddenly a sound came from heaven like the rush of a mighty wind, and it filled all the house where they were sitting. And there appeared to them tongues as of fire, distributed and resting on each one of them. And they were all filled with the Holy Spirit and began to speak in other tongues, as the Spirit gave them utterance. Now there were dwelling in Jerusalem Jews, devout men from every nation under heaven. And at this sound the multitude came together, and they were bewildered, because each one heard them speaking in his*

own language. . . . And all were amazed and perplexed, saying to one another, "What does this mean?" But others mocking said, "They are filled with new wine." (Acts 2:1 ff.)

Even the Pentecost miracle was for those who did not want to believe merely the result of alcoholic overindulgence. In other words, for the committed unbeliever, no event, even the most miraculous, is "miracle"; it does not help him to faith, it does not automatically make him a believer. Judas probably witnessed as many miracles as any of the other disciples, but this did not keep him from betraying Jesus to his enemies. These events did not open Judas' eyes to God. For him they were not miracles. On the other hand, some of the most ordinary events, the most explainable events, can be transfigured into miracles for a person who believes. There was a rather well-known eye specialist to whom the ordinary working of the human eye was the miracle of miracles; if you gave him the opportunity, he would explain to you in great detail how the structure and operation of the human eye had helped him to come to faith in God.

The Protestant Faith is not committed to the absoluteness of the causal chain or the absoluteness of any physical law. We assume that what has happened a million times in a certain sequence will happen in the same sequence the one millionth and first time. This seems a most reasonable assumption until something else happens. All the Protestant Faith asserts is that nothing in this universe, including the causal chain or the law of gravitation is independent of God. In fact, all events depend upon God; without Him the "miraculous" as well as the "nonmiraculous" event could not occur. The unusual event may in a very specific sense become an occasion for faith, but not all unusual events do become occasions for faith. From the point of view of the Protestant Faith the significance of an event is dependent upon the power it has to help man meet God.

However, faith in the reality of miracle in the Christian past, the Christian present, and the Christian future must not lead us into a very serious misunderstanding. This is the notion that, in general, events run without God, by themselves, so to speak, and only occasionally does God enter into the processes of nature and history and perform a miracle. Afterward He withdraws again and lets things run by themselves.

Such a position is deistic, even if defended by a good Protestant. It reduces God to a spectator to the processes of nature and history, a spectator who only occasionally takes any interest in these processes. In contrast to this view, the Protestant Faith asserts that God the Creator upholds the universe at all times. Whether the events which occur seem to us ordinary or extraordinary, they happen because of the creative and maintaining power of God. And any event, the most routine as well as the most spectacular from our human point of view, can become the occasion for faith if this is God's will.

5

The Doctrine of Man

We are now ready to begin a discussion of that part of God's creation which concerns us most. What does the Protestant Faith have to say about man? What is its doctrine of man?[36]

There are many different ways in which we can and do look at man. We can look at man from the point of view of what is generally called "common sense."From this point of view we recognize that man is different from the animals and things that surround him. He is *homo faber,* he makes tools, he uses language, he creates culture. Somehow, he knows himself to be different from the rest of creation, yet at the same time he knows also that he is a part of it. All

[36] To the following, cf. Robert L. Calhoun, *What Is Man* (New York: Association Press, 1939).

this is a pretty disorganized approach to the problem of man. Yet every man has some sort of anthropology, some idea about what it means to be a man. It may not be very scientific, it may not be very articulate, but almost anyone can give you some idea of what he thinks man is.

But, besides these disorganized, common-sense ideas, there is the scientific approach to the question "what is man?" But the answer will depend a good deal on what science you choose. Professor Arthur Eddington once said, "If a mathematical physicist were asked for his definition of a human being, he would probably reply: 'a rather complex differential equation.' "[37] This means that man is also, among other things, a physical object that can be studied like other physical objects. The biochemist might give us an even better description of man than the physicist, while a biologist, concerned with living cells, would have still a different approach. If we asked a psychologist to answer the question "what is man?" his answer would depend upon which school of psychology he happened to belong to—behavioristic, psychoanalytic, or Gestalt. In its own way, each of these different schools of psychology is trying to answer the question, "what is man?" If we look further, we will find that the economist offers an answer to this question: man is producer, distributor, consumer of goods. The political scientist says: man acquires, exercises, regulates, and is subjected to political power.

The answers to our question become even more complicated and varied when we turn to philosophy. The dualistic philosophers will tell us that man is an interesting and unique combination of body and soul. They have devised many fascinating theories about this body and this soul and how they act upon each other. Other philosophers will say that man is merely body, merely matter. "Mind" or "soul," they assert, are merely words, or perhaps the description of some special functions of the body. And then there are the idealists, who deny the reality of matter and body and

[37] Calhoun, *What Is Man*, p. 21.

claim that man is "really" mind, and the body merely an illusion.

It is easy to see that it would take us forever to find all the answers that have been given to the question, "what is man?" In a sense it is the most important question man can ask. The Protestant Faith asks this question also, but the answer is very different from all the views which we have listed because the Christian Faith sees man primarily in his relationship to God. For the Protestant Faith this relationship of man to God is the key to the understanding of man. Without knowing about this relationship we may have all sorts of interesting ideas about man, but we will not have that meaning which brings all other meanings together, the ultimate meaning of man.

Of course, this does not mean that these other views of man are without value. As far as their specific insights are concerned, each one of them is of the greatest importance. It is not only proper, but necessary, to study man from all these different points of view. But the answers which economics and political science, medicine and psychology give concerning man are only partial answers.

The Protestant Faith asserts that if any of these answers is made into the whole story, if man is considered merely a "political animal" or the "economic man" or a bundle of reflexes, then the true nature of man is seriously misinterpreted.

If these partial views are accepted, everything that is said about man and man's life is perverted and falsified. One example will suffice. Two human beings are in love and become engaged. This relationship is in a sense economic, for without it jewelers would have a hard time selling diamond rings. This relationship is political; it involves a power structure and the distribution of power. It has important physiological and biological aspects. It can be studied psychologically and philosophically. And yet we all know, at least those of us who have ever been in love, that it is all of these things and more. We can only smile at the person who is trying to understand this relationship of one human being to another in such narrowly limited ways.

MAN AS CREATURE

Christianity asserts that man is unique, that he cannot be contained and enclosed in any of these partial descriptions, because he alone of all the creatures of this earth is on speaking terms with God. God speaks to man and man can respond. This fact about man has been described by the theologians with the phrase the *imago dei,* the image of God. According to the witness of the Bible, man is created in the image of God, different from the rest of creation and uniquely responsible to God. *So God created man in his own image, in the image of God he created him; male and female he created them.* (*Genesis 1:27*) The reality of this image is expressed by the fact that man knows *agape* and God is *agape,* and by the fact that man knows freedom and God is freedom.

But before we become too proud about this *imago dei,* this image of God, the Protestant Faith says also that, although man is created in the image of God, this image has been effectively destroyed through sin. It has become a broken image. This means that man's knowledge of *agape* does not lead him to love God and his neighbor. Rather, though man knows of love, he hates; he does not know how to love. He wants to be loved, he wants everybody to love him, but this very desire creates hate. While man wants everybody to love him, he does not know how to love anybody. And the same tragedy occurs when man is trying to use his freedom. Because of sin, because man is in revolt against God, he cannot use freedom except to enslave everybody around himself and ultimately himself as well. The man who imagines himself to be free is in fact a slave.

To use a very simple example, the small child that is given absolute freedom tyrannizes and terrorizes the entire family—and in the process of doing so becomes terribly unhappy. The child is enslaved by his own so-called freedom.

Because of our alienation from our Creator, classical Protestantism asserts, we turn love into hate and freedom into slavery. Whatever we do works our destruction. Yet the destruction of the image of God in man does not turn man into an animal. Even the enslaved man is still man. Even man who is full of hate is still man. Man cannot escape his humanity. He can try to escape, but he never succeeds.

There are many attempts on record in which man has tried to be merely a part of nature. People have said, "Let us be animals. We are unhappy, miserable men; perhaps we can be simple and happy animals. Let's go back to nature!" But whenever man has tried to abandon his humanity, to take it off as one takes off uncomfortable clothes, the effort has failed.

It has failed, first of all, because man has never been merely a part of nature. As we said earlier, there has never been a time in which man was merely animal. We might have the impression that early man was merely animal if we depend upon comic strips and magazine cartoons for our information about him. Here he is portrayed as a dumb brute who rules his cave by striking his mate with a club and dragging her about by the hair. No doubt these caricatures are significant, but they tell us more about modern man and his repressions than about the cave man. (Could it be that modern American man, tired of being dragged through department stores and suburbia by his wife, is projecting some of his deepest wishes into the prehistoric past?) The drawings which really tell us something about the cave man are drawings such as those found in the caves in Dordogne, France. One of the oldest records we have of early man, they are beautiful pictures of animals. They reveal that early man was not a brute, but an artist. As G. K. Chesterton has put it:

> It is the simple truth that man does differ from the brutes in kind and not in degree; and the proof of it is here; that it sounds like a truism to say that the most primitive man drew a picture of a monkey and that it sounds like a joke to say that the most intelligent monkey drew a picture of a man.[38]

[38] Reprinted by permission of Dodd, Mead & Company from *The Everlasting Man* by G. K. Chesterton. Copyright 1925 by Dodd, Mead & Company.

Man is always unique. The reason is, according to the Protestant Faith, that he stands in a unique relationship to God. The fact that this relationship has been terribly disturbed does not make it any less unique. And the record of the cave man does not tell us at all that man is merely animal, that he has ever been merely animal. The cave man tells us that man has always been man. There is no escape from our humanity into some animal ancestor. The effort to escape our humanity by claiming that some contemporary primitives are not really human, and that humanity is therefore merely an acquired characteristic that we can abandon if we so desire, is equally doomed. As we said before, there is no noble savage; there is no contemporary primitive who is merely animal. The more we learn about the various patterns of culture among men today, the more we must realize that, in spite of all the variety, every group of people is human. None of them act like animals, none of them act as if they were merely nature. Like "civilized" man, the contemporary primitives, too, know love and practice hate, know freedom and are enslaved. Man is always man; there is no escape from our humanity.

The same rule holds for those forlorn efforts of eighteenth-century Europeans who dressed up as shepherds and shepherdesses in order to "go back to nature." It is equally valid for our contemporaries in Los Angeles who let their hair grow and wear animal skins and sandals. "Nature Boy" does not represent an escape from our humanity—he only illustrates how we are bothered by the fact that we are men who are not what men are supposed to be. The Protestant Faith claims that we are men alienated from our Creator. We are the broken image of God. It is always true that the perversion of the best is the worst. It is because of man's special destiny that the failure of man is so uniquely tragic. As we can see all about us, what is wrong with man does not only threaten other men but all creation. It is man in his estrangement from God who destroys the fish in the Pacific Ocean with his experiments in mass destruction. It is man who poisons the air and the water and places all life on earth in jeopardy because of, not in spite of, his brilliant potentialities.

MAN AS SINNER

Classical Protestantism asserts that man is a sinner. This is his tragedy! This is the source of *all* his problems. Created for free fellowship with God, he uses his freedom to make himself into God and thus revolts against his Creator and Heavenly Father. The desire to be God is man's basic sin. Nietzsche once said, "But that I may reveal my heart entirely unto you, my friends: *if* there were gods, how could I endure it to be no god! *Therefore* there are no gods."[39] Man wants to be God—he wants everything to turn around himself. He wants to be the center and the meaning of the universe. He resents the fact that he is marginal, the experience that he is finite. He knows that there was a time when he was not, and he dreads that there will be a time when he will not be!

What man resents most is that he is so dispensable. Life goes on without any of us. It would go on without all of us. Thus we do not want to die—but not because we will leave such a great vacuum that it will never be filled! On the contrary, we fear death because we know that life will go on as if we had never lived. It is man's obvious dispensability which terrifies him. He envies God his godhead. Man wants to be like God and therefore he revolts (Genesis 3:1–5). Sin is man's revolt against God.

But how does this revolt specifically express itself? What in particular is sin? Looking at it psychologically, sin is pride. The Greek word for this pride is *hybris,* and the ancient Greeks suspected that this *hybris* was the source of man's suffering. It was the flaw in the hero of the great tragedies. The Greeks saw in it both the expression of the hero's greatness, that is, his awareness of his affinity to the gods, and the expression of his enmity toward

[39] Friedrich Nietzsche, *The Philosophy of Nietzsche* (New York: Random House, The Modern Library, 1927) p. 91. Used by permission of original publishers, George Allen & Unwin, Ltd.

The Doctrine of Man 133

the gods, his defiance of their superiority. It is this *hybris* which causes man's downfall and destruction in the tragic view of life of the Greeks.

For the Christian, *hybris* means that man, who is created to live his life in grateful dependence upon God, who is supposed "to fear, love and trust God above all things," this man believes that he can manage without God. Sin is to fear, love, and trust other things besides God. And classical Protestantism says that we are sinners because we do in fact worship other gods. Turning away from the one true God, man chooses to worship idols. This means that in a sense all sins are sins against the First Commandment: "I am the Lord your God, . . . You shall have no other gods before me."

In fact, man has other gods. One could say that he makes up his gods as he goes along. He worships himself and does everything to please himself. He lives as if there were no God. This is sin. But it is also sin if he worships other idols, for example, his nation. He then acts as if his country or his "race" were the highest good—he hates and even murders to maintain the supremacy of his "race"—and sins. Or money can be the idol. There are many people who will do anything for money, because having money gives them the feeling of being independent, sovereign—like God. They will lie, deceive, betray, and murder for money. This is sin.

According to the Protestant Faith man is created to return his life as a living sacrifice to God; he is supposed to live in God and for God. But when he lives in fact apart from God and only for himself, glorifying his own happiness and his own pleasure, he sins.

Sin may find innumerable expressions. In the New Testament we find the so-called "catalogues of vices," which indicate the many forms in which sin appears. Thus St. Paul writes:

Now the works of the flesh are plain: immorality, impurity, licentiousness, idolatry, sorcery, enmity, strife, jealousy, anger, selfishness, dissension, party spirit, envy, murder, drunkenness, carousing, and the like. (*Galatians* 5:19)

All these specific sins are the result and the expression of man's revolt against God. Since the perversion of the best is the worst, it is in the sins of the spirit that man sins most profoundly.

It is through the mind that man is superior to all the animals. It is through his imagination that he can accomplish the particularly human tasks, yet it is the imagination which enables him to revolt against God in the most sophisticated manner. As far as the Protestant Faith is concerned, an action is sinful to the degree that it expresses man's revolt against God.

This is most movingly illustrated in Fëdor Dostoevski's famous novel *Crime and Punishment.* In this novel we meet a murderer and a prostitute. Dostoevski shows that it is the murderer, Raskolnikov, who sins in the most horrible manner. He murders a pawnbroker, because he is convinced that he, a brilliant student, will make a greater contribution to society than this worthless old woman. As Professor Jaroslav Pelikan has put it:

> The murder of the old pawnbroker was a sin, but not merely because it was a breach of conventional morality. This made it a crime, not a sin. Raskolnikov's sin was brought on by his egocentricity, his assumption that his position in the universe was so important that he could suspend the existence of another person to advance his own ends. . . . Sin, therefore, was not the violation of some precept or prohibition, it was the assumption: I Am God.[40]

In the same novel we meet Sonia. She is a girl who sells her body into prostitution to secure food for her stepmother and her small brothers and sisters who are starving. She sins; she transgresses the moral law knowingly and deliberately. But while Raskolnikov "acted out of an egocentric belief that he had a claim

[40] Jaroslav Pelikan, *Fools for Christ* (Philadelphia: Muhlenberg Press, 1955), p. 74.

upon another person's life," Sonia "acted out of the belief that her stepmother and the children had a claim upon her life."[41]

There are vast differences between the kinds of evil deeds men do. But the most terrible aspect of sin, according to the Protestant Faith, is that it is revolt against God. This is perhaps most shockingly illustrated in another of Dostoevski's novels, *The Brothers Karamazov.* Here the Grand Inquisitor of Seville is confronted by Jesus, who has come to this city in Spain during the time of the greatest power of the Inquisition. Christ is put in prison by the Church. The Church has become an institution for the acquisition of power. As such it has no use for Christ, and so the Grand Inquisitor can tell the very Christ in whose name he has usurped his power:

> I repeat, tomorrow Thou shalt see that obedient flock who at a sign from me will hasten to heap up the hot cinders about the pile on which I shall burn Thee for coming to hinder us. For if any one has ever deserved our fires, it is Thou. Tomorrow I shall burn Thee![42]

Here a man of the Church shows sin in its most severe and serious form. It is revolt against God which leads the Grand Inquisitor to burn the Christ, as it once led Caiaphas and Pilate to crucify Him. Because the Grand Inquisitor wants to be God, because he refuses to let God be God, he sins most profoundly of all. In the perversion of our highest aspirations we commit our worst sins.

Psychologically speaking, sin is pride. Theologically speaking, it is unbelief. Because man does not believe in God, because he believes in that which is not God, he is a sinner. If man analyses his life he discovers again and again that his actions are inspired by trust in other gods besides the Lord God. Man is a sinner because he has other gods before the Lord his God! The Old Testa-

---

[41] Pelikan, *Fools for Christ,* p. 76.

[42] Fedor Dostoyevsky, *The Brothers Karamazov* (New York: Random House, The Modern Library [1929]), p. 270.

ment supplies many illustrations. The Israelites trust the golden calf—and sin! They trust their own kings instead of God—and sin! They trust Egypt—and sin! They trust their wealth and prosperity—and sin!

What the Old Testament says about the Israelites is equally true of contemporary Americans. The Protestant Faith asserts that Americans sin when they trust their natural resources, or their economic prosperity, or their military strength, when they put their trust in anything besides God, when they have other gods besides the Lord God. There is a story in the New Testament which helps to show that sin is unbelief, the trust in things instead of God. It is a very simple story taken from the everyday life of a rural society.

> *The land of a rich man brought forth plentifully; and he thought to himself, "What shall I do, for I have nowhere to store my crops?" And he said, "I will do this: I will pull down my barns, and build larger ones; and there I will store all my grain and my goods. And I will say to my soul, Soul, you have ample goods laid up for many years; take your ease, eat, drink, be merry." But God said to him, "Fool! This night your soul is required of you; and the things you have prepared, whose will they be?" So is he who lays up treasure for himself, and is not rich toward God. (Luke 12:16–21)*

Because man does not believe in God, because he trusts in all sorts of false gods, in himself, in his family, in his wealth, because of his unbelief, man is a sinner.

The Protestant Faith asserts furthermore that sin is a responsible act. There is no doubt that sin has a long history. Our own deeds of injustice are conditioned to a large extent by deeds done long ago. Sin has a way of proliferating, of giving birth to more sin, that is truly frightening. This has led some people to say that there is indeed evil in the world, but man is rather to be pitied than censured. He is a victim of circumstances over which he has no control. Sin is never personal sin, these people say; it is always a social disease. Man as an individual is good; it is society that makes him bad.

This argument has a great deal of attraction because it is so obvious that our life in society aggravates all our shortcomings from the most superficial to the most profound. It also involves our pride and our revolt against God. It seems obvious that men are worse in society than as individuals. A mob will commit crimes that no individual member of the mob would do by himself. Perhaps the family supplies the most striking illustration of the fact that we act worse as members of a group than we would act as individuals. A mother will lie, cheat, and steal if need be in order to protect her children—even though she would never do any of these acts to protect herself. A college student who would never cheat in a test in order to obtain a better grade himself will condone and protect the cheating of his classmates. And there are many other illustrations of this fact that we act less responsibly as members of collectivities than we would act if we were all by ourselves. The excesses of the mass movements of our time have further substantiated this judgment.

This observation has led some to speak of evil as a product of society and its maladjustments. According to these people, there is no sin; there are only poorly designed societies. If we would correct the inadequate design of our society we would immediately eliminate evil.

In some sense this seems to be the assertion of the Marxists, who blame all the shortcomings of man upon the deficiencies of the capitalist system and who seem to think that evil will disappear if we redesign society according to a socialist pattern. But the Marxists are not the only voices proclaiming that man is good individually and that he is made evil by society.

Against all these views the Protestant Faith asserts that sin is a personal and a responsible act. It is a personal revolt against God, which is aggravated by society and its shortcomings but which is nevertheless our personal responsibility. In fact, the shortcomings of society are in turn the result of personal failures. And so we are involved in a vicious circle. Personal sin creates a corrupt society, and the corrupt society aggravates and encourages personal sin. But man remains responsible. Though he will always try to blame his moral failures on others, ultimately the responsibility is his own. In the story of Paradise Eve blames sin on the serpent, and Adam blames sin on Eve. This is a most human reaction; the pattern has continued ever since. Though we know deep down in our hearts that we are responsible, we will always find somebody to blame. Not only is man a sinner, but he is a sinner who cannot face his sin honestly and always needs a scapegoat.

But in addition to emphasizing the reality of personal responsibility, classical Protestantism says simultaneously that man is a sinner because of original sin. Here we see again the principle of complementarity in operation. Sin is at the same time personal and collective responsibility. For classical Protestantism, original sin describes the fact that man is born in revolt. The revolt against God is not something which he must gradually learn but is the pattern of human nature, because mankind collectively since the dawn of history has been in revolt against God. People living on a dirt road in the country will tell visiting drivers in the winter, "Choose your ruts carefully; you will be in them for a long time!" This illustrates the predicament of man. He is in a rut, says the Protestant Faith. Sin surrounds and embraces him. Not only individual human beings but the entire human race is in revolt against God. And this revolt afflicts everything he does. This is what is meant by the total depravity, a Protestant concept that has come in for much criticism. It does not mean that we cannot act like ladies and gentlemen. It does not mean that we are beasts, that we are animals. It does mean, however, that nothing we do is unaffected by sin, by our revolt against God. Our social life as well as our personal life is perverted by sin. It affects our relationship with our friends as well as with our enemies. There is no area, no nook, of human life where the fact that man is in revolt against God is not noticeable. In the moment when we think we have escaped it, it becomes most obvious. This is repeatedly illustrated by the Pharisees in the New Testament. These Pharisees were good people, solid citizens; and their very goodness and righteousness resulted in pride and conceit and made them sinners! Ironically, many a modern Protestant has contemplated the story of the Pharisee and the publican and completely missed the point of the story. Where the Pharisee says, "Lord, I thank thee that I am not like this publican," the modern Protestant has said, "Lord, I thank thee that I am not like this Pharisee," and in doing so he has indicated that he is just as much of a sinner as the Pharisee of old, even if his pride is not pride because of righteousness but rather pride because of his lack of pride!

There is nothing that cannot become sinful. Man's highest aspirations, even his loyalty to his family and his country, can become the source of pride and the point of revolt against God. Even religion can become the focus of sin. This was the problem of the Grand Inquisitor. The very zeal of the religious man who burns the unbeliever to the greater glory of God is the expression of sin. Nobody is safe from it, says the Protestant Faith, and no aspect of human life is untouched by it. Even man's awareness of sin can lead him to become careless about sin, to take it for granted and thus not to take it seriously.

This is a temptation which threatens with greatest subtlety those who take their religion seriously. Dealing with the concept of sin as part of the language of their daily worship, they may become so accustomed to the word as to forget the dangerous reality it describes. People who work with high explosives in their daily routine must be constantly reminded that familiarity dare not breed contempt. If that happens they may carelessly risk their lives. Similarly, those for whom sin is part of their daily religious speech must be on guard lest familiarity with the word breed contempt for the ever-dangerous reality. This is why Holy Scripture warns the Christians constantly against overconfidence.

Thus the Protestant Faith asserts that all men are sinners and that man expresses his alienation from God in all that he does. The facts thus described must not be taken for granted.

But one comment must here be added. When the Protestant Faith speaks of original sin, it does not state or imply that this sin is sexual. The notion seems to be quite prevalent that "original sin" is "sexual sin," and that sex is somehow the result of sin. Whatever its origin, this is not Protestant teaching. Any basic drive in man can be perverted and made sinful. This is just as true of the drive toward self-preservation as of the sexual urge. We should not forget that the commandment dealing with adultery is not the first of the ten; it is not the key to the understanding of sin. And the tendency of our age, probably not uninfluenced by Victorianism, which makes so many people identify sin and sex has quite obscured the pervasiveness and profundity of man's depravity.

The Protestant Faith asserts that sex is God's invention. He made man male and female. Thus nothing is wrong with the sexual urge as such, for it has been given to man by God. Of course it can be perverted, but so can every other basic drive of man.

Here the Protestant Faith wants to be clearly distinguished from what could be called the modern attitude of positive or negative pansexualism. Positive pansexualism is the effort to explain man entirely in sexual terms, making the libido, the sex urge, the center of the human personality. This is certainly a tendency in contemporary life. It has been brilliantly described and explained by various social scientists. David Riesmann in his book *The Lonely Crowd* has called sex "The Last Frontier." He claims that, for modern man, the so-called "other-directed person," "it [sex] provides a kind of defense against the threat of total apathy."[43] Whatever the reason for pre-eminence of sex in the thought of our age, the Protestant Faith asserts that sex is simply not that important. It is part of life, an important part of life, but not all

[43] David Riesmann, *The Lonely Crowd* (New Haven, Conn.: Yale University Press, 1950), p. 154.

of life. It is quite possible to be a sinner, a man in revolt against God, without focusing the revolt in the area of the relationship of the sexes. This tendency to think of sin in sexual terms, which has dominated our culture, has had the effect of making us take less seriously all the other ways in which man revolts against God. All sorts of people who have revolted against God "intellectually" or in the way in which they have made other people into means to their ends have felt deceptively secure from sin because their particular revolt was not "sexual."

We read in the Gospel of Mark that Jesus, when asked by a scribe, *Which is the first commandment of all?* answered:

> *The first is, "Hear, O Israel: The Lord our God, the Lord is one; and you shall love the Lord your God with all your heart, and with all your soul, and with all your mind, and with all your strength." The second is this, "You shall love your neighbor as yourself." (Mark 12:29–31)*

Man is a sinner because he has broken and is breaking these commandments. He has other gods whom he loves, and he does not love his neighbor as he loves himself. All the specific sins which ruin man's life are the result of this. Man is in revolt against his God—yet without this God he cannot live! Man has always been in revolt against God; he belongs to a revolting community, to a race in revolt. He is involved in the collective guilt of the human race. This is the meaning of the doctrine of original sin in classical Protestantism. But in the Protestant Faith, this revolt is always at the same time personal responsibility and collective guilt. The personal responsibility explains the collective guilt—and the collective guilt throws light upon the personal responsibility.

The clue to the understanding of the predicament of man in the world, according to the Protestant Faith, is the fact of sin. All man's troubles stem from this one source. None can be solved ultimately unless the relationship to God, broken through sin, is restored.

Perhaps it is now in order to say a few words about some theoretical questions which always arise when the subject of sin is discussed. How can we explain the origin of sin? Where does evil come from? How can a universe created by a good God have evil in it? These questions are not answered by simply attributing evil to the activities of the devil or other demonic powers, for the question arises immediately—how did the devil become evil? Is he not also the creature of a good God?

To ask for an explanation of evil is actually a fairly "unprotestant" question. Protestantism begins with the encounter of God and man. In this encounter man knows himself as evil. He says with Isaiah:

Woe is me! For I am lost; for I am a man of unclean lips; for my eyes have seen the King, the Lord of hosts! (Isaiah 6:5)

But while we experience ourselves as sinners, as alienated from God, and while this is an utterly personal experience which needs no explanation of the origin of evil as far as the individual is concerned, some explanations of the origin of evil which have been offered by Christian thinkers could be mentioned.

Perhaps one of the most brilliant efforts is the explanation that the origin of evil does not have to be explained because it is essentially *nothingness*. It is non-being. An evil man is not a man plus something, namely evil. Rather an evil man is not fully man. He is deficient man. Evil is nothingness, non-being, and the vile person is the person whose deficiencies have perverted him. This is the explanation offered by Plato, which Augustine adopted with minor modifications. For Augustine, evil is not nothingness, but rather the turning of man from God to nothingness. Nothingness in itself is not evil. But the movement of the man who turns from

God to nothingness is evil. Here no explanation of evil is needed because pure evil has no being. Human sin it to turn toward nothingness instead of turning toward God.

The other equally ingenious effort to explain evil has been suggested by men like Nicolaus Cusanus at the end of the medieval period and by the German philosopher-shoemaker, Jacob Boehme, in the post-Reformation period. They asserted that evil is a lack of balance. If all things are in perfect balance, there is no evil. These various aspects of being are in themselves good if they are properly balanced against all other aspects of being. However, when a part goes off by itself, leaves the whole and becomes an independent part—then we have evil.

Perhaps this could be best illustrated by the example of the red and the white corpuscles in our blood. Both are in themselves good. Both white and red are necessary for the well-being of man. Neither is evil. But if the number of white corpuscles rapidly increases and the number of red corpuscles rapidly decreases, the person is sick. And the same happens if the red corpuscles increase and the white corpuscles decrease. Health is not having white corpuscles or having red corpuscles but having both in proper balance. Similarly, nothing in the universe is in itself evil. Evil originates if something that is part of the whole separates itself, makes itself independent from the whole, and thus upsets the divine balance.

Ingenious as these explanations of the origin of evil are, from the point of view of the Protestant Faith they serve only to illustrate that it is revolt which is at the root of sin. The revolt that turns man from God to nothingness or that makes him forget the balance and go off by himself. Man is sinner because he is in revolt against his Creator. There is no intellectual answer to the problem of evil—the only Christian answer is repentance and faith.

THE RESULT OF SIN

Man's revolt makes God's judgment necessary. The holy God appears to the sinner as the God of wrath. The Protestant Faith insists that God takes sin seriously. Against all efforts to reduce God to an overindulgent grandfather who overlooks disobedience and ignores it, the Protestant Faith asserts that God is holy and righteous altogether. He does not ignore the revolt of man any more than a good physician would ignore disease in the body. God would not be God if evil and sin were not abhorrent to Him. This is the unanimous witness of the Old Testament prophets. Amos sings:

> *Seek the Lord and live, lest he break out like fire in the house of Joseph, and it devour, with none to quench it for Bethel, O you who turn justice to wormwood, and cast down righteousness to the earth! He who made the Pleiades and Orion, and turns deep darkness into the morning, and darkens the day into night, who calls for the waters of the sea, and pours them out upon the surface of the earth, the Lord is his name, who makes destruction flash forth against the strong, so that destruction comes upon the fortress. They hate him who reproves in the gate, and they abhor him who speaks the truth. Therefore because you trample upon the poor and take from him exactions of wheat, you have built houses of hewn stone, but you shall not dwell in them; you have planted pleasant vineyards, but you shall not drink their wine. For I know how many are your transgressions, and how great are your sins . . . (Amos 5:6–12)*

It is because God is holy, because He is the Creator of heaven and earth, because He is all that has been said so far, that the Protestant Faith insists that God cannot and will not tolerate the revolt, the pride, and the unbelief of men.

The meaning of God's punishment is the assertion of His authority. He has not abdicated as ruler of the universe and He does not intend to do so. Thus man's revolt results in punishment. The fact that God is Lord, which is here expressed, was not hard to understand for the people of biblical times. In our democratic age, this notion is not so obvious. The Protestant Faith proclaims it nevertheless. God is not a constitutional monarch. The manner in which some Protestants tend to speak of God in our day would lead one to believe that God is a little like an elected chairman of the board of a great corporation of which the Christians are the stockholders. For this reason Rabbi Liebman's argument in his book *Peace of Mind* has found willing listeners among Protestants. For Dr. Liebman advocated a democratic god, an American god when he wrote:

> The story of the human race, until the age of technological democracy, has really been the story of dependence and helplessness—of men really feeling impotent in the presence of poverty and disease, of tyranny and autocracy, before which they had to bow their heads in resignation. . . . America is different from Europe. In Europe the emphasis was too often upon obedience and dependence upon some strong power to whose will man had to submit. In America . . . the emphasis has been upon self-reliance, upon every new generation doing better than its fathers, on becoming more successful in human attainments. One of the great troubles is that in our religion we have continued to picture our relationship to God in terms of the helpless, poverty-stricken, powerless motifs in European culture. Now, a religion that will emphasize man's nothingness and God's omnipotence; that calls upon us to deny our own powers and to glorify His—that religion may have fitted the needs of many Europeans, but it will not satisfy the growing self-confident character of America. . . . We must be brave enough to declare that every culture must create its own God idea rather than rely on outworn tradition. . . . The religion of the future, for the first time, may become a partnership religion in which men will not only *say* but will *feel,* that they are indispensable to God.[44]

It is hard for modern man to remember that God is independent of us and not a democratic leader subject to re-election. He is absolute Lord with absolute power. This aspect of the Protestant Faith, which is so eloquently proclaimed by a man like Calvin,

[44] J. L. Liebmann, *Peace of Mind* (New York: Simon & Schuster, Inc., 1946), p. 172 f.

has been frequently forgotten by the descendants of the Reformation, yet it remains an essential aspect of the classical Protestant Faith.

God is holy, and human revolt, human sin, brings about punishment. But here it is important to understand the peculiar double character of sin within Protestant theology: because man is a sinner, he sins; and because he sins, he is a sinner. Sin is both cause and effect. Again, we should remember that the theologians are attempting to describe in words what is in fact part of the experience of the Christian. He knows himself separated from God, and he feels responsible for this separation.

This is clearly indicated through the liturgical service of most Protestant churches. Episcopalians, Lutherans, Presbyterians, and to some degree other Protestants have at the very beginning of their main religious service—if they use any kind of formal service —a section called "confession of sins." In the *Morning Prayer* of the Episcopal Church, it reads as follows:

> Almighty and most merciful Father: we have erred and strayed from thy ways like lost sheep. We have followed too much the devices and desires of our own hearts. We have offended against thy holy laws. We have left undone those things which we ought to have done; And we have done those things which we ought not to have done; And there is no health in us.

And here follows a request for forgiveness. The words in *The Service* of the Lutheran Church are very similar:

> Almighty God, our Maker and Redeemer, we poor sinners confess unto thee, that we are by nature sinful and unclean, and that we have sinned against thee by thought, word, and deed. Wherefore we flee for refuge to thine infinite mercy, seeking and imploring thy grace for the sake of our Lord Jesus Christ.

And it would not be difficult to quote similar confessions of sins from all those Protestant churches which use some sort of formal worship. Even among those Protestants who do not use any kind of formal service, the confession of sins forms an important part of the worship. It is one of the most universally held beliefs of Protestants that man is indeed a sinner. And this revolt against God, this pride and unbelief, has deserved God's punishment. This is also expressed in most of the popular and ancient hymns of Protestantism. It forms the introduction to all the other proclamations of the Protestant Faith. Thus Luther sings:

Out of the depths I cry to thee, O Lord, my sins bewailing!
Bow down thy gracious ear to me, Make thou my prayer availing.
Mark not my misdeeds in thy book, But on my sins in mercy look,
Or who can stand before thee?[45]

The Protestant Faith asserts that sin, in which all men are involved, has some very real and observable results. These results are real—even for those people who deny the cause. All mankind, Christians and non-Christians alike, indeed the entire created world in which man lives feels the consequences of sin. Briefly summarized, they are strife, meaninglessness, and death.

According to the Protestant Faith, the conflict between man and man in its many forms is the result of sin. This applies equally to the quarrels between individuals and the quarrels between nations. The murder of Abel by Cain is such an individual expression of sin (Genesis 4). It is the ancestor of all family strife. Sin is at the bottom of the quarrels between husband and wife and between parents and children. Wherever there is real anger and real revolt there is man in revolt against God. And the Protestant Faith insists that it is important to take these quarrels seriously and to reduce their incidence. This is beautifully illustrated with another story from the Sermon on the Mount. Jesus, speaking of a man who wants to worship God, but is angry with his fellow man, said:

So if you are offering your gift at the altar, and there remember that your brother has something against you, leave your gift there before the altar and go; first be recon-

[45] *The Service Book and Hymnal of the Lutheran Church in America,* No. 372.

ciled to your brother, and then come and offer your gift."
(*Matthew 5:23, 24*)

For Jesus, estrangement from our fellow man implies estrangement from God. And as long as we are willful in our hate of our fellow man we cannot worship God.

Sin leads to estrangement from those closest to us. It is at the root of all our personal difficulties. This is a significant insight of Christianity and clearly part of the Protestant Faith.

But this is true not only of individual strife. Collective hatred, the hatred of one family for another, or of one nation for another, or of one race for another, is part of this sinfulness of man. This is seen in the Old Testament story of the Tower of Babel. Here, people in revolt against God are cast into confusion and strife (Genesis 11). Because of their revolt, the various nations can no longer understand one another. The Bible proclaims that international conflict and interracial conflict are the result of sin. Here again sin is both cause and consequence! Sin is the cause of the hatred between Germans and Frenchmen, Russians and Americans, Englishmen and Irishmen—and all the other hatreds which embitter our international life. But the resulting hatred is in turn sinful! Because of man's estrangement from God, he hates, and because he hates, he is further estranged from God.

The Protestant Faith asserts quite simply that all our strife, all our conflict, be it between a husband and his wife or the Soviet Union and the United States, is rooted in man's revolt against God. This is the ultimate source of all strife and hatred. As long as this revolt lasts, strife and hatred will last. The results of sin might temporarily find other forms of expression—husband and wife may become reconciled and hate the neighbors or the mother-in-law. But it is naïve to assume that the "object" of hostility, be it the existence of the mother-in-law or of Russia, is the real source of hatred. Even if men had the power to make these hated "objects" disappear altogether, they would not be able to get rid of their hatred. They would have to find other objects of hatred, because their revolt will always find expression in strife. Furthermore, men not only hate God and revolt against Him, and hate the neighbor and try to do him harm—as long as their revolt against God persists, they even hate themselves. The result of sin is not only self-love but also self-hatred. We do not want to accept ourselves as children of God; we want either to be God and love ourselves idolatrously, or the devil and hate ourselves with a holy hatred. Sometimes it takes a psychoanalyst to reveal this deep-seated self-hatred, which is as much a result of sin as the idolatrous self-love. This self-hatred will drive men into suicide; it will make them hypercritical of their own achievements; it will make it impossible for them to accept themselves as children of God with all the personal limitations which are part of their life.

This is the story of Shakespeare's Hamlet, Goethe's Faust, and Ibsen's Peer Gynt. They all tell us that man is not able to accept himself as a child of God. He either loves himself with an idolatrous love or hates himself with demonic hatred. This is the result of sin: man is involved in strife—with God, with the neighbor, and with himself!

A further result of sin is that life does not make sense: it is meaningless, it is "the tale told by an idiot full of sound and fury, signifying nothing." The Protestant Faith asserts that man in revolt against God cannot find any meaning in life. Life for him has no source, no present meaning, and no ultimate purpose. The appearance of man on this earth is some ghastly cosmic joke. It is the result of the combination of some infinitely impossible accidents. Here we are—coming from nowhere and going no place.

This is how Bertrand Russell describes the mood:

> The endless praises of the choirs of angels had begun to grow wearisome; for, after all, did he not deserve their praise? Had he not given them endless joy? Would it not be more amusing to obtain undeserved praise, to be worshiped by beings whom he tortured? He smiled inwardly, and resolved that the great drama should be performed.
> For countless ages the hot nebula whirled aimlessly through space.

At length it began to take shape, the central mass threw off planets, the planets cooled, boiling seas and burning mountains heaved and tossed, from black masses of cloud hot sheets of rain deluged the barely solid crust. And now the first germ of life grew in the depths of the ocean, and developed rapidly in the fructifying warmth into vast forest trees, huge ferns springing from the damp mold, sea monsters breeding, fighting, devouring, and passing away. And from the monsters, as the play unfolded itself, Man was born, with the power of thought, the knowledge of good and evil, and the cruel thirst for worship. And Man saw that all is passing in this mad, monstrous world, that all is struggling to snatch, at any cost, a few brief moments of life before Death's inexorable decree. And Man said: "There is a hidden purpose, could we but fathom it, and the purpose is good; for we must reverence something, and in the visible world there is nothing worthy of reverence." And Man stood aside from the struggle, resolving that God intended harmony to come out of chaos by human efforts. And when he followed the instincts which God had transmitted to him from his ancestry of beasts of prey, he called it Sin, and asked God to forgive him. But he doubted whether he could be justly forgiven, until he invented a divine Plan by which God's wrath was to have been appeased. And seeing the present was bad, he made it yet worse, that thereby the future might be better. And he gave God thanks for the strength that enabled him to forgo even the joys that were possible. And God smiled; and when he saw that Man had become perfect in renunciation and worship, he sent another sun through the sky, which crashed into Man's sun; and all returned again to nebula.

"Yes," he murmured, "it was a good play; I will have it performed again." Such, in outline, but even more purposeless, more void of meaning, is the world which Science presents for our belief. Amid such a world, if anywhere, our ideals henceforth must find a home. That Man is the product of causes which had no prevision of the end they were achieving; that his origin, his growth, his hopes and fears, his loves and his beliefs, are but the outcome of accidental collocations of atoms; that no fire, no heroism, no intensity of thought and feeling, can preserve an individual life beyond the grave; that all the labors of the ages, all the devotion, all the inspiration, all the noonday brightness of human genius, are destined to extinction in the vast death of the solar system, and that the whole temple of Man's achievement must inevitably be buried beneath the débris of a universe in ruins— all these things, if not quite beyond dispute, are yet so nearly certain, that no philosophy which rejects them can hope to stand. Only within the scaffolding of these truths, only on the firm foundation of unyielding despair, can the soul's habitation henceforth be safely built.[46]

Here is an honest man speaking. This is what he honestly believes. And since this is apparently a universal reaction of man, the Protestant Faith asserts that the result of sin is meaninglessness. Whenever men have contemplated the human predicament in ruthless honesty, they have despaired. The oldest Greek Hedonists who tried to persuade men to live a life dedicated to the pursuit of pleasure finally turned into advocates of suicide (Hegesias) for the same reason that Bertrand Russell has here given—the ultimate meaninglessness of life. And who can read a Greek tragedy and fail to be overwhelmed by the brilliant clarity with which it proclaims the meaninglessness of all human efforts?

The Protestant Faith says that this is the result of sin. Because of his revolt against God man is separated from the one source of meaning and eventually overwhelmed by the meaninglessness. Even if the wise man can escape involvement in the strife and the bickering that wastes the time of the fool, he soon realizes that meaninglessness is the alternative to the foolishness of strife and conflict. Therefore the Preacher says,

> *Remember also your Creator in the days of your youth,*
> *before the evil days come, and the years draw nigh, when*
> *you will say, "I have no pleasure in them"; before the sun*
> *and the light, and the moon and the stars are darkened*
> *and the clouds return after the rain; in the day when the*
> *keepers of the house tremble, and the strong men are bent,*
> *and the grinders cease because they are few, and those that*

[46] Bertrand Russell, *Selected Papers of Bertrand Russell* (New York: Random House, The Modern Library, [1927]), pp. 1–3. Used by permission of original publisher, George Allen & Unwin Ltd.

*look through the windows are dimmed, and the doors on
the street are shut; when the sound of the grinding is low,
and one rises up at the voice of a bird, and all the daughters
of song are brought low; they are afraid also of what is
high, and terrors are in the way; the almond tree blossoms,
the grasshopper drags itself along and desire fails; because
man goes to his eternal home, and the mourners go about
the streets; before the silver cord is snapped, or the golden
bowl is broken, or the pitcher is broken at the fountain,
or the wheel broken at the cistern, and the dust returns to
the earth as it was, and the spirit returns to God who gave
it. Vanity of vanities, says the Preacher; all is vanity.*
(*Ecclesiastes 12:1-8*)

The other result of sin is death. This is stated briefly and strikingly in the New Testament in the sentence: *The wages of sin is
death.* (*Romans 6:23*) This is all there is to it! The universal revolt
of man against his Creator results in universal death. Everybody
dies; there are no exceptions. To live means to die and there is no
escape. The poets and sages of the human race have faithfully proclaimed this fact. Shakespeare declares:

> To-morrow, and to-morrow, and to-morrow,
> Creeps in this petty pace from day to day,
> To the last syllable of recorded time;
> And all our yesterdays have lighted fools
> The way to dusty death. Out, out, brief candle!
> Life's but a walking shadow, a poor player
> That struts and frets his hour upon the stage
> And then is heard no more: . . .[47]

Yet while death is the destiny of the human race, our entire culture
is so designed as to avoid the very mention of the word. Death is
simply not referred to in polite society, and we make every effort
to remain unaware of it. In his little story *The Loved One* Evelyn

[47] Shakespeare, *Macbeth,* Act V, sc. 5.

Waugh shows how far our civilization is willing to go in order to preserve the illusion that nobody we care about really dies, even to the establishment of mortuaries for household pets. But one does not have to get very old to realize that our own efforts are no more successful than the efforts of the ancient Egyptians, who tried to avoid the stark reality of death through embalming.

The wages of sin is death—and, asserts the Protestant Faith, as we are all sinners, we shall all, without exception, die.

There is nothing "subjective" about this result of sin. It is not merely the allegedly morbid imaginations of the religious which cause men to die. Death is real for every man. It is as objective as anything we experience. And in no way does it depend for its reality upon the individual's faith or unbelief. Obviously we do not have to "believe" in death in order to die. Everybody dies. And the same is true about the other results of sin. We do not have to "believe" in strife in order to have our life made miserable by strife and conflict. Strife and conflict are part of the given, part of the world in which we live. Even if we personally should make a heroic effort to avoid all strife, it is possible for others to involve us in their strife against our will. Again, there is nothing merely subjective about Hiroshima, where the first atom bomb killed thousands; this was not a state of mind. Strife is a reality which as a result of sin confronts us everywhere. In a less dramatic sense, the personal bickering and quarreling which may make the home life of an individual miserable is not merely a state of mind; it is often the most real experience a person has in his entire life.

To be sure, meaninglessness is more subjective. It is not as objectively demonstrable as death and strife. But it is real nevertheless. And in some ways it is worse than either strife or death. One can put up with a lot of conflict if one believes that the conflict has some ultimate meaning. It is not impossible to die courageously for one's country or for one's friends if one believes that country and friends are worth dying for. If one believes that such a death "makes sense," it is quite possible to face it with equanimity and to say, "I regret that I have but one life to give for my country!"

But if the acid of meaninglessness has destroyed all genuine friendship and all spontaneous loyalty and patriotism—then indeed we have become more miserable than those who have to fight or to die. Though perhaps the least objective of the effects of sin, meaninglessness may be the worst of all because it is the most difficult to face and the hardest to bear.

But whatever value judgment we may make, whatever our attitude, the Protestant Faith asserts that strife, meaninglessness, and death are all three the inevitable results of sin. To some degree all men are aware of them.

The Protestant Faith asserts that the entire world as we know it is involved in man's sin. The world which man knows participates in his sin and suffers the consequences. In a sense sin has cosmic significance. It does not merely affect the individual human being; it affects everything with which the race of man comes into contact. This again has been described by the Apostle Paul in a very colorful phrase: *We know that the whole creation has been groaning in travail together until now. (Romans 8:22)* As a result of man's revolt against God, he has the ability to inject his own failure and strife and meaninglessness into all the things he touches.

War, atomic death, genocide are ways in which man's sin involves the whole world of man. Men do not only destroy each other in war, they destroy nature as well. With ever more powerful bombs they poison the air and the water not only for other men but possibly for all life on earth. Through the increased radiation level, which is the result of experimental bombs, the heredity of hundreds of generations yet unborn may be jeopardized. At least this seems to be the view of some of the most competent experts. And all this is the result of sin for the entire world of man. But while it may be fairly easy to see these universal effects of man's revolt against God in case of war and atomic experimentation, the same harmful consequences, even if more subtly, result from man's greed. What men have done to their rivers and forests, to their soil and air, affects not only man but all those creatures who share this earth with him.

Because it means easy profit, because it is cheap for the politicians who administer our cities, we poison our rivers and turn them into sewers. The vile polluted smell of some of America's great rivers bears witness to the results of our greed. So does the land turned into a dust bowl, which should have never been touched by a plow, and the desert left behind by strip-mining operations. All the earth is involved in man's greed and has to pay the price. There are innumerable ways in which man's cruelty, man's selfishness, man's greed, in short, man's sin, affect all creation.

Even if Albert Schweitzer can hardly be considered an exponent of classical Protestantism, his doctrine of reverence for life, which insists that man has the obligation to respect all life, is derived from the witness of Scripture. This is not man's earth, he is not the owner but merely a steward and administrator of God's possessions. This insight is clearly a part of the Protestant Faith. The complete disregard and the sovereign selfishness with which man disposes of all those riches which he is supposed to administer are surely the result of sin. *The whole creation has been groaning in travail together until now.*

But what about the relationship of "natural" catastrophes and sin? Is there any special theological meaning to earthquakes and hurricanes, floods and other disturbances? There was a time in which Protestants, and probably all Christians, would have answered this question with an unambiguous yes! There wasn't a comet in the sky which was not believed to have religious significance. Every natural catastrophe was immediately explained as a direct act of divine punishment.

Here again, the Protestant Faith does not offer an abstract interpretation of meteorological or astronomical phenomena. Whenever this has been done under the cover of Christianity, Christians have forsaken their principal message, that God speaks to man personally and man must respond as a person. But if it is understood that the Church does not compete with the weather bureau or the observatory, all sorts of events can in fact become occasions for faith. A natural catastrophe may become the incident through which God speaks to me. Or the absence of such an expected catastrophe may become an incident which God uses to address me. But such an interpretation is vastly different from the glib explanations of earthquakes and floods as punishment for other people. The use of "natural catastrophes" to demonstrate the power of God to punish the people we don't like comes from a different spirit than the Spirit who reveals Himself in the New Testament. It is significant that Jesus rejects this easy, moralizing interpretation of natural catastrophes when it is suggested to Him in the Gospel of Luke:

> *There were some present at that very time who told him of the Galileans whose blood Pilate had mingled with their sacrifices. And he answered them, "Do you think that these Galileans were worse sinners than all the other Galileans, because they suffered thus? I tell you, No; but unless you repent you will all likewise perish."*

And then He continues, referring to a major accident:

> *"Or those eighteen upon whom the tower in Siloam fell and killed them, do you think that they were worse offenders than all the others who dwelt in Jerusalem? I tell you, No; but unless you repent you will all likewise perish."*
> *(Luke 13:1–5)*

In view of the clear-cut statement of Christ that such catastrophes are not to be used in a moralizing manner—and in the light of the entire Book of Job in the Old Testament which indicates that personal misfortune should not be used by the outsider in such a moralizing manner, it is hard to understand why occasionally Christians have insisted on drawing nice comforting lessons from the catastrophes that have befallen other people. This is certainly a sub-Christian way to look at God's dealings with man.

The Protestant Faith rejects simultaneously the idealistic theodicy, which claims that this is the "best of all possible worlds," as well as the "naturalistic" despair, which insists that we are "lost in the stars." Both views have been submitted. Those who have said that this is the best of all possible worlds have claimed that all the evil that we do in fact observe is merely the opportunity for God to show His goodness.

No less a philosopher than the great Gottfried Wilhelm Leibnitz defended the goodness of God against all attacks in this manner in his book *Theodicy*. But the underlying assumption of such an effort is that God needs such a defense. Because this means that He must appear before the judgment throne of human reason and morality, this is completely out of order as far as the Protestant Faith is concerned. The Protestant Faith confesses with the Apostle Paul: *Let God be true, but every man a liar. (Romans 3:4)* God does not need to be vindicated before the tribunal of men. It is rather man who needs to be justified before God.

On the other hand, the Protestant Faith rejects with equal vigor the despair of those who claim that the life of the universe and the life of man make no sense whatsoever. Such despair is for the Christian itself a result of sin. Indeed it is one of the most dangerous forms in which sin appears. Despair cuts men off from God's mercy more effectively than any other sin. There are those who would say that Judas Iscariot was doomed not for his betrayal of Jesus but because he despaired of God's mercy. Had he gone to the Cross after his betrayal when he repented of what he had done and asked the man hanging on the Cross for forgiveness—it would have been granted to him. What doomed Judas was not his crime but the despair that followed the crime. The Protestant Faith rejects this despair just as firmly as it rejects the shallow optimism of the men who assert that this is the best of all possible worlds. Those who speak optimistically of the best of all possible worlds seem to have far too shallow a view of sin and its ravages; those, on the other hand, who claim that despair is the only stance possible for man have far too limited a vision of the God who has spoken to man in Jesus Christ.

These false alternatives, an optimism out of touch with the seriousness of the human situation and a pessimism oblivious to the greatness of God's love, indicate that modern man has trouble with the basic Christian concepts of "sin" and "salvation."

Indeed, one of the major problems which an interpretation of the Protestant Faith confronts is the fact that the word "sin," which has been used so frequently in these pages is largely meaningless to modern man. Though it meant a great deal to Martin Luther and John Calvin, to John Wesley and Jonathan Edwards, it conveys little meaning to the men and women of our time. Is there a reason why this once powerful and lucid word has neither force nor clarity today?

A large number of factors have apparently contributed to this development. Three seem of sufficient importance to deserve some attention here. First, there is the general mood of relativism, which affects every aspect of our life. Many people no longer believe that "right" and "wrong" are words that make much sense. They say that "right" and "wrong" are completely "relative" to the situation and mean that it depends entirely on the prejudices of the group or the individual whether a particular action is considered right or its very opposite. In one society murder may be frowned upon, in another society murder may become a sign of distinction. Among some people the eating of human flesh may be considered terribly evil, while in another society it may be the condition for membership in the most distinguished group. Examples like this have been produced in large numbers, and all have tended to make the notion of sin appear obsolete. Of course, these examples are important to show that it is not easy to discover an "absolute norm." It is true that quite often in the history of mankind people have confused their particular way of doing things with the absolute norm. Observing this, the Greek philosopher Xenophanes commented 2,500 years ago,

Mortals fancy gods are born, and wear clothes, and have voice and form like themselves. Yet if oxen and lions had hands, and could paint with their hands, and fashion images, as men do, they would make the pictures and images of their gods in their own likeness; horses would make them like horses, oxen like oxen.[48]

Relativism has rendered an important service by showing that what was considered the absolute law in one society did not turn out to be very absolute when all societies were taken into consideration.

Even when this significant contribution of relativism to the clarification of human behavior is granted, it appears now that this idea of the relativity of all concepts of right and wrong can also be carried too far. But it is the popular, unscientific "poor man's relativism" which has subverted all moral standards. The belief that "right" and "wrong" are arbitrary has made it difficult to explain what the Protestant Faith means when it speaks of sin. Sin is revolt against God, but if God's will is not known to man or is even unknowable, the concept of sin does not make a great deal of sense.

We have discussed the Protestant Faith's answer to this problem previously. The Protestant Faith asserts that God's law is known and that there is right and wrong. No amount of statistics can change the facts that lying will make human communication eventually impossible and that homosexual behavior is sterile and if consistently and exclusively practiced dooms the human race to extinction. These are the facts of life which give the lie to those people who claim that all moral standards are equally valid or invalid, that they are in fact meaningless. Yet moral relativism has made it difficult for modern man to take sin as seriously as it must be taken according to the Protestant Faith.

The same can be said about naturalism. Here we have the assertion that all knowledge, even moral knowledge, is empirical. The key to the understanding of man is not his unique relationship to God but rather his relationship to nature. To the man on the street it means that man is no less and no more a part of nature

---

[48] C. M. Bakewell, *Source Book in Ancient Philosophy* (New York: Charles Scribner's Sons, 1939), p. 8.

than any other animal. Whatever he does he does as an animal and it is therefore natural. Just as one would not speak of the sinful behavior of dogs or cats, it would be equally senseless to speak of the sinful actions of man. The assumption is that man is merely animal. He is merely nature. This, of course, runs counter to the definition of man given by the Protestant Faith. Here man stands in a unique relationship to God. He is not merely animal; he is man. As man he is uniquely responsible to God. His relationship to the Creator is different from the relationship of a dog, a cat, or even a chimpanzee. The popular versions of naturalism, however, have obscured the difference, and as long as people believe that man is merely a highly developed animal the notion of sin cannot make much sense to them. The idea that man is in revolt against God is meaningful only if man stands in a unique relationship to God. This the Protestant Faith asserts. The notion of sin has to be understood from this point of view. Modern man, however, tends to ignore this unique relationship between himself and God, and thus his sense of sin is affected. If man is merely an animal it is no more reasonable to try him for his offenses, to blame him for his sins, than it would be to try a rattlesnake for striking, to blame a cat for chasing mice, a mouse for stealing cheese. It is because of the widely held view that we can explain man as merely animal apart from his origin and destiny in God that the notion of sin has become meaningless for many people in the twentieth century.

A third factor which has contributed to the difficulties of communicating the insights of the Protestant Faith to modern man is the superficial psychologizing and psychoanalyzing which have become part of our civilization. Sigmund Freud and his associates have made important contributions to man's understanding of himself. It would be foolish and obscurantist to deny the profound insights into the human mind which depth psychology in all its various forms has provided. But when accepted by modern man as a religion offering salvation by correcting the flaws in the relationship of man to himself, depth psychology can make it difficult for him to comprehend that sin describes the broken relationship between God and man.

For Freud religion is the result of the Oedipus complex. It is the result of man's guilt, traceable to the dim past, when, according to Freud, human beings traveled in herds, and the young men killed the father and took over the females.[49] This is not the place to debate the validity of these notions concerning the past history of man. Suffice it to say that most anthropologists and psychologists believe that Freud's theology is probably the weakest link in his system. But quite apart from the accuracy of his theories, their effect on the understanding of the Christian Faith among those who are influenced by Freud is considerable. Faith is reinterpreted into something quite different from trust; it becomes an expression of fear.

Religion is "neurotic" and prayer is "compulsive." All feelings of guilt and the consciousness of sin are considered dangerous. Especially when this kind of psychology has been popularized by novelists, amateur psychiatrists, and cocktail-party psychologists, the result has been that sin has become a "dangerous" notion which a healthy person must by all means throw overboard. These popularizers have tended to say that if a person is conscious of sin, it is dangerous for his mental health. They claim that every effort has to be made to free mankind from all feelings of guilt. It has become fashionable to speak disdainfully of the "repressed" people who worry about sin. In this frequently garbled form depth psychology has become the property of all literate Americans and of a good many illiterate Americans as well.

All these developments have made the interpretation of the concept of sin as held by the Protestant Faith very difficult. For many modern men it no longer makes any sense.

While the reality of sin has been denied or rationalized away, the consequences of sin have become ever more apparent. It is the

[49] Cf. "Totem and Taboo," *The Basic Writings of Sigmund Freud,* trans. and ed. by Dr. A. A. Brill (New York: Random House, The Modern Library, 1938), pp. 807 ff.

claim of the Protestant Faith that the biblical witness does in fact describe the human situation most accurately. Thus, regardless of our subjective views of the meaning of life, the actual, observable, empirical life of sinful man has been blighted. Modern man may be able to deny the *existence* of sin. He may be able to discard the very notion as old-fashioned and irrelevant. Yet it is the claim of the Protestant Faith that the *results* of sin are demonstrable, observable, and painfully apparent to anybody who looks at our age.

However successful modern man may have been in denying the existence of sin, he has been spectacularly unsuccessful in avoiding its consequences. This is not merely pious talk on the part of those who are committed to the Christian point of view. This is the universal witness of all those people who take time to observe our situation and then take the trouble of writing down their observations. It would take us too far afield to quote all the evidence adduced by those outside the Christian faith in support of this view. One example will have to suffice.

Nobody will accuse Jean-Paul Sartre of being a spokesman for Christianity, yet even a cursory reading of his plays and novels shows that he describes a situation identical with the human situation distorted by sin. The picture he shows is an accurate view of the situation of man without God according to the Protestant Faith. In his play *No Exit* Sartre shows three very modern and emancipated people who are being destroyed by sin. Significantly, the play takes place in hell. The three people are in a drawing room, two women, Estelle and Inez, and one man, Garcin. It is Garcin who finally discovers the secret of Sartre's hell. He says, "So this is hell, I'd never have believed it. You remember all we were told about torture-chambers, the fire and brimstone, the 'burning marl.' Old wives' tales! There is no need for red-hot pokers. Hell is—*other people!*"[50]

Sartre's pessimistic description of the human situation is elo-

---

[50] Jean-Paul Sartre, *No Exit and Three Other Plays* (New York: Vintage Books, Inc., 1955), p. 47. Reprinted by permission of Alfred A. Knopf, Inc. and Vintage Books, Inc.

quently supported by American authors. In every serious play, we encounter strife, meaninglessness, and death. This is the story of Willy Loman in Arthur Miller's *Death of a Salesman* and of Blanche in Tennessee Williams' *Streetcar Named Desire*. Everywhere the same message is being proclaimed. Modern man may have trouble understanding the theological concept of sin as used in the Protestant Faith, but the consequences of sin are all about him. Whether we like it or not, whether it makes sense to us or not, whether we approve of it or not—the Protestant Faith asserts: The wages of sin is death—and all the evidence seems to support this position.

6

The Doctrine of Christ

Because of his original and actual sin man is doomed to despair and eternal death. He experiences the wrath of God. This is not only the description of a future state but of a present experience. While the experience is universal, the explanation for it varies greatly. The non-Christian will attribute his feeling of anxiety and despair to circumstances over which he has no control. The Christian, however, sees this situation as the result of his revolt against God. Man's life is meaningless because he has torn himself away from the source of all being, from the power which alone can give direction and ultimate purpose to his life. The Christian knows that his hopeless state is his own responsibility and not God's.

THE REASONS FOR THE INCARNATION

Man has broken the father-child relationship by his revolt against God, and classical Protestantism asserts that he cannot re-establish it out of his own power. While man can break the relationship he cannot restore it. It is as if a man were held by a friend while climbing a high mountain. Beneath him yawns an abyss. In this situation he can push the helping hand of his friend away. He can free himself from this helping interference. But once he has done so, he falls, and now he cannot re-establish the connection which he could dissolve. While he was free to push the friend away, he is not free to get a hold on him again. Through the very act of pushing him away his situation has radically changed. He is now hurtling through space and will surely be smashed on the ground unless something happens. But this is something which he cannot produce or control. It is entirely outside of his power. Søren Kierkegaard, dealing with this problem in his *Philosophical Fragments,* used a very lucid illustration to make this point. He says:

> Suppose a child had been presented with a little sum of money, and could buy with it either a good book, for example, or a toy, both at the same price. If he buys the toy, can he then buy the book for the same money? Surely not, since the money is already spent. But perhaps he may go to the bookseller and ask him to make an exchange, letting him have the book in return for the toy. Will not the bookseller say: My dear child, your toy is not worth anything; it is true that when you still had the money you could have bought the book instead of the toy, but a toy is a peculiar kind of thing, for once it is bought it loses all value. Would not the child think that this was very strange? And so there was also a time when man could have bought either freedom or bondage at the same price, this being the soul's free choice and commitment in the choice. He chose bondage; but if he now comes forward with a proposal for an exchange, would not God reply: Undoubtedly there was a time when you could have bought whichever you pleased, but bondage is a very strange sort of thing; when it is bought it has absolutely no value, although the price

paid for it was originally the same. Would not such an individual think this very strange? Again, suppose two opposing armies drawn up in the field, and that a knight arrives whom both armies invite to fight on their side; he makes his choice, is vanquished and taken prisoner. As prisoner he is brought before the victor, to whom he foolishly presumes to offer his services on the same terms as were extended to him before the battle. Would not the victor say to him: My friend, you are now my prisoner; there was indeed a time when you could have chosen differently, but now everything is changed.[51]

Man's unenviable position is like that of the captured knight. He had a choice and he made the wrong choice. There is no way in which man out of his own resources can unmake this decision.

The Protestant Faith shares the awareness of the desperate predicament in which man finds himself with all other sensitive descriptions of the human situation. But, important as this insight is, it is only part of the story. It is the assertion of the Protestant Faith that God has become man in Jesus Christ in order to bridge the gap which man has established through his revolt. God has become man in Jesus Christ in order to save man. This translation of God into human form is called the "incarnation." It is a translation of God into human language. Without this incarnation God would be utterly incomprehensible to men. He must speak to them with words and symbols they can understand. Since they cannot understand God as *God*, God must translate Himself into their terms so that they may understand God as *man*. This is what happened in Jesus Christ. Here God speaks to us in our language. This is not the sophisticated language of philosophy and of theology. He has chosen to speak the simple language of action and words understandable to children and childlike minds and yet beyond the comprehension of even the most profound. This is the message of Christmas. In a sense even the smallest child can get some meaning out of the baby in the manger who was Christ the Lord, worshiped by shepherds, wise men, and angels. Yet that He who

[51] Soren Kierkegaard, *Philosophical Fragments,* trans. David F. Swenson (Princeton, N.J.: Princeton University Press, 1942), p. 11.

cannot be contained by the universe is now in the arms of Mary and that He who upholds with His power everything that is has become a baby—this message transcends all philosophical speculation.

Classical Protestantism asserts with one voice that Jesus Christ is both "very God of very God" and true man subject to all the frailties and temptations of other human beings. As true man and true God He is the mediator between God and man. For the Protestant Faith this term is reserved for Christ. As the Apostle Paul says: *For there is one God, and one mediator between God and men, the man Christ Jesus.* (*I Timothy 2:5*) While some Christians may consider other human beings as possible "mediators," on this point classical Protestantism is adamant. There is only one mediator, and he is Jesus Christ. He alone can translate God into our language, He alone can restore the relationship which man's revolt has destroyed. For He is not only the teacher but above all the Savior.

THE HUMANITY OF CHRIST

It is important to understand what is meant when the Protestant Faith asserts that Christ is truly man, for there have been times in the history of the Christian Church when His humanity has been called into question. In the early church there were many people who denied Christ's humanity. They claimed that He was God but denied that He was man. To buttress their claims, these people, who were called Docetists, asserted that Jesus' body was not a true body but merely looked like a body. They said that God merely *appeared* in human form. As early as the end of the first century Ignatius, Bishop of Antioch, wrote against those who denied the humanity of Jesus Christ: "Be deaf therefore when anyone speaks to you apart from Jesus Christ, who was of the family of David, and of Mary, who was truly born, both ate and drank, who was truly persecuted under Pontius Pilate, was truly crucified and died."[52]

[52] *Ignatius to the Trallians,* IX/1, *The Apostolic Fathers,* Kirsopp Lake,

Against the Docetists and all others who deny the humanity of Christ the Protestant Faith asserts that Jesus Christ was man, just as truly a human being as any one of us. He was conceived, was born, grew from infancy to manhood, was hungry and thirsty, was tired and sad, wept and rejoiced, suffered and died. For the Protestant Faith Jesus Christ is a person who was born when Quirinius was governor of Syria and who died under Pontius Pilate. He was bound in history and time, He was limited in knowledge. We read in the New Testament that Jesus said concerning the end of the world: *But of that day and hour no one knows, not even the angels of heaven, nor the Son, but the Father only.* (*Matthew 24:36*) This, say Protestant theologians, demonstrates that Jesus' humanity was so complete that it included such limitations in His knowledge of the future. However, this must not be understood as merely a piece of interesting information. Rather, this very humanity of Jesus Christ is a challenge and call to discipleship for the Christian. This is how the Apostle Paul interprets it:

Have this mind among yourselves which you have in Christ Jesus, who, though he was in the form of God, did not count equality with God a thing to be grasped, but emptied himself, taking the form of a servant, being born in the likeness of men. And being found in human form he humbled himself and became obedient unto death, even the death on the cross. (Philippians 2:5–8)

Not merely speculation but action, not merely thought but life, is the significance of Christ's humanity.

All this means that for the Protestant Faith Jesus Christ is no abstract philosophical ideal but a real historical person. He is as real and historical as any other person who ever walked on this

---

trans. (Cambridge: Harvard University Press, Loeb Classical Library, 1945), p. 211.

earth. He is no "ghost," no "poetic symbol," no "vision," but flesh of our flesh and blood of our blood. The humanity of Christ is also demonstrated in his relationship to the Father. He learns, He prays, He obeys, He is tempted and struggles, and finally exclaims, *Father, into thy hands I commit my spirit!* (*Luke 23:46*)

According to the Protestant Faith there is no pretense about any of these expressions of Jesus' humanity. His temptations are not play-acting; they are real temptations, as real as any other human temptations. Protestants take much comfort from these temptations of Christ because they illuminate our own temptations. Because God became man in Jesus Christ, the Protestant Faith asserts, temptation is not alien to Him; in Jesus Christ God has shared even our temptations with us.

And the man Jesus Christ truly suffers. His suffering is not a show, a game of "let's pretend." It is the most real suffering imaginable. What makes the Lenten season so profoundly moving is that we see God share our human suffering. He is no mere spectator of the human tragedy. It is not a show which God is watching. Rather, the human tragedy is experienced by God in Jesus Christ. He suffers with us; He suffers in us. And Christ shares not only man's physical suffering, when He is beaten and bleeding on the way to the Cross. He shares even our spiritual suffering, our loneliness and our despair. This is the meaning of Gethsemane. Here we see Jesus plead with His disciples that they should stay with Him in that terrible night before his arrest, trial, and execution. He wants them to stay awake with Him, to keep Him company, to comfort Him in these difficult hours. But the disciples fall asleep, and in these last hours Jesus is left all alone. He is not the conquering hero who knows exactly what he wants to do and how to do it, but a troubled man who knows anxiety and despair. This is what we read in the Gospel according to St. Matthew:

> *And taking with him Peter and the two sons of Zebedee, he began to be sorrowful and troubled. Then he said to*

*them, "My soul is very sorrowful, even to death; remain
here and watch with me." And going a little farther he
fell on his face and prayed, "My father, if it be possible,
let this cup pass from me; nevertheless not as I will, but
as thou wilt." And he came to the disciples and found
them sleeping. (Matthew 26:37-40)*

Here we meet a man who knows what trouble is and who needs
companionship in his troubles. This is the most profound conviction of the Protestant Faith and it is movingly expressed in some
of the hymns of the Church and also in the Negro spirituals when
they sing, "Nobody knows the trouble I've seen—Nobody knows
but Jesus!"[53] Here we find a profound awareness characteristic of
the Protestant Faith of the reality and the depth of the suffering
and despair which Jesus experienced and which He shared with
all men. No human suffering, no human anxiety, is alien to Him.

This is perhaps most profoundly expressed in the word from
the Cross: *My God, my God, why hast Thou forsaken me?*
(*Mark 15:34*) Here Jesus experiences in His person the profound
separation of man from God which is the result of sin and leads
to the catastrophe of man's life. For the Protestant Faith this means
that nobody is ever so forsaken by God that his experience is not
shared by God Himself in the man Jesus Christ, And this includes
even the ultimate human experience, the experience of death itself.
Jesus Christ suffered, was crucified, died, and was buried! Because
Jesus Christ is truly man, nothing human is alien to God.

Because of Christ's humanity all He does is relevant to us.
In the New Testament we are not confronted by a hero of Greek
mythology, a being which is half man and half god. The Greeks,
indeed, had many such hybrid beings. Achilles and Hercules, for
example, were not truly human nor truly divine, but somewhere
in between, a peculiar blend of humanity and divinity. Against
all these figures of Greek antiquity the Protestant Faith asserts

[53] Cf. also: *Service Book and Hymnal of the Lutheran Church in America,* Hymn No. 500, st. 1-3.

that Jesus Christ was true man. He is the son of Mary, our brother and our example.

THE DIVINITY OF CHRIST

But this is only one side of the story. Complementary to it and equally important is the assertion of the divinity of Christ. The same Jesus Christ who is truly man is also truly God. This confession has many and inexhaustible implications. For the Protestant Faith it means that when Jesus Christ speaks, God speaks. In Him we meet God the Creator, the Lord, the Judge, the Father. For the Protestant Faith there is no other way to meet God than in Jesus Christ. Apart from Christ we cannot know God. Apart from Christ God remains for us always the unknown God, the hidden God. In Christ we meet Him face to face. In Christ God reveals Himself to man.

It is in the very proclamation of Christ that we find described His unique relationship to the Father. *All things have been delivered to me by my Father; no one knows the Son except the Father, and no one knows the Father except the Son and any one to whom the Son chooses to reveal Him.* (*Matthew 11:27*) Or we read in John 14:9: *He who has seen me has seen the Father. . . . Believe me that I am in the Father and the Father in me.* It is Jesus Christ Himself who makes these claims, according to the New Testament. After His resurrection Jesus said to the disciples: *Where two or three are gathered in my name, there am I in the midst of them.* (*Matthew 18:20*) And a little later we read in the same Gospel: *All authority in heaven and on earth has been given to me. . . . Lo, I am with you always to the close of the age.* (*Matthew 28:20*)

The New Testament is full of the faith in Jesus Christ as true God. In Colossians 1:17 we read about Him: *He is before all things, and in Him all things consist.* In the Book of Revelation the Christ proclaims: *I am the Alpha and the Omega, who is and who was and who is to come the Almighty.* (*Revelation 1:8*) In other words, according to the proclamation of the Bible and thus as an integral part of the Protestant Faith the man Jesus Christ is at the same time the eternal God. In Hebrews 13:8, the Apostolic Church proclaims: *Jesus Christ is the same yesterday and today and forever*—thus confessing that this man Jesus Christ is at the same time the Immutable God.

It is in this context that the statements in the Gospel of John concerning the eternal Christ must be understood:

> *In the beginning was the Word, and the Word was with God and the Word was God. He was in the beginning with God; all things were made through him, and without him was not anything made that was made. (John 1:1-3)*

For the Protestant Faith this is not idle theological speculation concerning some abstract and theoretical proposition about Jesus Christ. On the contrary, it is the language of worship which adores the Savior. The Christian Church knows Him as free from the chains of time and space. His omnipotence and omnipresence are not logically derived from some theory concerning the nature of God; they are, rather, the way in which the Almighty Lord has always and everywhere confronted His people.

It is the fact that Jesus Christ is true God which suffuses and permeates everything that has been said about His humanity. At the same time it is the fact that Jesus Christ is true man which gives relevance to the worshipful confession of His divinity, making it a call to faith and love.

Therefore the Church sings:

> Thou art the King of Glory, O Christ;
> Thou art the everlasting Son of the Father.
> When thou tookest upon thee to deliver man:
> Thou didst humble thyself to be born of a Virgin.

When thou hadst overcome the sharpness of death:
Thou didst open the kingdom of heaven to all believers.

(From the *Te Deum Laudamus*)

Indeed Christ did humble Himself, but even in this humiliation, this voluntary giving up of the exercise of His divine power, the Protestant Faith confesses that Christ was truly God.

Thus the Christian Church will speak of Christ as having power to forgive sins and raise the dead. He is the object of faith and worship with the Father and the Holy Spirit. As the Gospel of John quotes Jesus: *I am the way, and the truth, and the life; no one comes to the Father, but by me.* (*John 14:6*)

For the Protestant Faith Jesus Christ is true God, the second person of the Holy Trinity, and classical Protestantism has been unanimous in this assertion. Luther's explanation of the Second Article of the Apostles' Creed is this: "I believe that Jesus Christ, true God, begotten of the Father from eternity, and also true man, born of the Virgin Mary, is my Lord." This is basically the faith of the main stream of Protestantism everywhere. However, it must be added that it is impossible to dissociate the message of Christ from the Christ who proclaims this message. It is the person of Christ, the fact that He is God speaking to man, which gives validity to the message. At the same time the message is in conformity with the messenger. It is a fitting message corresponding to the source.

For the Protestant Faith it is impossible to accept the message without accepting Him who proclaimed it. There have always been people who have liked what Christ had to say but who did not want to yield to Him who said it. While wanting to adopt the truths proclaimed by Christ, they rejected the claims which Christ made about Himself in connection with these truths. But the message cannot be separated from the spokesman. If the spokesman is a megalomaniac, a man who suffers from some mental disorder which makes him think he is the son of God, then it is neither intelligent nor safe to accept his message. This is the dilemma of those who like the message, except for what it says about the messenger. Whenever the faith in the person of Christ has been given up by Christians, the faith in His message has been discarded soon afterward. Without the authority of the person of Christ His message is of little value.

It is equally impossible to accept the Christ without accepting His message. This too has been tried. There have always been some people who have been fascinated by the idea of Christ, overwhelmed by the speculative grandeur of Christology, the doctrine of Christ, but who have ignored what Christ said or did. These people have been most willing to believe statements and propositions about Christ's humanity and divinity but have not seemed equally ready to follow Him, obey Him, and be His disciples. According to the Protestant Faith it is as impossible to accept the Christ without His Gospel as it is to accept the Gospel without the Christ.

Classical Protestantism has always emphasized that the Christ and His Gospel are inseparable. The validity of the Gospel depends upon the authority of the Christ, and the authority of the Christ in the life of the Christian depends upon the willingness of the Christian to let the Gospel transform his life. It is as futile to say "yes" to Christ and "no" to His Gospel as it is to say "yes" to His Gospel and "no" to the Christ. Although both of these confused responses have been tried, classical Protestantism has insisted that the "yes" to the Gospel depends upon the "yes" to the Christ and that "yes" to the Christ must find expression in a "yes" to His Gospel.

In the light of what has now been said about the divinity of Christ, is it really possible to maintain His true humanity? Does not the fact of His holiness and sinlessness detract from His true manhood? The letter to the Hebrews states that He is *holy, blameless, unstained, separated from sinners, exalted above the heavens.* (*Hebrews 7:26*) St. Paul writes that Christ *knew no sin.* (*II Corinthians 5:21*) The First Letter of Peter refers to Him symbolically as *a lamb without blemish or spot.* (*I Peter 1:19*) And in the Gospel of John we read that Jesus challenged His opponents to convict Him of sin (John 8:46). Grounded in the biblical witness the classical Protestant Faith proclaims that Jesus Christ is sinless. He is not in revolt against God—His life is a life of obedience, surrender, and fellowship with the Father. But rather than detracting from His humanity this holiness makes Jesus Christ the *true* man. Man in revolt against God is false man, man cut off from his roots. To see what God wants all men to be, one must look at Jesus Christ, the true man.

This is what the theologians of the Christian Church have meant when they called Jesus Christ the second Adam. He is the alternative to Adam. The Apostle Paul expressed it this way:

For as by a man came death, by a man has come also the resurrection of the dead. For as in Adam all die, so also in Christ shall all be made alive. (I Corinthians 15:21, 22)

Man knows now not only what the pattern of estrangement and revolt against God is like and will lead to; he also knows what the pattern of obedience to God is like and will lead to. Through Christ another alternative has come into human history. Christ has made the pattern of obedience and fellowship possible.

If a Protestant were to try to define what the human life is supposed to be, he would not point to any Christian, be he ever so outstanding; he would point to Christ, in whom the human possibilities under God have been fully revealed. This is what it means that Jesus Christ is "the second Adam." In Him we see man at his best. Jesus Christ is what man should be and can be according to God's holy will.

No Protestant discussion of the person of Christ would be complete without a reference to the climactic event of His earthly life, the resurrection. The resurrection of Christ is the deed of God which explains to the Christian the origin and destiny of the Church. If Christians did not believe in the resurrection, if Christ had not been raised from the dead—then all the things said initially about the tragedy of human existence would still be true. Christ's death would be the murder of another Socrates, a good man who was killed by an evil age. This would still only show that "you can't win," that "the dice are loaded." Life would still be only the tale told by the idiot full of sound and fury, signifying nothing.

But we are confronted by the fact of the Christian Church, which has proclaimed from the very beginning that God raised Jesus Christ from the dead. In other words, the crooked politicians and the corrupt ecclesiastical dignitaries who had Christ crucified were not victorious. The Cross is not the end—it is merely the beginning.

To a world which claimed that it had killed Christ the early Christians answered that Christ lives. They did not merely say that, they were willing to die for it. They knew it to be true, because they had experienced it in person. The fact that Christ had overcome death took away all the terror from death and made the Christians who believed in the resurrection invincible.

Every effort was made to destroy this message and to hush it up, for it had a demoralizing effect on the Roman Empire. If your power is built on the fact that you can exterminate people, then your power will be undermined if people learn that although you may be able to kill them, they will live again. This "good news" of the early Christians was the kind of message which could not be suppressed by force. Every effort was made—thousands and hundreds of thousands were killed throughout the centuries to suppress the message that death has no power. But for every Christian who was killed, others who saw him die without fear were converted to Christianity, so that the early Christians could say, "The blood of the martyrs is the seed of the Church!"

It is the faith in the resurrection of Christ which explains the existence of the Christian Church. Without this faith the Christian Church would never have come into being, and should it ever lose this faith it will not last very long. The resurrection and the message of Christ are mutually interdependent. The resurrection is God's confirmation of the Gospel. This is why the Apostle Paul says:

If Christ has not been raised, your faith is futile and you are still in your sins. . . . But in fact Christ has been raised from the dead, the first-fruits of those who have fallen asleep. (I Corinthians 15:17 ff.)

While it is generally admitted that the resurrection of Christ is the crowning event of His life, there are some Christians who would put equal stress upon His miraculous birth. In view of the fact that neither the Apostle Paul nor the Gospel of John even mentions the circumstances of His birth, such an emphasis seems unjustified. The tendency among some Christians to make the belief in the virgin birth into a theological shibboleth is unfortunate because it has effectively obscured the meaning of the Church's proclamation that Jesus Christ was born of the Virgin Mary. Yet it is part of the faith of an overwhelming majority of all Christians that this birth was extraordinary and different from all other human births. Most Protestants believe that in a unique sense God was the author of the human life of Jesus. Since this doctrine has become controversial among Protestants in the nineteenth and twentieth centuries, it might be in order to try to explain what this doctrine does and does not mean.

For the Protestant Faith the doctrine of the Virgin Birth does not imply a depreciation of sex, nor is it an attempt to provide a spectacular beginning for Jesus' life. If we remember the temper of the times in which Jesus was born, we will note that a virgin giving birth to a child was not particularly spectacular; in that age such events were considered quite possible. This was a pre-scientific age and the law of cause and effect was not held to be insurmountable. If the early Christians wanted to invent a spectacular origin for Christ, the virgin birth appears to have been a fairly unauspicious choice. It should be noted that according to Greek mythology Pallas Athene, a goddess of the Greeks, had jumped fully armed out of the head of Zeus. This was indeed a spectacular beginning, and in comparison with this type of story current in the Hellenistic world the virgin mother in the stable surrounded by the shepherds does not seem very spectacular.

Rather than a proof of the divinity of Christ, the doctrine of the virgin birth is for the Protestant Faith, at least for the many Protestants who take this doctrine seriously, a part of the emphasis on the central significance of "by grace alone," which we discussed at the very beginning. We said then, and we repeat now, that one of Protestantism's main theses is the assertion that man is saved and brought into fellowship with God through God's action and not because of anything man can do. The doctrine of the virgin birth underlines this sovereign grace of God. It proclaims that God gives the Savior to men. Christ is God's gift to mankind. Man cannot claim that he saved himself in Jesus Christ. God saved man in Jesus Christ "by grace alone," and this fact is safeguarded by the doctrine of the virgin birth.

For almost all Christians, however, the doctrine of the virgin birth is the result of faith in Christ and not its cause. Protestants, even those Protestants who greatly stress the importance of the virgin birth, will insist that they believe in the virgin birth because they believe in Christ and not that they believe in Christ because of the virgin birth. Belief in the virgin birth is the result of faith in Christ rather than its condition!

It should be added that ultimately the person of Christ is for the Protestant Faith a secret of God's grace. No theological statement can exhaustively describe what is essentially an experience of the Christian individual within the Christian community. If one listens carefully to the words of the Christmas hymns of the Church, one can gain some insight into the nature of the Christian Faith as faith in Christ. For adoration and worship are the only adequate response to God's gift. A Christmas hymn by Charles Wesley may sometimes communicate the faith better than any amount of theological analysis. Thus the Church sings:

Hark! The herald Angels sing, "Glory to the newborn King;
Peace on earth and mercy mild, God and sinners reconciled!"

Joyful all ye nations rise, Join the triumph of the skies,
With th'angelic host proclaim, "Christ is born in Bethlehem."
Hark! the herald Angels sing, "Glory to the new-born King."

Christ, by highest heaven adored, Christ the everlasting Lord;
Late in time behold Him come, Off-spring of a virgin's womb!
Veiled in flesh, the God-head see, Hail th'incarnate Deity!
Pleased as Man with men to appear, Jesus our Immanuel here!

Hail, the heavenly Prince of Peace, Hail the Sun of Righteousness!
Light and life to all He brings, Risen with healing in His wings.
Mild He lays His glory by, Born that Man no more may die:
Born to raise the sons of earth; Born to give them second birth.

Come, Desire of nations, come, Fix in us Thy humble home;
O, to all Thyself impart, Formed in each believing heart!
Hark! the herald Angels sing, "Glory to the new-born King;
Peace on earth, and mercy mild, God and sinners reconciled!"

Very briefly and very simply, and yet very profoundly, this is the
Protestant Faith as far as the person of Christ is concerned.

THE WORK OF CHRIST

What does the Protestant Faith teach about the work of
Christ? According to the teaching of classical Protestantism the
work of Christ has been divided into three parts: The work of
prophet, priest, and king. Christ's work is prophetic because He
proclaims uniquely and definitively the will and purpose of God
for man. According to the Protestant Faith there is no other proclamation which can possibly surpass or replace the proclamation
of God in Jesus Christ. Christ is the definitive and final expression of God's will for man; He is not merely a stage in the self-
disclosure of God, He is Himself the self-disclosure of God.

This is an assertion with significant implications. It makes it
impossible for Protestants to expect greater revelations or other
revelations which will contradict or surpass the revelation in Christ.
There are religious groups who accept all revelations as partially
valid, and all religions as true. For them Christ is one of many

inspired prophets who communicates some partial information about God. This position cannot be taken by the Protestant Faith. The Protestant Faith asserts: *No one has ever seen God; the only Son, who is in the bosom of the Father, he has made him known."* (*John 1:18*) The Protestant Faith asserts that Christ and His teaching are the standard or criterion by which all religious truth must be measured. Compared with the proclamation of Christ all other proclamations are of secondary importance. Christ gives the ultimate interpretation and revelation of God's will.

Next, what is the priestly work of Christ according to the Protestant Faith? Perhaps this question is best answered with the quotation from Isaiah 53 which was cited before: The priestly office of Christ was fulfilled when *he has borne our griefs and carried our sorrows; . . . he was wounded for our transgressions, he was bruised for our iniquities; upon him was the chastisement that made us whole, . . . the Lord has laid on him the iniquity of us all. (Isaiah 53:4–6)*

This idea, that through Christ's death on the Cross the abyss that separates man from God has been bridged, is known as the doctrine of the atonement. The atonement for man is Christ's work as priest. There are numerous passages in the New Testament which describe this aspect of the work of Christ. In Romans we read: *For if while we were enemies we were reconciled to God by the death of his Son, much more, now that we are reconciled, shall we be saved by his life. (Romans 5:10)* Perhaps the most profoundly simple passage expressing this doctrine of the atonement is the following:

> *Beloved, let us love one another; for love is of God, and he who loves is born of God and knows God. He who does not love does not know God; for God is love. In this the love of God was made manifest among us, that God sent his only Son into the world, so that we might live through him. In this is love, not that we loved God but that he loved us and sent his Son to be the expiation for*

our sins. Beloved, if God so loved us, we also ought to love one another. (John 4:7 ff.)

And there are innumerable other passages in which this notion of expiation, of Christ being the "ransom" and the reconciler between God and man, is expressed. That the Christian Church in general and the Protestant Faith in particular teaches that man is reconciled with God through the work of Christ, particularly His death on the cross, is evident. However, it is less evident how this atonement is to be interpreted. That Christ reconciles God and man is universally accepted by Christians. That he accomplishes this reconciliation through His death on the Cross is also generally agreed upon. The question that remains is how this death on the Cross is effective.

Essentially three interpretations of the atonement have been offered in the past two thousand years. Since the Protestant Faith has been influenced by all three, they all deserve our attention.

The oldest interpretation of the atonement has been called the *Christus Victor* interpretation. Here the conflict in which man is involved is seen as a conflict between the forces of God and the forces of evil. Man is in the middle. But as a result of sin man is now in the power of Satan as his victim and prisoner. Christ defeats Satan on the Cross and frees man from the power of evil, which has held him in bondage. Christ's death on the Cross is the victory of God over Satan, which frees man from his power. This interpretation of the atonement was first suggested by the great Christian theologian Ignatius. In its full sharpness it was stated by Rufinus of Aquileia as follows:

> The purpose of the Incarnation . . . was that the divine virtue of the Son of God might be as it were a hook hidden beneath the form of human flesh . . . to lure on the prince of this age [devil] to a contest; that the Son might offer him his flesh as a bait and that then the divinity which lay beneath might catch him and hold him fast with its hook. . . . Then, as a fish when it seizes a baited hook not only fails to drag off the bait but is itself dragged out of the water to serve as food for others; so he

that had the power of death seized the body of Jesus in death, unaware of the hook of the divinity concealed therein. Having swallowed it, he was caught straightway; the bars of hell were burst, and he was, as it were, drawn up from the pit, to become food for others.[54]

This view, picturesque and crude as it is, reveals a strong dualism. The atonement is seen as a struggle between good and evil, Christ and the devil. In this conflict the Cross becomes the great defeat of the forces of evil because in their encounter with Jesus Christ they overreach themselves. Having a right to kill those who are separated from God because they have become the slaves of Satan through sin, they have no right to kill the sinless Christ. By killing him they lose everything.

Here the atonement takes place against the background of a cosmic struggle. It is in a sense a cosmocentric view of the priestly office of Christ, and it operates with what we could call a limited dualism. Dualism is that view of reality which insists that everything must be explained against the background of a cosmic struggle between the forces of good and the forces of evil. Absolute dualism makes these forces coequal. They are two gods eternally at war with each other. Man and his world are in the middle in this struggle, with the option to choose one side or the other. This absolute dualism can be found in Persian religion, where Ormuzd or Ahura Mazda, the good god, is opposed by Ahriman, the evil spirit.

However, Christian dualism is never that absolute. Even the powers of evil are not independent of God, for they derive their power ultimately from the one and only God. Absolute evil would be sheer nothing. As Augustine stated it: "Everything which has form, in so far as it has form, and everything which has not yet form. in so far as it is capable of receiving form, holds what it has from God."[55] But, while an absolute dualism is inconsistent

[54] Bettenson, *Documents,* p. 49.
[55] "De vera religione," XVIII, 35–36, in Erich Przywara, *An Augustine Synthesis,* (New York: Harper Torchbook, 1958), p. 123.

with the Christian faith in God as Creator, limited dualism has been a permanent part of Christian teaching. The powers of evil are known as real powers. But these powers are defeated through Christ's death on the Cross. It is a victory over death and sin and devil, and Christ is the victor. An old Easter hymn puts it:

> The strife is o'er, the battle done;
> Now is the Victor's triumph won;
> Now be the song of praise begun,
> Alleluia!
> The powers of death have done their worst,
> But Christ their legions hath dispersed;
> Let shouts of holy joy outburst!
> Alleluia![56]

And Luther sings in one of his Easter hymns:

> It was a strange and dreadful strife
>   When Life and death contended;
> The victory remained with Life,
>   The reign of death was ended;
> Stripped of power, no more he reigns,
> An empty form alone remains;
>   His sting is lost forever!
>   Alleluia![57]

The element of Christus Victor is, indeed, a valid and persistent element in the Protestant Faith's understanding of the priestly work of Christ.

The most familiar interpretation of the atonement and Christ's priestly work, however, is known as the *satisfaction* interpretation. In his famous book *Cur Deus Homo* Anselm of Canterbury wrote:

> The problem is, how can God forgive man's sin? To clear our thought let us first consider what sin is, and what satisfaction for

[56] *Service Book and Hymnal of the Lutheran Church in America*, Hymn No. 90, st. 1.
[57] *Service Book and Hymnal of the Lutheran Church in America*, No. 98, st. 2.

sin is. . . . To sin is to fail to render God His due. What is due
to God? Righteousness, or rectitude of will. He who fails to render
this honor to God, robs God of that which belongs to Him, and
dishonors God. This is sin. . . . And what is satisfaction? It is
not enough simply to restore what has been taken away; but in
consideration of the insult offered, more than what was taken
away must be rendered back.
Let us consider whether God could properly remit sin by mercy
alone without satisfaction. So to remit sin would be simply to
abstain from punishing it. And since the only possible way of
correcting sin, for which no satisfaction has been made, is to
punish it; not to punish it, is to remit it uncorrected. But God
cannot properly leave anything uncorrected in His Kingdom.
Moreover, so to remit sin unpunished would be treating the sinful
and the sinless alike, which would be incongruous to God's nature.
And incongruity is injustice.
It is necessary, therefore, that either the honor taken away should
be repaid, or punishment should be inflicted. Otherwise one of
two things follows—either God is not just to Himself, or He is
powerless to do what He ought to do. A blasphemous supposition.
The satisfaction ought to be in proportion to the sin. . . .
And thou hast not yet duly estimated the gravity of sin. . . .
Thou canst not make satisfaction for it, unless thou payest something greater than the whole creation. All that is created, that is,
all that is not God, cannot compensate the sin.

And Anselm continues:

Satisfaction cannot be made unless there be some One able to
pay to God for man's sin something greater than all that is beside
God. . . . Now nothing is greater than all that is not God, except
God Himself. None therefore can make this satisfaction except
God. And none ought to make it except man. . . . If, then, it
be necessary that the kingdom of heaven be completed by man's
admission, and if man cannot be admitted unless the aforesaid
satisfaction for sin be first made, and if God only *can,* and man
only *ought* to make this satisfaction, then necessarily one must
make it who is both God and man.
He must have something to offer greater than all that is below
God, and something that He can give to God voluntarily, and
not as in duty bound. Mere obedience would not be a gift of this
kind; for every rational creature owes this obedience as a duty

to God. But *death* Christ was in no way bound to suffer, having never sinned. So death was an offering that He could make as of free will, and not of debt.

Now one who could freely offer so great a gift to God, clearly ought not to be without reward. . . . But what reward could be given to one who needed nothing—One who craved neither gift nor pardon? . . . If the Son chose to make over the claim He had on God to man, could the Father justly forbid Him doing so, or refuse to man what the Son willed to give him?

What greater mercy can be conceived than that God the Father should say to the sinner—condemned to eternal torment, and unable to redeem himself—"Receive my only Son, and offer Him for thyself," while the Son Himself said—"Take me, and redeem thyself"?

And what greater justice than that One who receives a payment far exceeding the amount due, should, if it be paid with a right intention, remit all that is due?[58]

Here we have the satisfaction interpretation of the atonement in its oldest and most concise form. Sin offends God's justice; if it were not punished, justice would be overthrown. It is through Christ's death on the Cross that God shows His mercy and His justice at the same time.

This satisfaction interpretation, though first developed in this rigorous form by Anselm, has, of course, its roots in New Testament teaching. Many times Jesus' death is described as propitiation for man's sin. He is called the "Lamb of God that taketh away the sins of the world." In classical Protestantism this satisfaction theory plays an important part. The emphasis of the Protestant Faith, however, is on the fact that *God* reconciles, that *God* satisfies, that *God* re-establishes the relationship with man which man has destroyed through his sin. While Anselm's interpretation permitted *man* to offer Christ to God, the Protestant Faith insists that it is God, not man, who reconciles fallen humanity by sacrificing His son.

Perhaps the Protestant understanding of this priestly work of Christ could be illustrated with this rather simple story. Let us

[58] Bettenson, *Documents*, p. 196 ff.

assume that there was once in some foreign country a tribe of people who were destroying their tribal existence through excessive drink. Everybody was brewing his own beverages and consuming them thirstily. Eventually no work was done and the tribe began to disintegrate. The chief finally decided something had to be done. Only very severe punishment would stop this road to destruction. He proclaimed that the next person who brewed some of this strong drink would be punished severely—fifty lashes over his back with a bull whip. This severity stopped the rioting. Slowly the village recovered and the tribe went back to work. And then, one day, there was another drunken riot. The chief tried to find out who had brewed the drink, but nobody wanted to tell him. Finally, he discovered that it was his old mother who had been responsible. What was he to do? If he did not punish her, he had lost the right to punish anybody else. Chaos would return and the tribe would be doomed to destruction. If he punished her, the old woman would not survive, and he would be responsible for the execution of his own mother. Well, when the hour of judgment approached and his mother was brought before him, the chief found her guilty as charged. But instead of having her punished, he stepped from his throne and ordered the executioner to give him the fifty lashes. In this way justice was preserved and his mother's life was saved. This is, of course, a rather superficial illustration, but it may help illustrate what is the basic concern of the interpretation of the atonement which emphasizes the justice of God. It is important to keep in mind that for the Protestant Faith it is God and God alone who does the reconciling. He does it through His death on the Cross. And He does it once and for all. While some Christians speak of the unbloody repetition of the bloody sacrifice on Golgotha every time the Holy Eucharist is celebrated, for the Protestant Faith the atonement has been effected once and for all. It is an accomplished fact. God, the Protestants say, has indeed reconciled the world unto Himself; it is now only a question of who will believe in what God has done. The sacrifice does not have to be repeated in any form or manner. For man does not sacrifice Christ to God; God has sacrificed Himself for man. This is an important emphasis in the Protestant interpretation of the atonement as satisfaction for man's sin.

As we called the first interpretation of the priestly office of Christ "cosmocentric," because it sees the atonement against the background of a cosmic struggle between the forces of death and sin against the forces of life and love, so might we label the Anselmian interpretation "theocentric." It is God who reconciles the world unto Himself.

Here it may be proper to mention briefly the third interpretation of the atonement, commonly associated with the medieval theologian Peter Abelard. This is known as the *moral influence* interpretation of the atonement. According to Abelard the significance of Christ's atoning death lies in the example it provides to the sinful human race. It reveals God's love and shows Christ to be our teacher and model. The result of such example and teaching is to produce faith and love in the believers. The forgiveness of sins is based upon the love aroused in the believer by Christ's teaching and example. Abelard put it:

> But to us it seems that by this means we are justified in the blood of Christ and reconciled to God; that through this particular favor manifested toward us, that his Son assumed our nature and persisted even until death in instructing us both by word and by example, he has very strongly drawn us to himself through love, so that, inflamed by this great benefaction of divine grace, true love now shrinks not from the endurance of anything whatsoever.[59]

Abelard's interpretation of the atonement was immediately attacked in the Middle Ages as reducing the work of Christ to the work of a teacher. In the form in which Abelard suggested it, classical Protestantism would also reject it categorically, since it placed the emphasis on what man would do under the moral influence of the life of Christ. This view was anthropocentric, since

[59] Reinhold Seeberg, *Textbook of the History of Doctrines,* trans. Charles E. Hay (2 vols.; Phildelphia: Lutheran Publication Society, 1905), I, 71.

it saw the meaning of the atonement in the transformation of the moral behavior of man. Yet, while classical Protestantism rejected this point of view, those later Protestants who saw in Jesus the great teacher who guides us to a better life through His inspired example found in Peter Abelard an early precursor.

If we want to summarize the understanding of the atonement of Christ as held by the main stream of Protestantism, we should say that it accepts both the Christus Victor interpretation and the satisfaction interpretation of Anselm as complementary to each other. This means that each has to be seen in the light of the other. Thus the Protestant Faith is certainly less crudely dualistic than Rufinus and less obviously legalistic than Anselm. The emphasis is here as everywhere else upon God's work in Jesus Christ. The atonement is Christ's priestly work; it is not man who reconciles himself to God but God who reconciles man to Himself. This is the dominating and significant emphasis of the Protestant Faith, here as everywhere else. Abelard's view represents a valid, though definitely and dangerously partial, insight into the nature of the atonement. Certainly man is involved in the atonement. The Christian Faith is never a spectator sport, and the atonement can never be merely a cosmic battle or a transaction within God. What God has done on the Cross must make a difference in the life of the believers. This element of Abelard's view is a valid element, which is preserved in the Protestant Faith. The insistence that sanctification is a necessary consequence of justification means that man is not merely a spectator of the drama of the atonement. On the contrary, he is involved. The atonement is bound to make a difference in his life. What Christ has accomplished on the Cross makes it possible for men and women to live the new life in Christ.

The Cross, therefore, is in the center of the Protestant proclamation. It is not possible to state the classical Protestant Faith apart from its message. For the central message of Protestantism is what God has done for man on the Cross and what man can now do through God's power thus made available to him.

In the Cross God's love is revealed. It is not Jesus' love which changes the Father's mind. It is not the man Jesus Christ who turns the wrath of God away from sinful man. The Protestant Faith insists that the Father sent His Son into the world to reconcile God and man and to defeat the powers of darkness. The Cross is not man's sacrifice to God, but God sacrificing Himself for the sake of man.

The Cross reveals the love of God so profoundly and dramatically that it makes faith possible. It reveals the importance of the Law and the seriousness of sin as revolt against the order and structure established by God. The Cross proclaims and preserves the holiness of God's Law, while at the same time revealing His boundless and overwhelming love. This means that it is impossible for those who take the Protestant Faith seriously to take the sinful revolt of man against God lightly. The Cross makes it apparent that God cannot forgive sin as an indulgent parent may forgive an offense. Forgiveness which is merely indulgence would subvert the order and structure of the universe. To understand what is at stake one could compare justice and mercy in the cosmic order with the problem of justice and mercy as it confronts men in the ordering of human society. It has been suggested, and some people advocate it vociferously, that it might be a good idea not to punish crimes. Since it appears that criminals do not generally become better through punishment and a crime cannot be undone by punishment, some say that we might as well abolish all prisons and courts and thus save a great deal of money. This is the indulgent-parent approach to crime, which advocates letting bygones be bygones and showing mercy instead of punishing the offender. If most people do not approve of such a procedure it may be that, knowing themselves, they realize that men are often deterred from illegal actions by the fear of punishment. This is, of course, not a very high motive; however, it helps to keep some sort of order in man's world. The evidence seems to indicate that people are not willing to obey the law because it is good for them; rather, they obey because punishment will follow. Since this has at times been questioned by learned men, let us look, for example, at the laws concerning speeding and drunken driving on the statute books of most states.

Of course, people should obey these laws because they are good for them. Punishment does not make people better. By paying a fine for speeding or going to jail for drunken driving, a man's character is not improved. Granted all that, the fact remains that speeding and drunken driving can be controlled by rigid law enforcement. The more strictly the law is enforced, the greater the chance that I might get caught and be punished, the more carefully I will drive. In other words, though law enforcement may not make me truly better, it makes me behave in a manner which is safer for me and for my fellow men. We have all no doubt observed what happens when a police car enters a stream of traffic. Cars slow down, and drivers meticulously observe the various traffic laws. It is doubtful whether anybody has become better because of the appearance of this police car, but everyone's behavior—poorly motivated as it may be—has become safer for everyone concerned. It is a truism that rigid law enforcement is necessary to achieve greater safety on the roads.

There is nothing commendable about a policeman who lets his friends go free when they break the law. Likewise, a judge is not exhibiting love or charity when, because of political pressure, he acquits offenders brought before him. The result is that the interests of criminals are more carefully protected than those of society and its law-abiding citizens. In fact, this kind of "law enforcement," which makes justice a joke under the mantle of mercy, is the surest way to chaos and anarchy.

There is likewise nothing praiseworthy about parents who do not restrain the destructive and antisocial impulses of their children, who bring up juvenile delinquents and claim that it is their love and mercy which keep them from punishing and restraining anti-social behavior. Ignoring the structures which maintain life and make society function is not mercy or love but sheer irresponsibility. It is against this background that Protestant assertions about the Cross must be understood. Through the Cross the holiness of God's law is preserved. This law protects all men and makes the life of society possible. At the same time the Cross also reveals God's boundless love.

Jesus Christ as the mediator between God and man suffers for man under the judgment. He takes upon himself man's sin, even to the moment of despair on the Cross. His priestly work is to re-establish the broken tie between God and man without doing violence to God's justice, which upholds the universe, or God's love, which gives it meaning.

Simone Weil has put it:

> When the whole universe weighs upon us, there is no other counterweight possible but God himself—the true God, for in this case false gods cannot do anything, not even under the name of the true one. Evil is infinite in the sense of being indefinite: matter, space, time. Nothing can overcome this kind of infinity except the true infinity. That is why on the balance of the cross a body which was frail and light, but which was God, lifted up the whole world. "Give me a point of leverage and I will lift up the world." This point of leverage is the cross. There can be no other. It has to be at the intersection of the world and that which is not the world. The cross is this intersection.[60]

In summary, it should be said that for the Protestant Faith there are many different elements in Christ's atoning work on the Cross which are all valid and complementary to each other. The Cross is *sacrifice,* in that it is God's sacrifice for the sake of man. The Cross is *punishment,* in that it reveals the seriousness of the offense against the divine law. It contains elements of *satisfaction.* In Paul's words: *Christ redeemed us from the curse of the law, having become a curse for us. (Galatians 3:13)* But the Cross is also *example.* Jesus said to His disciples, *If any man would come after me, let him deny himself and take up his cross and follow me. (Matthew 16:24)* And finally the Cross is *victory.* It is the sign of triumph over the forces that separate man from God. It

[60] Simone Weil, *Gravity and Grace.* Copyright 1952. Published by G. P. Putnam's Sons. Used by permission.

demontrates that suffering and death can, through the grace of God, become meaningful and lead to peace and joy and life. For the Protestant Faith all these elements of the atoning work of Christ are valid. Far from being mutually exclusive, they complement and supplement each other. For all the theories of the atonement are formulations in human language of the divine act which transcends all formulations. It is the divine act which saves, rather than its description, be it ever so precise. The Protestant Faith in its classical expressions is a Cross-centered faith. Thus it can be said that the theology of classical Protestantism is always the theology of the Cross.

It would, however, be an error to assume that Protestantism claims to be able to exhaust the meaning of the atonement and of the Cross by means of any or all of the interpretations here presented. After all is said and done, the Cross remains God's mystery. As the great mystery of the love of God for man it is in the center of the Protestant Faith.

The third office of Christ as defined by the theologians of Protestantism is His royal office. With the Apostles' Creed the Protestant Faith asserts that Christ "sitteth at the right hand of God the Father." This is, of course, not a geographical description but symbolic language expressing the faith that, through Christ, God the Father rules the universe. Or, as the Apostle Paul puts it: *That at the name of Jesus every knee should bow, in heaven and on earth and under the earth. (Philippians 2:10)* Christ is King, indeed, and He rules everywhere.

It is for this reason that Protestants like to speak of the "lordship of Christ." This means that when confronted by Christ the believer knows that he is face to face with Him who has *all authority in heaven and on earth.* (Matthew 28:19) In the words of Karl Barth, the famous Swiss Protestant theologian:

He [God] rules His people and cosmos as this man is at His right hand, i.e., as He is the concretion and manifestation of His power and righteousness. . . . His kingdom and lordship and dominion are concretely the kingdom and lordship and dominion of this man exalted by Him to fellowship with His being and work; of the man in whom He, God, humbling Himself in His Son, became a servant.[61]

For Protestantism this faith in Christ's work as King is based upon the biblical witness. The gospels are unanimous in their report that people were *amazed, so that they questioned among themselves, saying what is this? A new teaching! With authority he commands even the unclean spirits and they obey him* (Mark 1:27)

This royal authority of Christ is also expressed in the words which the New Testament uses for the proclamation of Jesus. He *proclaims the good news*. When John the Baptist sends his disciples to Jesus to ask, *Are you he who is to come or shall we look for another?* Jesus' answer is: *Go and tell John what you hear and see: the blind receive their sight and the lame walk, lepers are cleansed and the deaf hear, and the dead are raised up, and the poor have good news preached to them.* (Matthew 11:4)

Jesus *teaches*. But this is teaching with a difference. As the New Testament reports: *When Jesus finished these sayings, the crowds were astonished at his teaching, for he taught them as one who had authority, and not as their scribes.* (Matthew 7:28, 29) For He speaks as the Father has taught Him (John 8:28).

And Jesus *preaches*. The Greek word literally means "to cry or proclaim as a herald." It is the authoritative proclamation of the King which is here described: *And he went about all Galilee, teaching in their synagogues and preaching the gospel of the kingdom and healing every disease and every infirmity among the people.* (Matthew 4:23)

But this *proclaiming of the good news,* this *teaching with authority,* this *preaching the gospel of the kingdom* are not merely the articulation of words but the expression of royal power. They reveal Christ as the King who rules the destiny of man.

While the gospels bear witness to the fact that Jesus Christ is King, they are not alone in this proclamation. "Christ is King," is

[61] Karl Barth, *Church Dogmatics,* trans. G. W. Bromiley (Edinburgh: T. & T. Clark, 1958), Vol. IV, Part 2, p. 155.

the confession which unites the entire Christian community. It is this confession which separates Protestant Christians from all those who may believe in other rulers. The Protestant Faith proclaims that Christ has been King from all eternity. The Book of Revelation refers to Him as *Lord of Lords and King of Kings* (*Revelation 17:14 and 19:16*), and in the Gospel of John, Jesus prays: *Father glorify thou me in thy own presence with the glory which I had with thee before the world was made.* (*John 17:5*) And He rules His Church now. In the holy Christian Church Christ rules over all believers. He is present as the ruler of His people today, for he has promised, *Lo, I am with you always, to the close of the age.* (Matthew 28:20) He makes those who believe in Him into a new nation, a new people. *But you are a chosen race, a royal priesthood, a holy nation, God's own people.* (I Peter 2:9)

The Protestant Faith asserts that Christ rules directly and in person: *Where two or three are gathered in my name, there am I in the midst of them.* (*Matthew 18:20*) He is personally and really present in the Lord's Supper. He therefore cannot be represented by a vicar or deputy. Need for the rule of the Church through a "vicar of Christ," as some Christians believe, would deny the real presence in His Word and in the sacrament. The Protestant Faith asserts that Christ does not need such vicarious representation through some ecclesiastical dignitary because He rules in person. This is the central and distinguishing emphasis which is derived from faith in Christ as Lord and King.

Finally, Christ is King because his eternal kingdom is, according to the Protestant Faith, the ultimate destiny of the universe. This kingdom has begun but is not completed. It has been described in one of the most famous passages of the New Testament:

> *When the Son of man comes in his glory, and all the angels with him, then he will sit on his glorious throne. Before him will be gathered all the nations, and he will separate them one from another as a shepherd separates the sheep from the goats, and he will place the sheep at his right*

hand, but the goats at the left. Then the King will say to those at his right hand, "Come, O blessed of my Father, inherit the kingdom prepared for you from the foundation of the world; for I was hungry and you gave me food, I was thirsty and you gave me drink, I was a stranger and you welcomed me, I was naked and you clothed me, I was sick and you visited me, I was in prison and you came to me." Then the righteous will answer him, "Lord, when did we see thee hungry and feed thee, or thirsty and give thee drink? And when did we see thee a stranger and welcome thee, or naked and clothe thee? And when did we see thee sick or in prison, and visit thee?" And the King will answer them, "Truly, I say to you, as you did it to one of the least of these my brethren, you did it to me." (Matthew 25:31 ff.)

This kingdom of glory is the profound aspiration of the Protestant Faith. Thus, Protestants will speak of themselves as a pilgrim people of God, that is, a people who are marching toward a future kingdom. This has been brilliantly described in a great Protestant classic, John Bunyan's *Pilgrim's Progress*. In various forms this is a universal hope of Protestantism. In several periods in Church history Protestants have expected this kingdom in the very near future. Christians in the early church and again at the time of the Reformation, for example, hoped that the end of this world and Christ's kingdom of glory were impending. In a somewhat different sense liberal Protestantism in the early part of this century expected that this kingdom could be attained through the conversion of the world to the social gospel of Christ. A popular hymn of this period by William Pierson Merrill gives expression to this aspiration:

> Rise up, O men of God!
> Have done with lesser things;
> Give heart and soul and mind and strength
> To serve the King of kings.
> Rise up, O men of God!

His kingdom tarries long;
Bring in the day of brotherhood,
And end the night of wrong.
Rise up, O men of God!
The Church for you doth wait,
Her strength unequal to her task;
Rise up and make her great!
Lift high the Cross of Christ!
Tread where his feet have trod;
As brothers of the Son of Man,
Rise up, O men of God![62]

Even though most Protestants may be less confident today that it is in their power to bring in the kingdom of glory, the eager expectation of Christ's kingdom is an essential part of the Protestant Faith.

---

[62] *Service Book and Hymnal of the Lutheran Church in America,* No. 541. Words by permission of *The Presbyterian Outlook.*

7

The Holy Spirit and the Church

In our discussion of the Protestant Faith, we have now come to the Holy Spirit and the Church. While the atonement is the work of Christ, the appropriation of this work of Christ by the individual believer is the work of the Holy Spirit. It is through the power of the Holy Spirit that the Christian is brought to faith in Christ. In his explanation of the Third Article of the Apostles' Creed, Luther says:

> I believe that I cannot by my own reason or strength believe in Jesus Christ my Lord, or come to Him; but the Holy Spirit has called me through the Gospel, enlightened me with His gifts, and sanctified and preserved me in the true faith; in like manner as He calls, gathers, en-

lightens and sanctifies the whole Christian Church on earth, and preserves it in union with Jesus Christ in the true faith; in which Christian Church He daily forgives abundantly all my sins, and the sins of all believers, and at the last day will raise up me and all the dead, and will grant everlasting life to me and to all who believe in Christ.[63]

THE HOLY SPIRIT

This explanation of the creed shows that the task of the Holy Spirit is no minor task; the Holy Spirit is not, so to speak, an afterthought in Protestantism, although one might get this idea from much of contemporary Protestant worship. In classical Protestantism, the Holy Spirit is God at work in man, saving and transforming man according to His purpose. Of Luther, Professor Regin Prenter has said in a recent volume:

> The concept of the Holy Spirit completely dominates Luther's theology. In every decisive matter, whether it be the study of Luther's doctrine of justification, of his doctrine of the sacraments, of his ethics, or of any other fundamental teaching, we are forced to take into consideration this concept of the Holy Spirit.[64]

Congregationalists and Anglicans, Methodists and Presbyterians have written hymns in praise of the Holy Spirit. According to the Protestant Faith the doctrine of the Holy Spirit is deeply rooted in the proclamation of the early church. The New Testament abounds in references to the Holy Spirit and its power:

> *If you love me you will keep my commandments and I will pray the Father, and He will give you another counsellor to be with you forever, even the Spirit of Truth, whom the world cannot receive, because it neither sees Him nor knows Him; you know Him for He dwells with you and will be in you. (John 14:15–17)*

[63] *Book of Concord*, i, 367.
[64] Regin Prenter, *Spiritus Creator*, trans. John M. Jensen (Philadelphia: Muhlenberg Press, 1953), p. ix.

And the Apostle Paul says: *It is the Spirit himself bearing witness with our spirit that we are children of God.* (*Romans 8:16*)

According to the Protestant Faith, this Holy Spirit is God. As the Father is God and the Son is God so the Spirit is God. When Ananias in the Acts of the Apostles lies to the Apostles and to the Holy Spirit, Peter says: *You have not lied to men but to God.* (*Acts 5:1–6*) And the Holy Spirit is person. The whole Christian Church and the Protestant Faith assert that the Holy Spirit is not merely a divine "force" or divine "truth," but, rather, that the personal God confronts man personally in the Holy Spirit. Karl Barth puts it:

> According to the New Testament, the Holy Spirit is one of the objects of faith. The Creed too declares in conformity with the New Testament: I believe in the Holy Ghost. The Holy Spirit, object of faith, is also an object of prayer: We must not only pray that we may receive the Holy Spirit. We must pray to him.[65]

Though this may appear to be quibbling, the insistence on the part of classical Protestantism that the Holy Spirit is a person to whom we can pray protects the Protestant Faith against the tendency of man to identify himself with God. In mysticism, especially in its Oriental forms, divine force is understood in such impersonal terms that the result is the self-identification of the individual with God. Man and God run into each other, and it becomes ever more difficult to see where man ends and God begins. Man is God and God is man. This is impossible within biblical Christianity because of the insistence upon the Holy Spirit as person. He is not divine energy, He is not some undefined divine force; rather, He is the third person of the Trinity and He meets man personally. The meeting with the Holy Spirit is for the Protestant Faith a personal encounter. Again it is an I-Thou relationship rather than infiltration or emanation. Edward Cooper sings: "Eternal Spirit! By Whose

---

[65] Karl Barth, *The Faith of the Church*, trans. Gabriel Vaharian (New York: Meridian Press, Inc. Living Age Books, 1958), p. 130.

breath the soul is raised from sin and death, Before Thy throne we sinners bend: To us Thy quickening power extend."[66]

And in Whitfield's collection of 1757, we find this hymn: "Come, Holy Comforter, Thy sacred witness bear, In this glad hour! Thou Who almighty art, Now rule in every heart, And ne'er from us depart, Spirit of power!"[67]

THE HOLY TRINITY

On the basis of what we have said so far, we can now conclude that the Protestant Faith asserts that there is one God in three persons, Father, Son, and Holy Spirit. This is known as the doctrine of the Holy Trinity. Perhaps no other hymn is more popular than the so-called doxology: "Praise God, from whom all blessings flow; Praise Him, all creatures here below; Praise Him above, ye heavenly host; Praise Father, Son and Holy Ghost!" Though few Protestants are able to give a detailed definition of the doctrine of the Trinity, faith in God as Father, Son, and Holy Spirit is part of the common Protestant heritage.

Protestants believe in the Holy Trinity because the one God, the God of Abraham and Isaac and Jacob, as the Old Testament likes to call Him, has revealed Himself in Scripture as Father, Son, and Holy Spirit. However, this experience of the Trinity points to the eternal Trinity; classical Protestantism asserts that God was always three in one. This means that although the Son became man in Jesus Christ, this is not an evolution in God, but from all eternity God was Father, Son, and Holy Spirit. This assertion of the eternity of the Trinity safeguards the Christian understanding of God against all pantheistic and mystical notions which tend to make God dependent upon man.

The doctrine of the Trinity is an attempt to express the reality of God and guard it against certain obvious and historical mis-

[66] *The Hymnal*, The Protestant Episcopal Church in the U.S.A. (New York: Church Pension Fund, 1920), No. 206.
[67] *The Hymnal*, No. 209.

understandings. In its developed form it has been stated in defense of the Christian Faith against efforts to change and misinterpret it. It asserts the reality of the creative tension in God. Aristotle's God, we are told, is the unmoved mover, eternally beholding His own perfection—"and his thinking is a thinking on thinking." Christians confess that God is a living God—not the abstract keystone of a philosophical system.

Thus the I-Thou relationship, which is the basis of all relationships between God and man and men with each other, is a reflection or image of the primary I-Thou relationship in the very being of God. The doctrine of the Trinity testifies to the eternal encounter in the one living God, Father, Son, and Holy Spirit.

On the one hand, by confessing the Trinity the Protestant Faith rejects two prevalent interpretations as inadequate and false. One is *Unitarianism,* the assertion that there is one God, but only one, rather than three, persons. The Son is not God and neither is the Holy Spirit. This view was rejected very early in the history of the Christian Church, and the Protestant Faith has unanimously joined in this rejection. Even in such an inclusive organization of Christians as the World Council of Churches, the Unitarians are therefore not included. The other interpretation removing this tension in God is known as *Sabellianism,* which was also rejected early in the history of the Christian Church. Sabellianism asserts that there is one God and that the Father, Son, and Holy Spirit are three modes in which this one God appears. It is as if one would look at the sun through red and blue and yellow glasses and thus see three different suns or see the sun in three different colors. This view has also been rejected because it denies the living encounter in God.

On the other hand, the doctrine of the Trinity protects the Protestant Faith against any form of three theism. There are not three gods, but only one. Each person in the godhead is coeternal with the two other persons.

Probably no aspect of the Protestant Faith so far discussed in these pages seems as strange as the discussion of the Trinity. And yet, although the definitions may appear abstruse and complicated, the underlying reality is rather simple. The Protestant Faith asserts that there is one God and that Father, Son, and Holy Spirit are God. In the defense of these basic assertions of the Christian Faith, the admittedly complicated formulation of the doctrine of the Trinity became a necessity.

It appears that this doctrine helped a good deal to preserve the early Christian Church from the fate of the other Oriental religions, which had been amalgamated into the general religious chaos of the Hellenistic world. The doctrine of the Trinity does not dispel the mystery of God. It does not explain God. It is an effort on the part of the Christian Church to protect its witness to God against misinterpretation and perversion. The theologians of the early church who had a hand in defining these doctrines were not interested in mere speculation. They were not professors of philosophy or even theology—actually, they were veterans of persecution who had often demonstrated their willingness to live and die for their faith. They insisted on this definition of the Trinity because they saw in it the only way to preserve all the confessions of the Christian faith about God. However, in order to understand this attitude we ought to keep in mind that these confessions appear in the context of worship and adoration. As Horatius Bonar sings: "Glory be to God the Father! Glory be to God the Son! Glory be to God the Spirit! God Eternal, Three in One!"[68] It is impossible to understand any assertion of the Protestant Faith and, most especially, the confession of the Trinity, apart from the worshiping and praying community which makes the confession. The doctrine of the Trinity is for the Protestant Faith not abstract metaphysical speculation—but adoration and worship of the God who has revealed Himself in His Word: Father, Son, and Holy Spirit!

THE CHURCH

In our discussion of the Protestant Faith, we have now come to the doctrine of the Church and its task. The Christian Church

[68] *Service Book and Hymnal of the Lutheran Church in America*, No. 139.

is specifically the product of the Holy Spirit. The day of Pentecost, the day on which, according to the Acts of the Apostles, the Holy Spirit was given to the early Christians, is the birthday of the Church, for it is through the Holy Spirit that the risen Christ creates the Church. But what is the Church according to the Protestant Faith? It is the witnessing community, the people of God proclaiming its faith in its King to each other and to all the world.

If we want to understand the Protestant doctrine of the Church, it will be helpful to keep in mind the principle of complementarity which we have used frequently to interpret the Protestant Faith. For most assertions concerning the Church have to be made by making a number of statements which may appear contradictory but which taken together give the most adequate description of the Church.

First, the Church is both an institution and a fellowship. The assertion that it is an institution is necessary in order to convey the insight that here is a reality which transcends all individuals. It is made up of individuals but no individual is the Church. The reality of the Church surpasses all individuals and is greater than the sum of all individuals. In other words, the Protestant Faith asserts here that the sum total is more than the sum of its parts; the Church is more than the addition of individual members. It transcends and comprehends the individual members. But, at the same time, the Protestant Faith asserts that the Church is fellowship and communion. Never merely institution, it is people, the people of God living together in a personal fellowship. Whenever the Church is merely institution, organization, machinery—apart from people—it is no longer truly Church. And whenever the Church is only a collection of individuals who like each other, who meet because they like each other—it is no longer Church. Both extremes are temptations to the Protestant Faith. It would not be too difficult to give examples of Protestant churches which have much more in common with a well-run corporation like the General Motors Corporation than with the New Testament Church. Sometimes machinery for machinery's sake accumulates, and when the church meets, it seems like a stockholders' meeting. The Protestant Faith would assert that a church which is merely an efficiently run corporation designed for the preservation of its organizational life is no longer a Protestant church. Conversely, when the church becomes a group of like-minded individuals who have a good time together, who belong to the same race, the same nationality, the same income group, the same educational level, sometimes the same family—a group of individuals who meet because they enjoy each other's company—we see another aberration from the Protestant concept of the Church.

Secondly, the Church is a means and a goal at the same time. It is a means to an end. Through the Church the Gospel of Christ is proclaimed. Through the Church, men and women are confronted by Christ. It is God's tool and instrument for the proclamation of His Word and the administration of the sacraments. Through the Church, Christian love becomes effective in the missionary efforts, the relief work, the deeds of charity of the community. God uses the Church, say the Protestants, so that His message of salvation might be proclaimed to all people. Here the Church is a means to an end, the proclamation of the Christian Faith.

If one studies the life of the typical American Protestant church, it is not hard to see the instrumental character of the community. It is through the Church that the young and the old are instructed in the Christian Faith. It is through the Church that the insights of the Christian Faith are made available to the immediate community in which the Church is established and also to people in those parts of the country where there may be no churches and in foreign lands where the Christian message would otherwise not be proclaimed. It is through the Church that men, women, and children everywhere are given the opportunity to worship God. From this point of view it is not difficult to see how the Church functions as a means to an end and as a tool and instrument in the hands of God.

However, the Protestant Faith makes the complementary assertion that the Church is an end, a goal, and the purpose of God's plan with man. The proclamation of the message creates a community of believers, a people of God, which is an end in itself. In the New Testament word, it makes people members of the body of Christ. According to the Protestant Faith it is the purpose of man's existence to be grafted into the body of Christ. While it is not difficult to see the Church as a means to an end, it is generally harder for the average Protestant to understand how this church is also the product and objective of the divine will. Yet, the Protestant Faith asserts that if these tasks of teaching and preaching and serving are taken seriously, God creates a fellowship of love and worship. When people love God with all their being and the neighbor as themselves, the kingdom of God is among them. For the Protestant Faith the love and service which is part of the life in and for the Church is not merely a way to God, it *is* fellowship with God. This life of fellowship with God, which is the ultimate purpose of human existence, is not entirely in the future; it is at least partially anticipated in the present. To be sure, as the Apostle Paul says: *Now we see in a mirror dimly, but then face to face. Now I know in part; then I shall understand fully.* (*I Corinthians 13:12*) However, even now we see! The Protestant Faith asserts that in every deed done in the service of God, in every word spoken through the power of God's love, in every thought that goes through a human mind under the influence of the Holy Spirit, there is a foretaste, an anticipation, of the ultimate fulfillment. It is therefore an error, according to the Protestant Faith, to see in the Church merely a tool of God's purpose, an instrument which will eventually be cast away. It is rather an instrument which God is perfecting. The Church is the great creative effort of the Creator of heaven and earth and the Savior of mankind.

The Church is means as well as end, tool as well as product, yet these functions are complementary and must not be disjoined. Whenever the Church is merely a means to an end it is no longer the Church at all. Sometimes this happens. The Church may become a means to build a better community, to reduce juvenile delinquency, to send relief to hungry people abroad, or to safeguard the American way of life. Whenever the life of the Church exhausts itself in being a means to ever-so-worthy ends, it is no longer the Church of Christ. The Church is also failing if it is merely an end in itself. Sometimes churches act as if they were the resting place of people who have arrived. When Christians sit quietly in their corner or in their church "content to let the world go by," they no longer can be considered the Christian Church. The Church of Christ according to the Protestant Faith is not a mutual-admiration society of those who consider themselves perfect Christians. It can never be a static gathering of those who merely observe and criticize human society from a safe haven. Only when the Church is both means and end, tool and product, is it truly the Church of Christ according to the Protestant Faith.

Thirdly, the Protestant Faith asserts that the Church is both the proclamation of God and the people of God. Here again it is necessary to maintain both assertions as complementary to each other. The Church is a proclaiming Church, a community with a message. When we read the New Testament, we are impressed by the urgency of the message which this Church proclaims in season and out of season. The Church has been defined as a witnessing community, and this witness is of the essence. If this witness is lost, what is left is not the Church but a social club, sometimes, indeed, an a-social club. No other community, no other institution, depends as much on what it proclaims as the Christian Church. Take away the message of Christ and of the Cross, discussed in detail in previous chapters, and buildings, budgets, membership lists, and able leadership cannot make up for it. According to the Protestant Faith, the Church depends on its proclamation. The Church is where the proclamation is or, perhaps in even simpler terms, the Church is where the Word is—and where the Word is not proclaimed, there is only machinery, stone and bricks, but no Church. But it is of the greatest importance not to lose sight of the other half of the assertion. The Church is the people of God. The Word is not disembodied, it is spoken by people and for people, it is a living Word. And it remakes and transforms living people. The Church is people—men and women who have heard this Word, obey this Word, and who are transformed by this Word. The Protestant Faith asserts, therefore, that the Church must be judged by the life it produces. This is the new life in Christ. This is how Jesus Christ describes this new possibility: *I came that they may have life, and have it abundantly.* (*John 10:10*) And the Apostle Paul asks in the same vein:

> *Do you not know that all of us who have been baptized into Christ Jesus were baptized into his death? We were buried therefore with him by baptism into death, so that as Christ was raised from the dead by the glory of the Father, we too might walk in newness of life.* (*Romans 6:3, 4*)

And we can also read:

> *And this is the testimony, that God gave us eternal life, and this life is in his Son. He who has the Son has life; he who has not the Son has not life.* (*I John 5:11*)

A philosophical system may stand on the coherence or persuasiveness of its propositions. A philosopher may be personally a scoundrel, a thief, and a murderer; this does not affect the validity of the theories which he has uttered. They stand on their own merits and are neither proved by his charm nor disproved by his obnoxious behavior. The Church is otherwise. It is not a collection of propositions or sayings; but a people transformed by the Word, the people of God. There is a vital link between the life and the thought of Christian people, according to the Protestant Faith. In the Church this vital connection must be obvious. The Church is both proclamation of God and people of God. And this can also be expressed by saying that the Church is both Word and flesh. Just as in Jesus Christ, the Word became flesh, so, in dependence upon this incarnation of God, the Word must ever become flesh in the Church. This means that the Word must grasp men and women so that they live their faith in love. The Protestant Faith insists that it is not sufficient to tell the story of God's incarnation in Jesus Christ; this story must bear fruit in the life of the Church, so that the Christian can say with the Apostle Paul: *It is no longer I who live, but Christ who lives in me.* (*Galatians 2:20*)

The link between life and thought explains also the famous distinction between the invisible and the visible Church. The Protestant Faith almost universally uses these two terms to express the belief that the Church as an ecclesiastical institution, the empirical Church, is not coextensive with the Church as the people of God. As there was a Judas even among the twelve disciples of Jesus, Protestants would say that mere membership in the visible Church does not guarantee membership in the kingdom of God. And the reverse statement would be almost as widely accepted: The mere fact that a person does not belong to any particular ecclesiastical organization does not necessarily exclude him from membership in the kingdom of God. If Judas is the spectacular example of the member who did not truly belong, the thief on the Cross, who died on Jesus' side and to whom Jesus said, *Truly, I say to you, today you will be with me in Paradise* (Luke 23:43), is an equally spectacular example of a man who belonged to Christ although he was never baptized or formally a disciple.

It would be an error to assume from these two examples that the Protestant Faith considers membership in the visible Church irrelevant and immaterial. On the contrary, the Church is in a sense always visible—but visible to faith. In the creed most Protestants will say that they "believe in the one holy universal church." It is part of the Protestant Faith to see the true Church of Christ in the motley collection of "butchers and bakers and candlestick makers" who make up the visible Church. The invisible Church does not exist apart from the visible Church, but within it. It would indicate a serious misunderstanding of the Protestant Faith to claim that it teaches an invisible Church to which people can belong apart from the visible Church. It rather teaches that the Church of Christ is the people of God, and *The Lord knows those who are his.* (*II Timothy 2:19*) Whenever the notion of the visible and the invisible Church is used as an excuse by an individual to separate himself from the visible Church, the rejection of this excuse by Protestantism has been universal and sometimes scathing. The great Protestant evangelist Dwight L. Moody was once told by a person who had not joined a church that he could not do so because there were too many hypocrites in the Church. Moody looked at him for a while and then said, "Friend, don't mind that; there is always room for one more." The Protestant Faith sees the reality of the Church as visible and invisible. Again, these two concepts are best understood if we say the Protestant Faith teaches that the Church is both visible and invisible. The invisible Church is visible to faith and the visible Church is invisible—as the Church of Christ—to unbelief. Here, too, it is dangerous to dissolve the complementarity of the two assertions.

The Church is not merely a message nor merely a fellowship, but a fellowship with a message and a message which creates a fellowship. Both are essential for the understanding of the Protestant Faith when it speaks about the Church. And here the oldest of the Protestant definitions of the Church may be illuminating. In Article VII of the Augsburg Confession it is stated: "The Church is the congregation of saints, in which the Gospel is rightly taught and the sacraments rightly administered." The fellowship, which is the congregation of saints, the message, which is the true proclamation of the Gospel, and the right administration of the sacraments are of the essence of the Church. Similar definitions can be found in almost all Protestant confessions.

This brings us to a discussion of the common characteristics of the Church, the characteristics generally accepted by the Protestant Faith. First of all, the Protestant Faith asserts that the Church is both *militant* and *triumphant*. This is an ancient distinction that describes the Church in this world as the militant Church, the Church at war with the powers of evil, which obstruct the purpose of God. The Church must always be "militant." It cannot be at rest in this world as long as there is injustice and hate, conflict and strife. Anybody who is even superficially familiar with the Protestant Faith and the Protestant churches in America knows that its prophetic leaders have often been in the forefront in the fight for social betterment, sometimes to the great annoyance of some of their more conservative members. It is obvious that sometimes the causes were poorly conceived and the goals were not attained, but regardless of setbacks and failures, the Protestant Faith sees in the Church a fighting force which tries to bring about changes for the better in the world. From the establishment of the republic to the abolition of slavery and the struggle for social justice, the Protestant Faith has supplied inspiration and leadership. This participation in the struggle against evil is colorfully expressed in Julia Ward Howe's famous "Battle Hymn of the Republic":

> Mine eyes have seen the glory of the coming of the Lord;
> He is trampling out the vintage where the grapes of wrath
>   are stored;
> He hath loosed the fateful lightning of his terrible swift
>   sword:
> His truth is marching on.
> He has sounded forth the trumpet that shall never call retreat;
> He is sifting out the hearts of men before his judgment-seat;
> O be swift, my soul, to answer him; be jubilant, my feet!
> Our God is marching on.
> In the beauty of the lilies Christ was born across the sea,
> With a glory in his bosom that transfigures you and me:
> As he died to make men holy, let us die to make men free,
> While God is marching on.[69]

The militancy of the Protestant Faith is not reserved for enemies without. Protestants historically have been always ready to fight the enemy within the gates as well as the enemies outside. This

[69] *Service Book and Hymnal of the Lutheran Church in America*, No. 356.

is one of the reasons for the many divisions within Protestantism. The Protestant Faith asserts that the fight must be carried into the midst of the Church, when good reason exists to believe that the enemy has infiltrated. While this militancy has been divisive, it has also been corrective. Evil has not remained unpunished, and the most severe and acute criticism of Protestantism's failures has come from its own ranks.

But while the Protestant Faith interprets the Church as militant, it also speaks of the Church triumphant. These are "the saints who from their labors rest." It is that part of the Church which is no longer fighting but which, according to the Protestant Faith, participates in the triumph which was won for the whole Church on the Cross. For the Church consists not only of those few Christians who happen to live on this earth at one particular time but of all believers from the beginning of the world to its end. For this reason the author of Hebrews writes: *Since we are surrounded by so great a cloud of witnesses, let us lay aside every weight and sin which clings so closely and let us run with perseverance the race that is set before us.* (*Hebrews 12:1*) The Church militant lives supported and encompassed by the Church triumphant. The concept "Church," however, includes both realities: The Church still involved in battle and the Church which even now participates in God's victory.

Furthermore, the Church is *one.* This seems a very strange assertion coming from people so obviously divided as Protestants are. Yet in spite of their many denominations they will by and large be united in the claim that the Church is one. The obvious divisions in the ecclesiastical organization of the empirical Church do not affect the ultimate unity. The Church is in fact one because Christ is one: *There is one body and one Spirit, just as you were called to the one hope that belongs to your call, one Lord, one faith, one baptism, one God and father of us all, who is above all and through all and in all.* (*Ephesians 4:5*) This is the source of the Church's unity, which is not dependent upon a unified organization. There seems to be no evidence that the Christian Church was ever organizationally one. Such unity was apparently of no concern to the early Christians. For them the oneness of the Church is the oneness in faith, hope, and love. The Apostle Paul indicates that there were divisions in the church of Corinth (I Corinthians 1:10–17). No superorganization controlled the various Christian groups in the earliest centuries of church history. Soon there were Armenian, Indian, Syrian, and Coptic churches. In 867 the church of the Roman Empire was divided into an Eastern and a Western church. In 1054 A.D. Pope Leo IX excommunicated the patriarch of Constantinople, Michael Cerularius, who quite naturally returned the anathema a little later. This major division took place almost five hundred years before Luther and has never been healed. And, of course, long before the better-known Protestants, there were Protestants such as John Wycliffe and John Hus who preferred faithfulness to the Bible to organizational unity. Now, in spite of all these acknowledged divisions—and the Protestant Faith does not deny or ignore these divisions—Protestants assert that the Church is one. It was Luther who stated in 1520 against the claims of the Roman leadership that "the Moscovites, the White Russians, the Greeks, the Bohemians and many others, believe as we do, baptize as we do and preach as we do."[70] Though there was no organizational unity, the oneness of the Church transcended the disunity of the churches. The unity of the Church, according to the Protestant Faith, is a unity which has its roots in the oneness in Christ. It is founded upon the common Lord of the Christians, nor their common organization. To assure the oneness of the Church, the Protestant Faith relies on the one Lord. Where this Christ is Lord, there the Church is one and united. Protestants are therefore generally suspicious of those who insist that organizational unity is the condition for the oneness of the Church. The Church is one because Christ is one. To make the oneness depend upon the consent of ecclesiastical dignitaries and the efficiency of ecclesiastical machinery would contradict the Protestant assertion that man is justified by grace. For this reason all move-

[70] *Luther's Works* (Weimarer Ausgabe), 6, 287, (Von dem Papsttum in Rom, 1520).

ments toward organizational unity are for Protestants to be justified on pragmatic grounds. No amount of human efficiency and organizational skill will ever improve on the unity which Christians have even now through the *one Lord, one faith, one baptism, one God and Father of us all who is above all and through all and in all.* (*Ephesians 4:5*)

With all other Christians the Protestant Faith asserts the holiness of the Church. The Church is *holy* because it shares in the holiness of Christ, its head. This does not mean for the Protestant Faith that the members or leaders of the Church automatically possess a special holiness which should exempt them from the common duties and obligations which are the responsibilities of other citizens. While other Christians have claimed tax exemption for their clergy and even insisted on their exemption from the jurisdiction of the civil and criminal courts,[71] Protestants have been ready and willing to assume all their civic duties. Even the exemption of the clergy from military service is hardly in line with the Protestant understanding of the holiness of the Church. And this holiness does not imply that the message of the Church is invalidated because of moral lapses of individual members or leaders of the Church. With most of Christendom the great majority of Protestants take the side of Augustine in the Donatist controversy. The Donatists asserted that the preaching and the administration of the sacraments by people who were living in sin invalidated what they did. For example, a man baptized by a priest who had committed a murder would not truly be baptized. Against this position the ancient Church, and with it the Protestant Faith, asserts that the holiness of the Church is not dependent upon the holiness of the members—though this is very desirable—but rather on the holiness of the Christ who is the head of the Church. In the words of St. Augustine:

> Wherefore, anyone who is on the devil's side cannot defile the sacrament, which is of Christ. . . . When baptism is administered

[71] See the Bull "Clericis Laicos," in Bettenson, *Documents*, p. 159.

in the words of the gospel, however great be the perverseness of either minister or recipient, the sacrament itself is holy on his account whose sacrament it is.[72]

And the Church is *universal*. In his epistle to the Galatians, the Apostle Paul writes:

> *For as many of you as were baptized into Christ have put on Christ. There is neither Jew nor Greek, there is neither slave nor free, there is neither male nor female; for you are all one in Christ Jesus.* (*Galatians 3:27, 28*)

The universality of the Church means to the Protestant Faith that it includes all kinds and conditions of men and women. Most Protestants would say that being a man or woman is not religiously significant. One is not closer to God by belonging to one sex or the other. Similarly, one's nationality or race has no theological significance. The Church of Christ is not "white" or "colored," "American" or "European," and such distinctions must not be allowed to divide the Church. In other words, the Church of Christ is by definition "integrated," and while hell may indeed be segregated, the Protestant Faith asserts that heaven is not! Similarly, all social distinctions are meaningless in the universal Church. Though Protestantism in America has undoubtedly tended to organize along national and social lines,[73] the assertion of the universality of the Church makes this type of organization not only useless but actually godless. To the degree to which the living Christ is the Lord of the Protestant churches, the universality of the Church will also be realized. This is the reason why the conflict over racial integration in the churches is of such profound significance. While in other institutions segregation may be harmful or expensive, in the Church segregation is subversive to its very nature. A medical school which advocates segregation may remain

[72] St. Augustine, "De baptismo," in Bettenson, *Documents,* pp. 109 ff.
[73] Cf. Helmut R. Niebuhr, *The Social Sources of Denominationalism* (New York: Meridian Press, Inc., Living Age Books, 1957).

a good medical school, but a church which does the same ceases to be the Church.

The Church is furthermore *apostolic*. This means for Protestants that the Church is based upon the preaching and teaching of the Apostles. The Church is where the *kerygma* is, that is, where the witness to the Christ given by the Apostles and evangelists can be found. Most Protestants are highly suspicious of those efforts which try to establish the authenticity of the Church upon some two-thousand-year supergenealogy, although some few Protestants are actually engaged in efforts to base the validity of their Christian proclamation upon an uninterrupted chain of ecclesiastical dignitaries dating back to the Apostles. The main stream of Protestantism seems to have little use for this so-called "apostolic succession," but rather insists that the Church must have the apostolic preaching. It is the "faith which was once for all delivered to the saints" which must be apostolic. If this is the case, most Protestants will pay little attention to the hierarchical genealogies. But if this apostolic proclamation is absent, no genealogy can possibly make up for it.

Once the Church has been defined in the manner here described, the Protestant Faith can also say that *outside the Church there is no salvation*. It does not mean, as has been said before, that any human institution has exclusive rights to Christ. And subjection to an ecclesiastical dignitary can never be made a condition for salvation.

But what about the organization of the Church? Does the Protestant Faith have anything to say concerning the manner in which the churches have been or should be organized? Actually, three basic patterns have appeared and been adopted by Protestantism. They are somewhat similar to the familiar patterns of ancient political philosophy: monarchy, aristocracy, and democracy. The pattern of church government most similar to monarchy is the episcopal pattern. Many Protestants have organized their churches in this manner. In Protestantism, however, the bishop is usually elected rather than appointed, although there are also important

Protestant churches where the bishop is appointed by some lay authority, frequently the crown. The pattern of church government most similar to aristocracy is the presbyterian pattern. Here a body of selectmen, both laymen and clergy, rules the church. The pattern most similar to democracy is the congregational form of government. The church is here controlled locally and by all the members in good standing. Any larger association of churches has only as much power as has been delegated to it by the individual congregations.

The episcopal, the presbyterian, and the congregational patterns can be found among Protestants. There is a tendency to claim that one or the other pattern is *the* pattern of the New Testament Church. But it seems hard or even impossible to establish which was the exact pattern, if a universal pattern existed in New Testament times. Few Protestants, however, would insist that any particular organization is of the essence of the Church. The manner in which the institutional church is to be administered is for them a pragmatic concern and should be adjusted to the needs of the contemporary situation. Thus in one situation the congregational system may offer the best machinery for an effective church. In another situation an episcopal system might prove more efficient. But since it is Christ, the Lord, who saves, it is inconsistent with the basic proclamation of Protestantism to attribute saving significance to the administrative method chosen for the direction of the Church.

Perhaps the most significant difference in the conception of the Church that can be found in Protestantism has little to do with the episcopal, congregational, or presbyterian form of organization but rather concerns what has been called the "inclusive" or "exclusive" view of the Church. Certain Protestant churches tend to emphasize that the Church in the world is inclusive. This means that it includes both the true believers and the hypocrites. It is impossible for human beings to tell them apart, and men must therefore wait until the Lord of the Church Himself separates those who belong to Him and those who do not. This position is taken by the Protestant defenders of the established church or a folk church. Such Protestant churches can be found today in the Scandinavian countries, in Finland, Sweden, Norway, and Denmark, in Scotland, and to a certain extent in England. In the United States the Puritan fathers were advocates of the idea of "establishment," and historically there have been various establishments in this country. It is significant that followers of the congregationalist as well as the presbyterian and the episcopal pattern of church organization have at times advocated the establishment of their churches. The favorite parable of those who support this inclusive view of the Church is the parable of the wheat and the tares:

> *The kingdom of heaven may be compared to a man who sowed good seed in his field; but while men were sleeping, his enemy came and sowed weeds among the wheat, and went away. So when the plants came up and bore grain, then the weeds appeared also. And the servants of the householder came and said to him, "Sir, did you not sow good seed in your field? How then has it weeds?" He said to them, "An enemy has done this." The servants said to him, "Then do you want us to go and gather them?" But he said, "No; lest in gathering the weeds you root up the wheat along with them. Let both grow together until the harvest; and at harvest time I will tell the reapers, Gather the weeds first and bind them in bundles to be burned, but gather the wheat into my barn. (Matthew 13:24–43)*

And a little later Jesus tells a very similar parable when he says:

> *Again, the kingdom of heaven is like a net which was thrown into the sea and gathered fish of every kind; when it was full, men drew it ashore and sat down and sorted the good into vessels but threw away the bad. (Matthew 13:47)*

218   *The Holy Spirit and the Church*

The other point of view considers the Church a "gathered people," a "holy minority," and adherents of this view make every effort to separate the true believers from the unbelievers even now. This point of view has perhaps been most clearly expressed by Menno Simons, a leader of the Mennonites:

> Christ's Church consists of the Chosen of God, His saints and beloved who have washed their robes in the blood of the Lamb, who are born of God and led by Christ's Spirit, who are in Christ and Christ in them, who hear and believe His word, live in their weakness according to His commandments and in patience and meekness follow in His footsteps, who hate evil and love the good, earnestly desiring to apprehend Christ as they are apprehended of Him. For all who are in Christ are new creatures, flesh of His flesh, bone of His bone and members of His body. . . . Some of the parables, as of the net in which the good and bad fishes are caught; of the wise and foolish virgins and their lamps; of the wedding of the king's son and the guests, and of the threshing floor with wheat and chaff, although the Lord spoke them in allusion to the Church, yet they were not spoken for the purpose that the Church should knowingly and willfully accept and suffer open transgressors in its communion; because in that case, Christ and Paul would differ in doctrine, for Paul says that such should be disciplined and avoided. But they were spoken because many intermingle with the Christians in a Christian semblance, and place themselves under the Word and its sacraments who in fact are no Christians, but are hypocrites and dissemblers before their God.[74]

Historically, Lutherans, Anglicans, Presbyterians, and Congregationalists have tended toward the inclusive view of the Church, while Mennonites, Baptists, and Methodists have tended toward the exclusive view. However, in the peculiar denominational pattern of the American church these distinctions are no longer particularly meaningful, and all Protestant churches have adopted a more voluntary pattern than was the case with the established Protestant

[74] Harold S. Bender, *Menno Simons' Life and Writings* (Scottdale, Pa.: Mennonite Publishing House).

churches of Europe. This adjustment to the conditions of the New World was made easy by the relative unimportance of the organizational pattern of the Church for the Protestant Faith.

Here it may be in order to mention the relationship of *the* Church and the churches in Protestant thought. This problem is particularly significant since in recent decades Protestants have been involved in a fairly comprehensive process of examining the reasons for their diversities and discovering the basis for greater co-operation and unity. These examinations have led to the development of agencies through which many Protestant churches in the world as well as in the United States have worked together in various areas in which the Church must express its concern. Much of the relief, for example, which Protestants have offered to the needy of the world since World War II has been given through co-operative agencies which represented most of the major Protestant denominations in America. The most famous agencies for such inter-Protestant co-operation are probably the NCCUSA, the National Council of the Churches of Christ in the United States of America, and the WCC, the World Council of Churches. The latter also includes prominently the representatives of various Greek and Russian Orthodox traditions. The areas in which the WCC has been working are the following:

(1) A group has been engaged in studies of *faith and order,* discussing the subject under the heading "Our Oneness in Christ and Our Disunity as Churches." Representatives of the various Protestant and Orthodox traditions have studied together and explained to each other the meaning of the Church. This process is still going on and is one of the most significant developments in contemporary Christendom.

(2) A second area of concern has been *evangelism.* This has been summarized as "the mission of the Church to those outside her life." By mutual consultation Protestants have attempted to understand their responsibility for the proclamation of the Gospel to the whole world.

(3) A third area of concern in which the WCC has given

leadership and has supplied a forum for discussion for Protestantism is the field of *social questions*. Protestants have discussed with each other the implications of the social revolution going on all over the world for their various churches and for the Church.

(4) *International* affairs is a fourth concern of the WCC. Difficult and controversial as any discussion of international affairs is bound to be if the participants represent people on both sides of the various "curtains" which have divided the world, it has been carried on. Protestant and Orthodox Christians have asked themselves, "What is the responsibility of Christians in the struggle for world community?" The answers they have found have hardly pleased everybody, but the very fact that the questions were asked has awakened Protestants to some of their political responsibilities.

(5) The discussion of *intergroup relations* is an effort to study the Church's responsibility in racial and ethnic tensions. While some individual Protestants have been leaders in the fight for greater justice in the relationship between the races, the WCC attempts to call all churches to responsible participation in this struggle.

(6) The sixth area of concern of the WCC is *the laity*. Here the discussion centers around the responsibility of the Christian in his daily work. Working together, Protestants are trying to find ways to implement in daily life their common faith in the priesthood of all believers.

These six concerns of the WCC indicate that many Protestants are seriously concerned with the problems which confront the Protestant Faith in the world today. They apparently realize that they will have to work together to make an impact commensurate with the scope of the problems. Not all Protestants co-operate in these joint efforts. Even those who do not co-operate, however, are indirectly influenced by this twentieth-century development.

In recent years Protestants have begun to discuss frankly many of the nontheological factors which have separated the various Protestant denominations from each other. It is obvious that especially here in the United States many divisions among Protestants, one could almost say most divisions among Protestants, have their roots in sociology rather than theology. For example, it would be difficult to see why there should be more than one Lutheran church —were it not for the fact that some Lutherans came originally from Sweden and others from Norway, some from Germany and others from Denmark. Similarly, many divisions among Calvinists are traceable to differences in the country of origin of the ancestors of the present members of these churches. Furthermore, the Civil War split many churches, and some of these schisms have still not been healed.

Another nontheological factor which has proven disruptive is income bracket and social status. It seems that in American Protestantism, a tendency has developed to assemble together according to the members' place in the social structure.

Since the reason for the existence of different denominations is often found to be national background, history, or sociological status, it seems obvious that efforts should be made to overcome these rifts. Attempts to unite Protestants into larger denominations crossing the nontheological divisions are characteristic of contemporary Protestantism.

In the discussion of the Protestant Faith, one must be careful to separate these nontheological factors from "Faith." For the Protestant Faith, the Church is not identical with the churches, but the Church does not exist apart from the churches. The Church and the churches exist in creative tension. But this tension can only be creative if it is understood. Today the Protestant Faith is seriously attempting to understand all the aspects of this tension in order to overcome them where they are sterile and to utilize them where they may contribute to greater vitality.

THE SIGNIFICANCE OF THE WORD AND THE SACRAMENTS FOR THE PROTESTANT FAITH

The task of the Church is to be the witnessing community. This means that the Church must proclaim the apostolic witness concerning Jesus Christ, the Son of God, the Savior. For the Protestant

Faith the proclamation of the Church is thus bound to the witness of Scripture; it is essentially and primarily the exposition of Scripture. In other words, whatever the Protestant Faith claims that it has to say to men today or in the past or in the future must be related to the events experienced and proclaimed by the early Christians. The message of the Protestant Faith is inescapably bound up with these events of the first century: with the birth, life, death, and resurrection of Christ. Take these events away, ignore these events, and the Protestant Faith has nothing to say. This is not idle conjecture because, actually, in the history of Protestantism there have been times and places when the Protestant Faith was separated from this *kerygma,* from the proclamation of the Christ event, from what we have called previously "Holy History." The resulting proclamation was always irrelevant and fruitless. During the period of rationalism in Germany, for example, an effort was made by some preachers to proclaim a useful message to the world—apart from the Christ event and apart from what we have called the *kerygma* and the message of the early church.

The results were sometimes amusing, frequently boring, always utterly irrelevant. For example, while rationalism flourished, a minister of a country parish might begin his Christmas sermon by reading the Christmas Gospel which mentions the fact that at Jesus' birth there was no room in the inn and that he was born in a stable (Luke 2:1 ff.). At this point the preacher would launch forth into a discussion of the advantages of feeding animals in a stable in the winter time over keeping them out in the open air. For almost an hour his farm audience would have to listen to his more or less expert opinion on this fascinating agricultural problem. Such sermons represented an effort to get away from the so-called "supernatural" or "irrational" elements of the Christmas story and make its lessons useful to the parishioner. If it happened to be Easter, the minister might read the story of the women who got up early to go to the tomb of Jesus and found the tomb empty (cf. John 20:1 ff.). At this point the preacher would hold forth on the advantages of getting up early in the morning. He would explain how this makes for a longer day in which to accomplish one's tasks and how "early to bed and early to rise keeps a man healthy, wealthy, and wise." This, then, would be the Easter sermon.

Of course, it was not only the late seventeenth and early eighteenth centuries that suffered from this peculiar understanding of the Christian proclamation. It has always been a temptation in Christendom to separate the proclamation from the person whom the Christians are supposed to proclaim. Historically, Christians have at times proclaimed interesting philosophical views, sage moral advice, and brilliant oratorical masterpieces. Indeed, almost every concern has at some time or other been proclaimed by Christians as the Christian Faith. Breathing exercises, health fads, dietary idiosyncrasies, racial and political prejudices, and other substitutes have all been preached in Christian churches and from Christian pulpits as the Christian message. But if classical Protestantism is used to supply the standards for the evaluation of the Protestant proclamation, one discovers that in Luther and Calvin, for example, preaching is always the proclamation of God's deeds for men as recorded in the Old or the New Testament. It is always followed by an explanation and application of the meaning of these events, their significance for the listeners, whoever they might be.

Perhaps the following illustration will help to show how this was done. In one of Luther's Christmas sermons, as quoted by Professor Bainton in his book *Here I Stand,* we read:

> How unobtrusively and simply do those events take place on earth that are so heralded in heaven! On earth it happened in this wise: There was a poor young wife, Mary of Nazareth, among the meanest dwellers of the town, so little esteemed that none noticed the great wonder that she carried. She was silent, did not vaunt herself, but served her husband, who had no man or maid. They simply left the house. Perhaps they had a donkey for Mary to ride upon, though the Gospels say nothing about it, and we may well believe that she went on foot. The journey was certainly more than a day from Nazareth in Galilee to Bethlehem, which lies on the farther side of Jerusalem. Joseph had thought, "When we get to Bethlehem, we shall be among relatives and can

borrow everything." A fine idea that was! Bad enough that a young bride married only a year could not have had her baby at Nazareth in her own house instead of making all that journey of three days when heavy with child! How much worse that when she arrived there was no room for her! The inn was full. No one would release a room to this pregnant woman. She had to go to a cow stall and there bring forth the Maker of all creatures because nobody would give way. Shame on you, wretched Bethlehem! The inn ought to have been burned with brimstone, for even though Mary had been a beggar maid or unwed, anybody at such a time should have been glad to give her a hand. There are many of you in this congregation who think to yourselves: "If only I had been there! How quick I would have been to help the Baby! I would have washed his linen. How happy I would have been to go with the shepherds to see the Lord lying in the manger!" Yes, you would! You say that because you know how great Christ is, but if you had been there at that time you would have done no better than the people of Bethlehem. Childish and silly thoughts are these! Why don't you do it now? You have Christ in your neighbor. You ought to serve him, for what you do to your neighbor in need you do to the Lord Christ himself. The birth was still more pitiable. No one regarded this young wife bringing forth her first-born. No one took her condition to heart. No one noticed that in a strange place she had not the very least thing needful in childbirth. There she was without preparation: no light, no fire, in the dead of night, in thick darkness. No one came to give the customary assistance. The guests swarming in the inn were carousing, and no one attended to this woman. I think myself if Joseph and Mary had realized that her time was so close she might perhaps have been left in Nazareth. And now think what she could use for swaddling clothes—some garment she could spare, perhaps her veil—certainly not Joseph's breeches, which are now on exhibition at Aachen.

Think, women, there was no one there to bathe the Baby. No warm water, nor even cold. No fire, no light. The mother was herself midwife and the maid. The cold manger was the bed and the bathtub. Who showed the poor girl what to do? She had never had a baby before. I am amazed that the little one did not freeze. Do not make of Mary a stone. For the higher people are in the favor of God, the more tender are they.

Let us then meditate upon the Nativity just as we see it happening in our own babies. Behold Christ lying in the lap of his young mother. What can be sweeter than the babe, what more lovely than the mother! What fairer than her youth! What more gracious than her virginity! Look at the Child, knowing nothing. Yet all that is belongs to him, that your conscience should not fear but take comfort in him. Doubt nothing. To me there is no greater consolation given to mankind than this, that Christ became man, a child, a babe, playing in the lap and at the breast of his most gracious mother. Who is there whom this sight would not comfort? Now is overcome the power of sin, death, hell, conscience, and guilt, if you come to this gurgling Babe and believe that he is come, not to judge you, but to save.[75]

We have given this quotation at such length in order to illustrate how the proclamation of classical Protestantism is bound up with Scripture. It is expository in that it explains the Scriptures and their message to the Church. This quotation from Luther, however, should also show that such proclamation is not merely the retelling of past events but also the living witness to the present generation on the basis of the Christ event. The Word as proclaimed by the Church is not ancient history but a relevant witness to the men and women of today. It is supposed to speak to their situation and make the events of Holy History speak meaningfully to their own lives. There is nothing particularly Christian about a boring sermon, although it is indubitably true that a good many sermons are boring. It is the claim of the Protestant Faith that the Word if truly preached is always meaningful, that it is a "means of grace," that is, a way in which God reaches men. It is for this reason that the sermon occupies a central place in Protestant worship. It is through the Word of God, as it is preached by the minister and proclaimed by the entire Christian community that God speaks to men today.

His message is primarily the good news, the gospel of His deeds for men in Jesus Christ. Secondarily, this message is the exhortation to discipleship, the explanation of what it means to trust in the

[75] Translated by Roland H. Bainton in *Here I Stand*, pp. 355 ff. Copyright 1950 by Pierce & Smith. By permission of Abingdon Press.

Gospel. But the sermon is primarily means of grace. This means that its main function is to tell what God has done for man and then indicate what man can do in grateful reply.

It is the result of an inadequate proclamation of the Protestant Faith if one sometimes gets the impression when listening to Protestant preaching that the sermon is only supposed to show people how evil they are and to tell them that they should try to do better. Looking at the preaching of classical Protestantism, one must conclude that this negative preaching is not Protestant at all. It represents a mistaken understanding of the proclamation of the Word as a means of grace. The primary function of the sermon is to tell the good news, to proclaim the *kerygma,* to recount God's deeds for man. This is the reason why the proclamation of the Word is indeed means of grace.

An examination of the proclamation of the Word as means of grace further reveals that such preaching is subject to the same tensions which have repeatedly become apparent as the key to the understanding of the Protestant Faith. Two complementary statements have to be made simultaneously, for this proclamation is at the same time the word of man *and* the Word of God.

The sermon is the word of man; indeed it is the word of one particular man. This individual may be very eloquent or rather inarticulate. Actually, it does not matter how eloquent he is, for according to the Protestant Faith God can use the eloquence of the eloquent and the stammering of the inarticulate speaker as a vehicle of His grace. The effectiveness of the preaching does not ultimately depend upon the fluency of the speaker. What matters is that the Holy Spirit must use the words to address the listener. Church history is full of reports which illustrate how great orators like St. Ambrose of Milan have been vehicles of the Holy Spirit and also how simple, unlearned revival preachers have been used in the same manner. As far as the Protestant Faith is concerned, it does not even have to be a clergyman who becomes the medium of God's address. The Sunday school teacher who explains the Bible to her pupils, the parent who leads his family in devotions may become instruments of God's grace through the power of the Holy Spirit. For such proclamation can always become the Word of God. He uses it to speak to the human heart. It is the power of the Holy Spirit which addresses man through human words. But it is important to remember that God does not *abolish* the man He so uses. It is still the word of man through which the Word of God reaches other men. Thus the proclamation of the Word is simultaneously human and divine.

But what is the relationship of the sacraments to this proclamation? For most Protestants the sacraments are a uniquely effective type of the ministry of the Word. The sacraments are not some other form of proclamation in addition or superior to the proclamation of the Word. On the contrary, in the sacraments the Word is proclaimed in a uniquely effective manner. The sacraments are, in the phrase of Augustine, *verbum visibile,* visible word. Words are means of communication. We use words to tell other people what we think and want and hope. But it is possible to use other means of communication to convey these innermost feelings. These other means of communication are visible words. The most obvious example that comes to mind is the kiss. Whether a parent kisses his child or a man kisses the woman he loves, we are dealing with a visible word, an action that "speaks louder than words." This action may convey our meaning more effectively and more profoundly than any number of words.

There are other visible words. Let us assume you have received the news that your best friend has lost his mother. You know that he was very close to her and loved her very much. Now, the first time you meet him, you may not know what to say. Everything that comes to mind seems platitudinous, meaningless, and empty. So you may just take his hand and grasp it firmly and look at him. It is quite possible that such an action may convey your sympathy as effectively, perhaps more effectively, than any number of well-chosen words.

In 1945, just after World War II, there was a meeting of Protestant churchmen in Geneva. Among the men invited were Bishop

Eivind Berggrav and the German pastor, Martin Niemoeller. Berggrav was a Norwegian who had just spent a long time in a Nazi prison in Norway. Pastor Niemoeller was much worried how he would be able to meet this man who had suffered so much from the Nazis. How would he react to a German? As soon as Niemoeller came into the room, old Bishop Berggrav went up to him and embraced him. This was an action that spoke louder than words; it was a true *verbum visibile,* a visible word.

For classical Protestantism, the sacraments are such divine actions, mediated through the Church, by which God speaks to men. While for some Christians the sacraments are actions that are effective *by the outward act (ex opere operato),* Protestants are unanimous in their assertion that the visible words are no more effective by the outward act alone than are any other words. If words of comfort and help are to do you some good, you must believe them. So the Protestant Faith asserts that the sacraments proclaim God's saving Word to the believers, to those who do not harden their hearts to the message, not in the sense, however, that their validity is dependent upon the faith of the recipient, but only their saving power. The efficacy of the means of grace, both Word and sacraments, is similar to the efficacy of a check. The validity of the check does not depend on the faith of the recipient in its soundness. Yet, unless the recipient trusts in the signature, he will not deposit and use it. Thus a perfectly good check could be discarded because the person to whom it was issued did not believe in it. Faith, while unable to make the check valid, can make it worthless. Similarly, the means of grace, while objectively valid, may become useless to the man who refuses to accept them in faith.

However, while all Protestants agree that the means of grace are received in faith, the exact understanding of the sacraments tends to divide Lutheran Christians from Christians of the Reformed tradition, for example, Presbyterians, Congregationalists, and Baptists. In this controversy the Episcopalians and the Methodists are hard to classify. Their tradition allows for great breadth in the interpretation of the sacraments, so that some hold views very similar to the Lutheran position, while others accept a Reformed interpretation.

The difference between the Lutheran understanding of the sacraments and the Reformed understanding is that the former would emphasize the objective effectiveness of the sacraments, while the latter would interpret the sacraments more as symbolic actions. These differences will become clearer a little later, when the sacraments of Baptism and the sacrament of the Lord's Supper are discussed.

Of both sacraments, however, it can be said that as divinely instituted actions they guard the Protestant Faith against a false intellectualism. The God of the Bible is a God who acts. It is always important to distinguish the Christian God from the unmoved mover of the philosophers. Aristotle's unmoved mover could not possibly establish sacraments. The God of the Bible does. Thus the sacraments demonstrate again that the God whom the Protestant Faith proclaims is no mere intellect, power, or even morality, but a personal God who acts in history. Furthermore, the sacraments as physical actions, involving the physical elements of water, bread, and wine, guard the Protestant Faith against a false spiritualism which depreciates matter. As has been shown before, the God of the Bible is the God of spirit *and* matter. Christians insist that He created matter. The sacraments, with their use of the material to convey God's grace to men, emphasize the significance of matter and thus protect the Protestant Faith against a spiritualism which would make matter evil and somehow opposed to God.

But what is the specific function of the sacraments in the Protestant Faith? The first important assertion of Protestantism is that there are only two sacraments: Baptism and the Lord's Supper. Other Christians have more sacraments; they are Confirmation, Penance, Extreme Unction, Holy Orders, and Matrimony, in addition to Baptism and the Lord's Supper. Protestantism knows only these last two. The reason for the smaller number of sacraments administered by Protestants is that only Baptism and the Lord's Supper are described by the Protestant definition of a sacrament as an action instituted by Christ, using an earthly element and conveying grace. The Protestant conviction that a sacrament must be instituted by Christ means that Christ Himself must have told His followers to use the sacrament. Furthermore, the sacrament must use a physical element like water or bread and wine and promise to convey grace. The churches of the Reformation claim that only Baptism and the Lord's Supper meet these specifications. Marriage, for example, is accepted as an extremely important divine order by all Christians, but, since it was this also in Old Testament times and even among those people who have never heard of Christianity, it cannot be said to have been instituted by Christ. Therefore, for Protestants, marriage is not a sacrament.

Baptism, however, is clearly an action instituted by Christ, using an earthly element and conveying grace. Baptism describes through action the meaning of membership in the Church of Christ. It expresses purification, since water has always been used for washing. In Baptism it is used to express the washing away of sin. Especially when immersion is practiced, it clearly expresses death and the new life, the immersion expressing the dying of the old man and the rising out of the water expressing the birth of the new man.

Baptism is for most Protestants an act of God, mediated through the Church. It is the Word of God in action. Baptism is, so to speak, the seal of God's love applied to the person being baptized. Just as a seal expresses the power and authority of the person whose seal is being affixed, so Baptism expresses the power and authority of God, whose seal it is.

Baptism could also be described as the kiss of God applied to the person being baptized. A kiss is an expression of love. And most Protestants would say in applying this figure to Baptism that, when a father kisses his baby, this kiss is an expression of love whether the baby fully understands the meaning of the kiss or not. What matters is the love of the father expressed in the kiss rather than the comprehension of the baby who receives the kiss. Thus a child may be baptized in early infancy.

However, infant Baptism is one of the most controversial subjects among Protestants, and there are many Protestants of the Baptist tradition who will insist that Baptism is not really Baptism unless the person being baptized clearly understands what Baptism implies. He must have acknowledged his allegiance to Christ.

It appears that the attitude toward infant or adult Baptism depends largely upon the sacramental understanding of Baptism. Those Protestant churches which emphasize that Baptism is really an act of God, an act in which God shows His love and mercy to man in a visible word, will practice infant Baptism. Those Protestant churches who see in Baptism essentially an opportunity to confess the Christian Faith and an expression of this confession will emphasize adult Baptism.

For those who will baptize children, Baptism has its antecedent in the Old Testament rite of circumcision. This operation was supposed to establish and express the covenant relationship between God and His people. It was performed on all male infants on the eighth day after birth. For most Protestants, Baptism establishes the covenant relationship for the people of the New Covenant, where there is neither male nor female, neither Jew nor Greek (Galatians 3:28). It is therefore to be applied to all.

Those who insist on adult Baptism object that infant Baptism leads to an understanding of Baptism as a meaningless rite, which has often merely superstitious connotations and thus counteracts the very message of the Christian Gospel. While this is certainly often the case, the advocates of infant Baptism assert that its abuses and misunderstandings should lead not to its abolition but to a clearer teaching concerning its true meaning.

For our purposes it may suffice to point out that Protestants, especially in America, are thoroughly divided on the subject of Baptism. Yet they are almost universally agreed that all Christians ought to be baptized, either in infancy or when they are able to express the desire themselves. But, while all Christians ought to be baptized, most Protestants hold that not the lack but the contempt of Baptism separates man from God. There is no special place between heaven and hell for unbaptized children. They are committed to the mercy of God.

All that is necessary for a valid Baptism are the words of institution:

> *Go therefore, and make disciples of all nations, baptizing them in the name of the Father, and of the Son, and of the Holy Spirit, teaching them to observe all that I have commanded you; and lo I am with you always, even to the close of the age. (Matthew 28:19, 20)*

And with these words the application of water in the name of the Father and of the Son and of the Holy Spirit. Though many Protestants do not believe that emergency baptisms are necessary, those who do, insist that in an emergency a Baptism can be performed by anyone. It is not even necessary that the person performing the Baptism be a Christian.

The second sacrament, and the only other sacrament accepted by Protestants, is the Lord's Supper. It has many other names; sometimes it is called Holy Communion, or the Holy Eucharist. It is the sacrament which was established by Christ for the forgiveness of sins of the believers. The institution of this sacrament is described in the Gospel of Matthew in the following words:

> *Now as they were eating, Jesus took bread, and blessed, and broke it, and gave it to the disciples and said, "Take, eat; this is my body." And he took a cup, and when he had given thanks he gave it to them, saying, "Drink of it, all of you; for this is my blood of the covenant, which is poured out for many for the forgiveness of sins. I tell you I shall not drink again of this fruit of the vine until that day when I drink it new with you in my Father's kingdom." (Matthew 26:26–29)*

The Holy Spirit and the Church 233

The Old Testament antecedent of the Lord's Supper is the Jewish feast of the Passover. In the spring of every year the Jews, celebrating their deliverance from Egypt, recalled how Pharaoh permitted the Jewish people to leave after the Lord had slain the first-born in every Egyptian family but passed over the Jewish homes, where the blood of a sacrificial lamb was placed on the doorposts. Jesus seems to have instituted the Lord's Supper in connection with a Passover celebration with His disciples. For the Protestant Faith, Jesus is the Passover lamb of the Christians. In the Gospel of John we read, *The next day John saw Jesus coming toward him, and said, "Behold, the Lamb of God, who takes away the sin of the world!" (John 1:29)* And the Book of Revelation is full of allusions to Christ as the Lamb of God.

While the Lord's Supper is an expression of the divine love and mercy and of the communion of the Christian Church with its Lord, it is also the sacrament which divides Christians most deeply. One could almost say that the Lord's Supper is the most controversial subject in the Christian Faith. Understood differently by Protestants and Roman Catholics, it has also led to considerable disagreement among Protestants.

It would lead beyond the scope of this volume to discuss in detail the various positions in regard to the Lord's Supper, yet the four basic positions can be described quite easily. They are usually known as (1) transubstantiation; (2) real presence; (3) symbolic presence; (4) memorial. What do these different terms mean?

The Roman Catholic Church teaches transubstantiation. This means that Roman Catholics believe that, after the priest has consecrated the elements of the Eucharist, the substance of bread has changed into the body of Christ and the substance of the wine has changed into the blood of Christ. In order to understand what this means, one must keep in mind that the Roman Catholic doctrine assumes the soundness of the Aristotelian distinction between substance and accidents. According to this philosopher everything consists of substance and accidents. A dog, for example, may have certain "accidents"—it may be white, have four legs, two eyes, a certain weight, and so forth. These characteristics are called "accidents" because the animal would still be a dog even if it lost one eye or one leg, or were dyed a different color, or changed its weight. But in addition to these accidents a dog has a "substance"—its "dogness," so to speak. If this changes, it would no longer be a dog, but something else. Now according to Aristotle the same could be said about an apple or a watch—or any other object. All have accidents and a substance. For example, an apple may be red, but if it were yellow it would still be an apple. Chalk may be white and round, but, if it were blue and square, it would still be chalk. But what has all this to do with the Roman Catholic doctrine of transubstantiation? Simply this: The Roman Catholic Church teaches that after the consecration of the elements, the accidents of the wine and the bread remain. In other words, the wine still looks like wine and smells like wine and tastes like wine, for these are accidents. But the *substance* has changed. Instead of the substance of wine it is now the substance of blood, and instead of the substance of bread the bread is now the substance of flesh. This is the meaning of the doctrine of transubstantiation. Every time the mass is said the miracle of the incarnation is repeated by the priest. This is the one extreme of the various positions concerning the Lord's Supper taken by Christians.

On the other extreme we find the memorial view of the Lord's Supper. Most Christians who hold this position are what has been called "left-wing Protestants." They assert that the elements are in no way affected by anything that is said or done at Holy Communion. The Lord's Supper is entirely a memorial feast. Christians come together to remember what Jesus did for them two thousand years ago. Just as Americans may come together on the Fourth of July in order to remember the Fourth of July, 1776, so Christians meet at the Lord's table to remember the first Lord's Supper and what this event has meant to the Church ever since.

Most Protestants' understanding of the Lord's Supper is somewhere between the doctrine of transubstantiation on the one hand and the memorial view on the other. Calvinists believe in the symbolic presence of Christ in the Lord's Supper. This is how Calvin himself describes the significance of the Lord's Supper:

> After God receives us into his family, and not only so as to admit us among his servants, but to number us with his children, —in order to fulfil the part of a most excellent father, solicitous for his offspring, he also undertakes to sustain and to nourish us as long as we live; and not content with this, he has been pleased to give us a pledge, as a further assurance of this never-ceasing liberality. For this purpose, therefore, by the hand of his only begotten Son, he has favored his Church with another sacrament, a spiritual banquet, in which Christ testifies himself to be the bread of life, to feed our souls for a true and blessed immortality. . . . Now, the only food of our souls is Christ; and to him, therefore, our heavenly Father invites us, that being refreshed by a participation of him, we may gain fresh vigor from day to day, till we arrive at the heavenly immortality. And because this mystery of the secret union of Christ with believers is incomprehensible by nature, he exhibits a figure and image of it in visible signs, peculiarly adapted to our feeble capacity; and, as it were, by giving tokens and pledges, renders it equally as certain to us as if we beheld it with our eyes.[76]

And Calvin believed that this sacrament was so important that it should be celebrated "at least once in every week."

The Lutherans and most Anglicans believe in the real presence of Christ with the elements of the Lord's Supper. The Christ, "through whom all things were made and in whom all things hold together," to use the New Testament phrase, is believed to be present everywhere and in everything.

> *For in him all things were created, in heaven and on earth, visible and invisible, whether thrones or dominions or principalities or authorities—all things were created through him and for him. He is before all things and in him all things hold together. (Colossians 1:16, 17)*

[76] John Calvin, *Institutes of the Christian Religion* (Philadelphia: Presbyterian Board of Education, 1936), Book IV, 17, 1, Vol. II, pp. 641 f.

It is this Christ who is truly present for the believer in the sacrament of Holy Communion. He allows Himself to be found here because He has given His word that in these elements man may find Him. Luther says:

> What is the Sacrament of the Altar? It is the true Body and Blood of our Lord Jesus Christ, under the bread and wine, given unto us Christians to eat and to drink, as it was instituted by Christ Himself. . . . What is the benefit of such eating and drinking? It is pointed out in these words: Given and shed for you for the remission of sins. Through these words, the remission of sin, life and salvation are given unto us in the Sacrament; for where there is remission of sins, there is also life and salvation.

And then Luther continues by asking:

> How can bodily eating and drinking produce such great benefits? The eating and drinking, indeed, do not produce them, but the words: Given and shed for you for the remission of sins. For besides the bodily eating and drinking, these words are the chief thing in the sacrament; and he who believes them, has what they say and declare, namely, the "remission of sins."[77]

Finally, it should be added that while the overwhelming majority of Protestants accept and use the sacraments of Baptism and the Lord's Supper, some Protestants, for example the Quakers, do not use any sacraments at all. Though they admit that such practices were at one time used in the Church, they claim that they were only "the shadows of better things" and that "they cease in such as have obtained the substance."[78]

Though this short discussion by no means exhausts the complexity of the Protestant preaching concerning the sacraments, it may show that probably no other area of the Protestant Faith is so full of conflict and disagreement as this particular field. The very sacrament which Protestants believe was instituted to establish and express the unity of the Christian people has in fact caused innu-

[77] "Small Catechism," *Book of Concord,* I, 374.
[78] Robert Barclay, "Apology for the Quakers" (1678). See Appendix, p. 279.

merable divisions. This has been for many Protestants a sure sign that evil is not only a force outside of the Church but has deeply infiltrated its ranks.

THE MINISTRY

Closely associated with the means of grace, the Word and the sacraments, are the men to whom the Church has entrusted the administration of these means, the ministers. What is the Protestant understanding of the ministry?

To Protestants the ministry is a functional office, not a sacrament. Some Christians believe that a man who has been ordained to the ministry will always be a priest; ordination puts an indelible mark on his person. He can become an unfaithful and evil priest, but he will always stand in a special relationship to God. Since ordination is for them a sacrament, one can never lose this mark. For the Protestant Faith the ministry is a functional office instituted by God for the sake of the Church. While God uses the ministry for the proclamation of His message and the guidance and care of His people, a man is a minister only as long as he exercises the functions of the ministry. Classical Protestantism immediately rejected the notion of the *character indelibilis*, the indelible mark which ordination imprints on the minister. If a man exercises the functions of the ministry, if he has a call from God and the Church, he is a minister. If he starts doing something else and gives up the functions of the ministry, no longer preaches and administers the sacraments—he may still be a very fine Christian, but he is no longer a minister in the eyes of Protestants.

Being a minister does not place a person any closer to God than other Christians. The minister can approach God by virtue of the fact that he is a priest. But this is true of every other Christian, for according to the Bible and the Protestant Faith all believers are priests and all have direct access to God without any mediation except the mediation of Christ. The minister, or pastor, serves an essential function of the Church—he preaches, he administers the sacraments, he administers the discipline of the Church—but all these are functions of the Church. The minister is a servant of God in the Church, no closer to God than any other equally faithful Christian and fellow priest in the priesthood of all believers.

For most Protestants this understanding of the ministry as a functional office makes the form and particular organization of the ministry of secondary importance. The ministry is instituted by God in many forms, assert the Protestants:

> *And his gifts were that some should be apostles, some prophets, some evangelists, some pastors and teachers, for the equipment of the saints, for the work of ministry, for building up the body of Christ. (Ephesians 4:11, 12)*

It appears that the various titles such as bishop and presbyter are used interchangeably in the New Testament. As far as the Protestant Faith is concerned, these terms make little difference, but the following words still apply to all who seek to serve the Church in any office of leadership:

> *If any one aspires to the office of bishop, he desires a noble task. Now a bishop must be above reproach, the husband of one wife, temperate, sensible, dignified, hospitable, an apt teacher, no drunkard, not violent but gentle, not quarrelsome, and no lover of money. He must manage his own household well, keeping his children submissive and respectful in every way; for if a man does not know how to manage his own household how can he care for God's church? (I Timothy 3:1)*

It is the care for God's Church which is the primary task of the ministry. The Protestant Faith considers all other aspects of the ministry as secondary to it. There is little concern with the specific manner of selection and appointment to this office. Most Protestants, however, would agree with Calvin, who said:

Though there is no express precept for the imposition of hands [in ordination], yet since we find it to have been constantly used by the apostles, such a punctual observance of it by them ought to have the force of a precept with us. And certainly this ceremony is highly useful both to recommend to the people the dignity of the ministry, and to admonish the person ordained that he is no longer his own master, but devoted to the service of God and the Church.[79]

[79] Calvin, *Institutes,* Book IV, 3, 16, Vol. II, p. 331.

8

Eschatology

No description of the Protestant Faith would be complete without a discussion of the subject of eschatology. The word itself comes from the Greek word for "the furthest," "the last." Thus eschatology deals with the ultimate destiny of man and the world.

As the teaching concerning the end, the last things, the goal of life and history, eschatology is a part of all religions. Every major religious movement has something to say about man's ultimate destiny. Thus Buddhists teach about Nirvana and the ancient Greeks believed in Hades. The ultimate goal of existence is of concern not only to Protestants but to all people.

This is most strikingly demonstrated by the great secular religions of our time. Communism and fascism in all their forms have well-developed eschatologies. They have a great deal to say about the ultimate outcome of history. Some of the fascination which these pseudo-religions exert upon modern man is apparently the result of this very concern with eschatology. They appeal because they claim to be the "wave of the future" and because they assert that they are able to foretell what the future will bring. This is clearly expressed in some of the Fascist and Communist songs. The notorious *Horst Wessel Lied,* the hymn of the Nazi movement, spoke about the *last* battle and promised that the future would belong to the *Führer.* Similarly the Communist *International* calls the workers to the *last* fight. Communism predicts that after the revolution the state will disappear and the classless paradise will dawn. It would seem that the success of communism in so many parts of the world is hardly the result of its economic theories, which few people read and even fewer understand, but rather the result of its eschatology. Its promise of a glorious future is attractive and easily understood.

But the eschatology of the great secular mass movements of our time is utterly different from the biblical eschatology of the Protestant Faith. Protestant eschatology derives its uniqueness from the fact that it sees the ultimate destiny of man and the world as dependent upon their relationship to God, the Father, Son, and Holy Spirit.

Some of the subjects with which Christian eschatology concerns itself are those which Protestants have considered the most stirring aspects of their faith. It deals with death, resurrection, judgment, life after death, and God's eternal kingdom. Its appearance at the end of a description of the Protestant Faith must not be construed as a value judgment. Without its particular eschatology the Christian Faith would not be Christian at all. Thus eschatology is actually the keystone of everything that has been said so far rather than a more or less superfluous final chapter.

At the beginning of this book it was stated that the Protestant Faith is derived from the confession that God was in Christ reconciling the world to Himself. Eschatology is the explication of this confession in regard to the future. It asserts that the future as well as the past is the Lord's. It is just as impossible to escape God in time as it is impossible to escape Him in space. The Psalmist says about space:

> *If I ascend to heaven, thou art there! If I make my bed in Sheol, thou art there! If I take the wings of the morning and dwell in the uttermost parts of the sea, even there thy hand shall lead me, and thy right hand shall hold me. (Psalm 139:8–10)*

In the Book of Revelation the Lord makes the very same assertion in regard to time: *I am the Alpha and the Omega, the first and the last, the beginning and the end. (Revelation 22:13)* Christian eschatology speaks from the perspective of time about this sovereign majesty of God as revealed in Jesus Christ.

THE KINGDOM OF GOD

If the sovereignty of God over time is taken seriously, the kingdom of God is seen as the purpose and goal of history. It is the realm where *God* rules in power and glory, and thus it is utterly different from all human Utopias which glorify man. In this kingdom the powers of evil have been destroyed and can no longer disrupt God's plan for man. Satan, who is often called the prince of this world, has been overcome on the Cross, but it is in the coming kingdom that this defeat of the evil powers will be apparent to all. The coming kingdom is reserved for God's people. Only those who are the subjects of the King will inherit His kingdom.

This kingdom of God has always been the hope of Christian people. The New Testament is dominated by this expectation, as are the writings of some of the greatest theologians in the history of the Christian Church. But while this hope has been uppermost in the minds of Christians at certain times and in certain places, there have been other periods in which this hope has not been as vital a part of the Christian life. Within the Protestant Faith the expectation of the kingdom of God has ranged from a position as the central doctrine to one of marginal concern largely buried in the textbooks on theology.

Whenever eschatology was in the forefront of Protestant thinking, certain books of the Bible were studied with particular zeal. The two books which have always been the favorites of eschatological ages are the Book of Daniel in the Old Testament and the Book of Revelation in the New Testament. The reason is obvious: both deal with the future and the outcome of history, and both are written in periods of persecution and distress.

A study of church history indicates that eschatology becomes a burning concern of Christians whenever people are no longer sure that the foundations upon which their society is built are sound. In ages of great turmoil and confusion and in countries which have experienced revolution and catastrophe, eschatological thought begins to dominate the thinking of the Church.

Protestant Christians have therefore differed widely in their understanding of the significance of eschatology. On the one hand those movements which are generally described as modernism or liberalism have been largely noneschatological in their outlook. Orthodoxy and fundamentalism, on the other hand, while taking eschatology more seriously, have tended to separate it from the totality of the Christian message and sometimes to pervert it through wild and materialistic speculation. Today many Protestant theologians in Europe place eschatology in the center of their theology. American Protestants, however, are still slightly uncomfortable with this subject. Caught between the humanistic utopianism of the liberals and the materialistic speculations of the fundamentalists, they have not been able to make full use of the Christian assertion that the coming Christ is the hope of the world.

While certain shifts in the emphasis on eschatology can be easily understood in the light of the changing pressures upon the Church, it must be said that a complete disregard of the Christian hope for the coming of God's kingdom would actually abolish the Protestant Faith. The prayer "Thy kingdom come" cannot be abandoned without abandoning the faith itself.

DEATH AND TIME

But what are some of the specific assertions which the Protestant Faith makes about the "last things"? What does it have to say about death and time? Classical Protestantism accepts the reality of death. Death is not an illusion which can be banished by wishful thinking. Because it is *the* fact which faces every human being, it must be taken seriously. Every effort to ignore it will only lead to self-deception. Classical Protestantism has little use for the elaborate modern efforts to devise methods which make it possible for men and women to deceive themselves about the reality of death. The illusion of modern man that he will live forever misleads him in regard to the seriousness of his predicament. Protestantism must point out to those lulled into a false security by the flood of statistics concerning life expectancy that regardless of the real accomplishments of the medical profession, the mortality rate remains a constant 100 percent. It does not ultimately matter that we may be able to reduce the percentage of people who die from heart disease or cancer. Finally, when all the figures are added up, they will invariably show that 100 percent of all men die. The Protestant Faith takes this fact very seriously.

But, while death is *the* fact of human existence, it is not the last word. In a sense it is the first word that must be said about man. From the moment he is born, man goes toward his death. In the words of the German philosopher Martin Heidegger, man's existence is a "being unto death." It is this fact which gives urgency and significance to his life. Time is not merely the endless repetition of identical moments; it has an end. Endless time could not be wasted. But man's time is not endless; it ends in death. Thus what happens while it lasts is of the utmost significance.

Especially because death, according to the Protestant Faith, is not the end at all, the life that ends in death receives ultimate importance. *It is appointed for men to die, and after that comes judgment.* (*Hebrews 9:27*) This judgment after death is the result of the resurrection of the dead. Most religions base their hope for a life after death upon the somewhat vague notion of the immortality of the soul. But, while many Christians believe also in the immortality of the soul, this is not the category which the Bible uses to describe life after death. Immortality of the soul seems to rest the life after death in some indestructible part of man, namely, his soul. Many who believe in it seem to think that man possesses some immortal quality which death cannot destroy.

Against this man-centered notion of a life after death the Protestant Faith asserts the biblical teaching of the resurrection of the body. This doctrine, which can be found in all the great creeds of Christendom, grounds the Christian Faith in an eternal life in fellowship with God in God's creative sovereignty rather than in any particular quality in man. While the emphasis on the immortality of the soul seems to suggest that there is something in man which is of necessity immortal, the doctrine of the resurrection asserts that the God who created man in the first place can recreate him in the second place.

You are here in this world. This is a fact which you cannot deny. You had no choice about being placed in this world. God placed you here according to His purpose. Indeed, you will die, but who are you to say that the God who put you into this world cannot raise you from the dead, recreate you whenever and however He desires? According to the Protestant Faith God desires to do so. This is His sovereign decision, no more and no less sovereign than the decision which places you in this world now. If you say that God cannot do it or that it is impossible or highly improbable, the Protestant Faith asserts that your existence here and now is also logically impossible or at least highly improbable. But God has placed you in this world nevertheless. Look at yourself; you are here, you exist! Who are you to say that you will not exist again if the sovereign Creator so chooses?

The emphasis in the doctrine of the resurrection in the Protestant Faith is entirely on *God's* creative power rather than on any innate quality of man which may prevent his extinction. Even the continuity between man's life now and his new life in the world to come is guaranteed by God rather than by any human quality. The Gospel of Luke reports that when the disciples of Jesus had returned from a successful missionary journey during which they had been able to subdue the powers of evil, they were full of joy and gratitude. It was on this occasion that Jesus said to them that while such authority over evil was indeed reason for gratitude they should rejoice rather because they were known by God. In the words of the New Testament: *Nevertheless do not rejoice in this, that the spirits are subject to you; but rejoice that your names are written in heaven. (Luke 10:20)* In the language of the Bible the word "name" stands for the "I," the person. To know God's name is to know God personally. And if God knows my name, He knows me personally.

Because the believer is known by God, because he has encountered God and God has established a personal relationship with him, he has become a "thou" to God's "I" and has hope for eternal life. The Christian hope for eternal life is thus rooted in the nature of God rather than in the nature and equipment of man. This is the meaning of the Protestant doctrine of the resurrection of the body.

THE INTERMEDIATE STAGE

While the faith in the resurrection has always been a basic part of the Protestant Faith, the state between the death of a person and his resurrection has been widely and inconclusively debated by theologians. The fundamental problem in all these discussions is the assumption that time is not only a category of the human mind but also a reality in God. The problem disappears, however, if one is prepared to take seriously the scriptural evidence that in God there is no time. He is *the same yesterday and today and for ever (Hebrews 13:8)*. Of Him the Psalmist says: *For a thousand years in thy sight are but as yesterday when it is past, or as a watch in the night.* (*Psalm 90:4*) And the Second Letter of Peter states: *But do not ignore this one fact, beloved, that with the Lord one day is as a thousand years, and a thousand years as one day.* (*II Peter 3:8*) Thus Jesus Christ can say to the thief on the cross: *Truly, I say to you, today you will be with me in Paradise.* (*Luke 23:43*) All this seems to indicate that it is an error to project human time into God and to subject God to the limitations of the human concept of time.

In line with the biblical witness it appears to be more accurate to assert that death means confrontation with the living God. Thus man is confronted by eternity at the moment of his death and no longer subject to the limitations of human time. However, while this seems to be a solution for the problems which a crude understanding of time creates for the Protestant Faith, it is by no means unanimously accepted by Protestants. Time and eternity have been much debated, but at present it is impossible to present a common teaching which would do justice to all the points of view which have been proposed.

While the understanding of time in relation to God is controversial, Protestants unanimously and categorically reject the notion of purgatory as a state which is neither heaven nor hell in which the souls of men are purged and prepared for fellowship with God. Protestants have always rejected especially the idea that the souls there imprisoned can be released by the prayers and offerings of the living. It was, in fact, a question of this sort which produced the occasion for the Reformation,

Since the Protestant Faith insists that fellowship with God is solely the result of God's grace and not in any way dependent upon human merit, the notion of purgatory is incongruous to one of the fundamental axioms of this faith. Luther himself, who accepted the existence of a purgatory for a long time after the Reformation, finally abandoned it since he could not find any scriptural evidence for this doctrine.

THE MILLENNIUM

Another controversial issue in the area of eschatology is the so-called "millennium." This is a period of one thousand years at the end of history when, according to some, Christ will return to earth and rule the world with his saints. Millennialism is based on a somewhat obscure passage in the Book of Revelation which reads as follows:

> *Then I saw an angel coming down from heaven, holding in his hand the key of the bottomless pit and a great chain. And he seized the dragon, that ancient serpent, who is the Devil and Satan, and bound him for a thousand years, and threw him into the pit, and shut it and sealed it over him, that he should deceive the nations no more, till the thousand years were ended. After that he must be loosed a little while. Then I saw thrones, and seated on them were those to whom judgment was committed. Also I saw the souls of those who had been beheaded for their testimony to Jesus and for the word of God, and who had not worshipped the beast or its image and had not received its mark on their foreheads or their hands. They came to life again, and reigned with Christ a thousand years"* (*Revelation 20:1–4*).

This quotation shows that we are dealing with a vision. The interpretation of such visions is never very easy and obviously gives great leeway to those who love to speculate. Some Protestants have become very much attached to these few verses and have exaggerated their significance out of all proportion to the total Christian message. They eagerly await the literal fulfillment of this prophecy of a thousand-year rule of the saints. However, like most literalists, they are somewhat selective about the passages they are going to take literally. For example, while this text seems to limit the rule to those who have been "beheaded for their testimony to Jesus and for the word of God," most millennialists teach that all true believers share in this rule.

Because of the obscurity of the passage there are a great many differences among those Protestants who have made the millennium part of their faith. Classical Protestantism has rejected all these speculations. For the main stream of the descendants of the Reformation the position of the Augsburg Confession is typical:

> They [the signers of the Augsburg Confession] condemn others also who now scatter Jewish opinions, that, before the resurrection of the dead, the godly shall occupy the kingdom of the world, the wicked being everywhere suppressed.[80]

Following Augustine, Luther and Calvin understood the millennium as a period of church history which began with Christ's victory over death. The left-wing Protestants generally interpreted it as a golden age at the end of history, either before (postmillennialism) or after (premillennialism) Christ's return. In the modernism of the nineteenth and twentieth centuries the millennial hope was transformed into the expectation of God's rule on earth through the application of Christian moral insights to the social order.

While the millennium has fascinated Christians through the ages, no consensus has ever been achieved. But, whenever speculation concerning the coming rule of the saints leads Protestants to neglect their responsibilities to God and the neighbor here and now, it must be rejected as worthless and dangerous on the basis of the principles of the Protestant Faith.

Even this short review of the Protestant Faith and eschatology has shown that this is an area of great concern and tension. But in spite of the many real disagreements concerning various aspects of eschatology, Protestants do agree on the source of the ultimate Christian hope. God has created mankind for His purpose. He *desires all men to be saved and to come to the knowledge of the truth (I Timothy 2:4)*. He has called them to fellowship with

[80] *Augsburg Confession*, Art. XVII, see Appendix, p. 262.

Him and service in His kingdom. This goal is achieved as the result of God's creative grace in Jesus Christ. It is a life which His people live eternally out of the power of His love with and for each other.

To the Protestant Faith this eternal fellowship is a personal fellowship with a personal God, bestowed through a personal promise. The Protestant Faith rejects the absorption of the individual "I" into some undifferentiated world soul. It asserts the life everlasting as a personal possession.

But, if this is a personal relationship which God establishes with man, it must be possible to reject it. If it could be forced on man it would not be the free relationship of God's "I" to man's "thou." Such a forced fellowship would abolish man as man. It is for this reason that the Protestant Faith proclaims not only eternal salvation but also eternal damnation. Hell is the result of the unlimited possibility of man to say "no" to God. Man can resist the love of God forever, for the God of the Bible cannot and will not force His love upon anybody. For this reason most Protestants reject universalism, that is, the teaching that eventually all men will be saved.

Nothing in the Scriptures would justify such a claim. When taken seriously, universalism tends to detract from the importance of the decision to which all men are called when confronted by God. If universalism is accepted, then man is saved by some automatic process rather than by the free and sovereign grace of God. And it is this free and sovereign grace of God which according to Protestantism is the center of the biblical witness.

Thus at the end of this study it is important to repeat what was said in the beginning. The Protestant Faith in its classical expressions glorifies the sovereign grace of God. It is God who creates, it is God who saves, it is God who preserves, it is God who alone guarantees eternal life. The underlying conviction of Protestantism concerning the "first things" as well as the "last things" is expressed most accurately in a hymn written by the Apostle Paul:

What then shall we say to this? If God is for us, who is against us? He who did not spare his own Son but gave him up for us all, will he not also give us all things with him? Who shall bring any charge against God's elect? It is God who justifies; who is to condemn? It is Christ Jesus, who died, yes, who was raised from the dead, who is at the right hand of God, who indeed intercedes for us. Who shall separate us from the love of Christ? Shall tribulation, or distress, or persecution, or famine, or nakedness, or peril, or sword? As it is written, "For thy sake we are being killed all the day long; we are regarded as sheep to be slaughtered." No, in all these things we are more than conquerors through him who loved us. For I am sure that neither death, nor life, nor angels, nor principalities, nor things present, nor things to come, nor powers, nor height, nor depth, nor anything else in all creation, will be able to separate us from the love of God in Christ Jesus our Lord. (Romans 8:31–39)

This, essentially, is the Protestant Faith.

Appendix

THE APOSTLES' CREED

I believe in God the Father Almighty; Maker of heaven and earth. And in Jesus Christ his only (begotten) Son our Lord; who was conceived by the Holy Ghost, born of the Virgin Mary; suffered under Pontius Pilate, was crucified, dead, and buried; he descended into hell; the third day he rose from the dead; he ascended into heaven; and sitteth at the right hand of God the Father Almighty; from thence he shall come to judge the quick and the dead.

I believe in the Holy Ghost; the holy catholic Church; the communion of saints; the forgiveness of sins; the resurrection of the body; and the life everlasting. Amen.

Philip Schaff, *The Creeds of Christendom* (New York: Harper & Brothers, 1877), II, 45.

THE NICENE CREED*

I believe in one God the Father Almighty; Maker of heaven and earth, and of all things visible and invisible.

And in one Lord Jesus Christ, the only-begotten Son of God, begotten of the Father before all worlds [God of God], Light of Light, very God of very God, begotten, not made, being of one substance

---

* The Western additions, of which the *Filioque* is the most important, are enclosed in brackets.

[essence] with the Father; by whom all things were made; who, for us men and for our salvation, came down from heaven, and was incarnate by the Holy Ghost of the Virgin Mary, and was made man; and was crucified also for us under Pontius Pilate; he suffered and was buried; and the third day he rose again, according to the Scriptures; and ascended into heaven, and sitteth on the right hand of the Father; and he shall come again, with glory, to judge both the quick and the dead; whose kingdom shall have no end.

And [I believe] in the Holy Ghost, the Lord and Giver of Life; who proceedeth from the Father [and the Son]; who with the Father and the Son together is worshiped and glorified; who spake by the Prophets. And [I believe] one Holy Catholic and Apostolic Church. I acknowledge one Baptism for the remission of sins; and I look for the resurrection of the dead, and the life of the world to come. Amen.

Schaff, *Creeds*, II, 58.

THE ATHANASIAN CREED

1. Whosoever will be saved: before all things it is necessary that he hold the Catholic Faith:

2. Which Faith except every one do keep whole and undefiled: without doubt he shall perish everlastingly.

3. And the Catholic Faith is this: That we worship one God in Trinity, and Trinity in Unity;

4. Neither confounding the Persons: nor dividing the Substance [Essence].

5. For there is one Person of the Father: another of the Son: and another of the Holy Ghost.

6. But the Godhead of the Father, of the Son, and of the Holy Ghost, is all one: the Glory equal, the Majesty coeternal.

7. Such as the Father is: such is the Son: and such is the Holy Ghost.

8. The Father uncreate [uncreated]: the Son uncreate [uncreated]: and the Holy Ghost uncreate [uncreated].

9. The Father incomprehensible [unlimited]: the Son incomprehensible [unlimited]: and the Holy Ghost incomprehensible [unlimited, or infinite].

10. The Father eternal: the Son eternal: and the Holy Ghost eternal.

11. And yet they are not three eternals: but one eternal.

12. As also there are not three uncreated: nor three incomprehensibles [infinites], but one uncreated: and one incomprehensible [infinite].

13. So likewise the Father is Almighty: the Son Almighty: and the Holy Ghost Almighty.

14. And yet they are not three Almighties: but one Almighty.

15. So the Father is God: the Son is God: and the Holy Ghost is God.

16. And yet they are not three Gods: but one God.

17. So likewise the Father is Lord: the Son Lord: and the Holy Ghost Lord.

18. And yet not three Lords: but one Lord.

19. For like as we are compelled by the Christian verity: to acknowledge every Person by himself to be God and Lord:

20. So are we forbidden by the Catholic Religion: to say, There be [are] three Gods, or three Lords.

21. The Father is made of none: neither created, nor begotten.

22. The Son is of the Father alone: not made, nor created: but begotten.

23. The Holy Ghost is of the Father and of the Son: neither made, nor created, nor begotten: but proceeding.

24. So there is one Father, not three Fathers: one Son, not three Sons: one Holy Ghost, not three Holy Ghosts.

25. And in this Trinity none is afore, or after another: none is greater, or less than another [there is nothing before, or after: nothing greater or less].

26. But the whole three Persons are coeternal, and coequal.

27. So that in all things, as aforesaid: the Unity in Trinity, and the Trinity in Unity, is to be worshiped.

28. He therefore that will be saved, must [let him] thus think of the Trinity.

29. Furthermore it is necessary to everlasting salvation: that he also believe rightly [faithfully] the Incarnation of our Lord Jesus Christ.

30. For the right Faith is, that we believe and confess: that our Lord Jesus Christ, the Son of God, is God and Man;

31. God, of the Substance [Essence] of the Father; begotten before the worlds: and Man, of the Substance [Essence] of his Mother, born in the world.

32. Perfect God: and perfect Man, of a reasonable soul and human flesh subsisting.

33. Equal to the Father, as touching his Godhead: and inferior to the Father as touching his Manhood.

34. Who although he be [is] God and Man; yet he is not two, but one Christ.

35. One; not by conversion of the Godhead into flesh: but by taking [assumption] of the Manhood into God.

36. One altogether; not by confusion of Substance [Essence]: but by unity of Person.

37. For as the reasonable soul and flesh is one man: so God and Man is one Christ;

38. Who suffered for our salvation: descended into hell [Hades, spirit-world]: rose again the third day from the dead.

39. He ascended into heaven, he sitteth on the right hand of the Father God [God the Father] Almighty.

40. From whence [thence] he shall come to judge the quick and the dead.

41. At whose coming all men shall rise again with their bodies;

42. And shall give account for their own works.

43. And they that have done good shall go into life everlasting: and they that have done evil, into everlasting fire.

44. This is the Catholic Faith: which except a man believe faithfully [truly and firmly], he can not be saved.

Schaff, Creeds, II, 66.

THE AUGSBURG CONFESSION

CHIEF ARTICLES OF FAITH

Article I. Of God

The churches, with common consent among us, do teach that the decree of the Nicene Synod concerning the unity of the divine essence and of the three persons is true, and without doubt to be believed: to wit, that there is one divine essence which is called and is God, eternal, without body, indivisible [without part], of infinite power, wisdom goodness, the Creator and Preserver of all things, visible and invisible;

and that yet there are three persons of the same essence and power, who also are co-eternal, the Father, the Son, and the Holy Ghost. And they use the name of person in that signification in which the ecclesiastical writers [the fathers] have used it in this cause, to signify, not a part or quality in another, but that which properly subsists.

They condemn all heresies which have sprung up against this Article, as the Manichees, who set down two principles, good and evil; in the same manner the Valentinians, Arians, Eunomians, Mohammedans, and all such like. They condemn also the Samosatenes, old and new; who, when they earnestly contend that there is but one person, do craftily and wickedly trifle, after the manner of rhetoricians, about the Word and Holy Ghost, that they are not distinct persons, but that the Word signifieth a vocal word, and the Spirit a motion created in things.

Article II. Of Original Sin

Also they teach that, after Adam's fall, all men begotten after the common course of nature are born with sin; that is, without the fear of God, without trust in him, and with fleshly appetite; and that this disease, or original fault, is truly sin, condemning and bringing eternal death now also upon all that are not born again by baptism and the Holy Spirit.

They condemn the Pelagians, and others, who deny this original fault to be sin indeed; and who, so as to lessen the glory of the merits and benefits of Christ, argue that a man may, by the strength of his own reason, be justified before God.

Article III. Of the Son of God

Also they teach that the Word, that is, the Son of God, took unto him man's nature in the womb of the blessed Virgin Mary, so that there are two natures, the divine and the human, inseparably joined together in unity of person; one Christ, true God and true man: who was born of the Virgin Mary, truly suffered, was crucified, dead, and buried, that he might reconcile the Father unto us, and might be a sacrifice, not only for original guilt, but also for all actual sins of men.

The same also descended into hell, and truly rose again the third day. Afterward he ascended into the heavens, that he might sit at the right hand of the Father; and reign forever, and have dominion over all creatures; might sanctify those that believe in him, by sending the Holy Spirit into their hearts, who shall rule [sanctify, purify, strengthen], comfort, and quicken them, and shall defend them against the devil, and the power of sin.

The same Christ shall openly come again, to judge the quick and the dead, according as the Apostles' Creed declareth these and other things.

Article IV. Of Justification

Also they teach that men can not be justified [obtain forgiveness of sins and righteousness] before God by their own powers, merits, or works; but are justified freely [of grace] for Christ's sake through faith, when they believe that they are received into favor, and their sins forgiven for Christ's sake, who by his death hath satisfied for our sins. This faith doth God impute for righteousness before him.

Article V. Of the Ministry of the Church

For the obtaining of this faith, the ministry of teaching the Gospel and administering the Sacraments was instituted.

For by the Word and Sacraments, as by instruments, the Holy Spirit is given: who worketh faith, where and when it pleaseth God, in those that hear the Gospel, to wit, that God, not for our merit's sake, but for Christ's sake, doth justify those who believe that they for Christ's sake are received into favor.

They condemn the Anabaptists and others, who imagine that the Holy Spirit is given to men without the outward word, through their own preparations and works.

Article VI. Of New Obedience

Also they teach that this faith should bring forth good fruits, and that men ought to do the good works commanded of God, because it is God's will, and not on any confidence of meriting justification before God by their works.

For remission of sins and justification is apprehended by faith, as also the voice of Christ witnesseth: 'When ye have done all these things, say, We are unprofitable servants.'

The same also do the ancient writers of the Church teach; for Ambrose saith: 'This is ordained of God, that he that believeth in Christ shall be saved, without works, by faith alone, freely receiving remission of sins.'

Article VII. Of the Church

Also they teach that one holy Church is to continue forever. But the Church is the congregation of saints [the assembly of all believers], in which the Gospel is rightly taught [purely preached] and the Sacraments rightly administered [according to the Gospel].

And unto the true unity of the Church, it is sufficient to agree concerning the doctrine of the Gospel and the administration of the Sacraments. Nor is it necessary that human traditions, rites, or ceremonies instituted by men should be alike every where, as St. Paul saith: 'There is one faith, one baptism, One God and Father of all.'

Article VIII. What the Church is

Though the Church be properly the congregation of saints and true believers, yet seeing that in this life many hypocrites and evil persons are mingled with it, it is lawful to use the Sacraments administered by evil men, according to the voice of Christ (Matt. xxiii.2): 'The Scribes and the Pharisees sit in Moses' seat,' and the words following. And the Sacraments and the Word are effectual, by reason of the institution and commandment of Christ, though they be delivered by evil men.

They condemn the Donatists and the like, who denied that it was lawful to use the ministry of evil men in the Church, and held that the ministry of evil men is useless and without effect.

Article IX. Of Baptism

Of Baptism they teach that it is necessary to salvation, and that by Baptism the grace of God is offered, and that children are to be baptized, who by Baptism, being offered to God, are received into God's favor.

They condemn the Anabaptists who allow not the Baptism of children, and affirm that children are saved without Baptism.

Article X. Of the Lord's Supper

Of the Supper of the Lord they teach that the [true] body and blood of Christ are truly present [under the form of bread and wine], and are [there] communicated to those that eat in the Lord's Supper [and received]. And they disapprove of those that teach otherwise [wherefore also the opposite doctrine is rejected].

Article XI. Of Confession

Concerning confession, they teach that private absolution be retained in the churches, though enumeration of all offenses be not necessary in confession. For it is impossible; according to the Psalm: 'Who can understand his errors?'

Article XII. Of Repentance

Touching repentance, they teach that such as have fallen after baptism may find remission of sins, at what time they are converted [whenever they come to repentance], and that the Church should give absolution unto such as return to repentance.

Now repentance consisteth properly of those two parts: One is contrition, or terrors stricken into the conscience through the acknowledgment of sin; the other is faith, which is conceived by the Gospel, or absolution, and doth believe that for Christ's sake sins be forgiven, and comforteth the conscience, and freeth it from terrors. Then should follow good works, which are fruits of repentance.

They condemn the Anabaptists, who deny that men once justified can lose the Spirit of God, and do contend that some men may attain to such a perfection in this life that they can not sin. [Here are rejected those who teach that those who have once been holy can not fall again.] The Novatians are also condemned, who would not absolve such as had fallen after baptism, though they returned to repentance. They also that do not teach that remission of sins is obtained by faith, and who command us to merit grace by satisfactions, are rejected.

Article XIII. Of the Use of Sacraments

Concerning the use of the Sacraments, they teach that they were ordained not only to be marks of profession among men, but rather that they should be signs and testimonies of the will of God towards us, set forth unto us to stir up and confirm faith in such as use them. Therefore men must use Sacraments so as to join faith with them, which believes the promises that are offered and declared unto us by the Sacraments.

Wherefore they condemn those that teach that the Sacraments do justify by the work done, and do not teach that faith which believes the remission of sins is requisite in the use of Sacraments.

Article XIV. Of Ecclesiastical Orders

Concerning Ecclesiastical Orders [Church Government], they teach that no man should publicly in the Church teach, or administer the Sacraments, except he be rightly called [without a regular call].

Article XV. Of Ecclesiastical Rites

Concerning Ecclesiastical rites [made by men], they teach that those rites are to be observed which may be observed without sin, and are profitable for tranquility and good order in the Church; such as are set holidays, feasts, and such like. Yet concerning such things, men are to be admonished that consciences are not to be burdened as if such service were necessary to salvation.

They are also to be admonished that human traditions, instituted to propitiate God, to merit grace, and make satisfaction for sins, are opposed to the Gospel and the doctrine of faith. Wherefore vows and traditions concerning foods and days, and such like, instituted to merit grace and make satisfaction for sins, are useless and contrary to the Gospel.

Article XVI. Of Civil Affairs

Concerning civil affairs, they teach that such civil ordinances as are lawful are good works of God; that Christians may lawfully bear civil office, sit in judgment, determine matters by the imperial laws, and other laws in present force, appoint just punishments, engage in just war, act as soldiers, make legal bargains and contracts, hold property, take an oath when the magistrates require it, marry a wife, or be given in marriage. They condemn the Anabaptists who forbid Christians these civil offices. They condemn also those that place the perfection of the Gospel, not in the fear of God and in faith, but in forsaking civil offices, inasmuch as the Gospel teacheth an everlasting righteousness of the heart. In the mean time, it doth not disallow order and government of commonwealths or families, but requireth especially the preservation and maintenance thereof, as of God's own ordinances, and that in such ordinances we should exercise love. Christians, therefore, must necessarily obey their magistrates and laws, save only when they command any sin; for then they must rather obey God than men (Acts v. 29).

Article XVII. Of Christ's Return to Judgment

Also they teach that, in the consummation of the world [at the last day], Christ shall appear to judge, and shall raise up all the dead, and shall give unto the godly and elect eternal life and everlasting joy; but ungodly men and the devils shall he condemn unto endless torments.

They condemn the Anabaptists who think that to condemned men and the devils shall be an end of torments. They condemn others also, who now scatter Jewish opinions, that, before the resurrection of the dead, the godly shall occupy the kingdom of the world, the wicked being every where suppressed [the saints alone, the pious, shall have a worldly kingdom, and shall exterminate all the godless].

Article XVIII. Of Free Will

Concerning free will, they teach that man's will hath some liberty to work a civil righteousness, and to choose such things as reason can reach unto; but that it hath no power to work the righteousness of God, or a spiritual righteousness, without the Spirit of God; because that the natural man receiveth not the things of the Spirit of God (I Cor. ii.14). But this is wrought in the heart when men do receive the Spirit of God through the Word.

These things are in as many words affirmed by St. Augustine, *Hypognosticon*, lib.iii.: 'We confess that there is in all men a free will, which hath indeed the judgment of reason; not that it is thereby fitted, without God, either to begin or to perform any thing in matters pertaining to God, but only in works belonging to this present life, whether they be good or evil. By good works, I mean those which are of the goodness of nature; as to will to labor in the field, to desire meat or drink, to desire to have a friend, to desire apparel, to desire to build a house, to marry a wife, to nourish cattle, to learn the art of divers good things, to desire any good thing pertaining to this present life; all which are not without God's government, yea, they are, and had their beginning from God and by God. Among evil things, I account such as these: to will to worship an image; to will manslaughter, and such like.'

They condemn the Pelagians and others, who teach that by the powers of nature alone, without the Spirit of God, we are able to love God above all things; also to perform the commandments of God, as touching the substance of our actions. For although nature be able in some sort to do the external work (for it is able to withhold the hands from theft and murder), yet it can not work the inward motions, such as the fear of God, trust in God, chastity, patience, and such like.

Article XIX. Of the Cause of Sin

Touching the cause of sin, they teach that, although God doth create and preserve nature, yet the cause of sin is the will of the wicked; to wit, of the devil and ungodly men; which will, God not aiding, turneth itself from God, as Christ saith: 'When he speaketh a lie, he speaketh of his own' (John viii.44).

Article XX. Of Good Works

Ours are falsely accused of forbidding good works. For their writings extant upon the Ten Commandments, and others of the like argument, do bear witness that they have to good purpose taught concerning every kind of life, and its duties; what kinds of life, and what works in every calling, do please God. Of which things preachers in former times taught little or nothing: only they urged certain childish and needless works; as, keeping of holidays, set fasts, fraternities, pilgrimages, worshiping of saints, the use of rosaries, monkery, and such like things. Whereof our adversaries having had warning, they do now unlearn them, and do not preach concerning these unprofitable works, as they were wont. Besides, they begin now to make mention of faith, concerning which there was formerly a deep silence. They teach that we are not justified by works alone; but they conjoin faith and works, and say we are justified by faith and works. Which doctrine is more tolerable than the former one, and can afford more consolation than their old doctrine.

Whereas, therefore, the doctrine of faith, which should be the chief one in the Church, hath been so long unknown, as all men must needs grant, that there was the deepest silence about the righteousness of faith in their sermons, and that the doctrine of works was usual in the churches; for this cause our divines did thus admonish the churches:

First, that our works can not reconcile God, or deserve remission of sins, grace, and justification at his hands, but that these we obtain by faith only, when we believe that we are received into favor for Christ's sake, who alone is appointed the Mediator and Propitiatory, by whom the Father is reconciled. He, therefore, that trusteth by his works to merit grace, doth despise the merit and grace of Christ, and seeketh by his own power, without Christ, to come unto the Father; whereas Christ hath said expressly of himself, 'I am the way, the truth, and the life' (John xiv.6).

This doctrine of faith is handled by Paul almost every where: 'By grace ye are saved through faith, and that not of yourselves: it is the gift of God, not of works' (Eph. ii.8, 9). And lest any here should cavil, that we bring in a new-found interpretation, this whole cause is sustained by testimonies of the Fathers. Augustine doth in many volumes defend grace, and the righteousness of faith, against the merit of works. The like doth Ambrose teach in his book, *De Vocatione Gentium,* and elsewhere; for thus he saith of the calling of the Gentiles: 'The redemption made by the blood of Christ would be of small account, and the prerogative of man's works would not give place to the mercy of God, if the justification which is by grace were due to merits going before; so as it should not be the liberality of the giver, but the wages or hire of the laborer.'

This doctrine, though it be contemned of the unskillful, yet godly and fearful consciences find by experience that it bringeth very great comfort: because that consciences can not be quieted by any works, but by faith alone, when they believe assuredly that they have a God who is propitiated for Christ's sake; as St. Paul teacheth, 'Being justified by faith, we have peace with God' (Rom. v.1). This doctrine doth wholly belong to the conflict of a troubled conscience; and can not be understood, but where the conscience hath felt that conflict. Wherefore, all such as have had no experience thereof, and all that are profane men, who dream that Christian righteousness is naught else but a civil and philosophical righteousness, are poor judges of this matter.

Formerly men's consciences were vexed with the doctrine of works; they did not hear any comfort out of the Gospel. Whereupon conscience drove some into the desert, into monasteries, hoping there to merit grace by a monastical life. Others devised other works, whereby to merit grace, and to satisfy for sin. There was very great need, therefore, to teach and renew this doctrine of faith in Christ; to the end that fearful consciences might not want comfort, but might know that grace, and forgiveness of sins, and justification, are received by faith in Christ.

Another thing, which we teach men, is that in this place the name of *Faith* doth not only signify a knowledge of the history, which may be in the wicked, and in the devil, but that it signifieth a faith which believeth, not only the history, but also the effect of the history; to wit, the article of remission of sins; namely, that by Christ we have grace, righteousness, and remission of sins. Now he that knoweth that he hath the Father merciful to him through Christ, this man knoweth God truly; he knoweth that God hath a care of him; he loveth God, and calleth upon him; in a word, he is not without God, as the Gentiles are. For the devils and the wicked can never believe this article of the remission of sins; and therefore they hate God as their enemy; they call not upon him, they look for no good thing at his hands. After this manner doth Augustine admonish the reader touching the name of Faith; and teacheth that this word Faith is taken in Scriptures, not for such a knowledge as is in the wicked, but for a trust, which doth comfort and lift up disquieted minds.

Moreover, ours teach that it is necessary to do good works; not that we may trust that we deserve grace by them, but because it is the will of God that we should do them. By faith alone is apprehended remission of sins and grace. And because the Holy Spirit is received by faith, our hearts are now renewed, and so put on new affections, so that they are able to bring forth good works. For thus saith Ambrose: 'Faith is the begetter of a good will and of good actions.' For man's powers, without the Holy Spirit, are full of wicked affections, and are too weak to perform any good deed before God. Besides, they are in the devil's power, who driveth men forward into divers sins, into profane opinions, and into heinous crimes; as was to be seen in the philosophers, who, assaying to live an honest life, could not attain unto it, but were defiled with many heinous crimes. Such is the weakness of man, when he is without faith and the Holy Spirit, and hath no other guide but the natural powers of man.

Hereby every man may see that this doctrine is not to be accused, as forbidding good works; but rather is much to be commended, because it showeth after what sort we must do good works. For without faith the nature of man can by no means perform the works of the First or Second Table. Without faith, it can not call upon God, hope in God, bear the cross; but seeketh help from man, and trusteth in man's help. So it cometh to pass that all lusts and human counsel bear sway in the heart so long as faith and trust in God are absent.

Wherefore, also, Christ saith, 'Without me ye can do nothing' (John xv.5), and the Church singeth, 'Without thy power is naught in man, naught that is innocent.'

Article XXI. Of the Worship of Saints

Touching the worship of saints, they teach that the memory of saints may be set before us, that we may follow their faith and good works according to our calling; as the Emperor may follow David's example in making war to drive away the Turks from his country; for either of them is a king. But the Scripture teacheth not to invocate saints, or to ask help of saints, because it propoundeth unto us one Christ the Mediator, Propitiatory, High-Priest, and Intercessor. This Christ is to be invocated, and he hath promised that he will hear our prayers, and liketh this worship especially, to wit, that he be invocated in all afflictions. 'If any man sin, we have an advocate with God, Jesus Christ the righteous' (I John ii.1).

Article XXII

This is about the sum of doctrine among us, in which can be seen that there is nothing which is discrepant with the Scriptures, or with the Church Catholic, or even with the Roman Church, so far as that Church is known from writers [the writings of the Fathers]. This being the case, they judge us harshly who insist that we shall be regarded as heretics. But the dissension is concerning certain [traditions and] abuses, which without any certain authority have crept into the churches; in which things, even if there were some difference, yet would it be a becoming lenity on the part of the bishops that, on account of the Confession which we have now presented, they should bear with us, since not even the Canons are so severe as to demand the same rites every where, nor were the rites of all churches at any time the same. Although among us in large part the ancient rites are diligently observed. For it is a calumnious falsehood, that all the ceremonies, all the things instituted of old, are abolished in our churches. But the public complaint was that certain abuses were connected with the rites in common use. These, because they could not with good conscience be approved, have to some extent been corrected.

Schaff, *Creeds*, III, 7–27.

THE ARTICLES OF RELIGION OF THE PROTESTANT EPISCOPAL CHURCH*

I. Of Faith in the Holy Trinity

There is but one living and true God, everlasting, without body, parts, [or passions]; of infinite power, wisdom, and goodness; the Maker, and Preserver of all things [both] visible and invisible. And in the unity of this Godhead there be three Persons, of one substance, power, and eternity; the Father, the Son, and the Holy Ghost.

II. Of the Word or Son of God, which was made very Man

The Son, which is the Word of the Father, [begotten from everlasting of the Father,] the very and eternal God, and of one substance with the Father, took Man's nature in the womb of the blessed Virgin, [of her substance:] so that two whole and perfect Natures, that is to say, the Godhead and Manhood, were joined together in one Person, never to be divided, whereof is one Christ, very God, and very Man; who truly suffered, was crucified, dead, and buried, to reconcile his Father to us, and to be a sacrifice, not only for original guilt, but also for actual sins of men.

[III. Of the going down of Christ into Hell

As Christ died for us, and was buried; so also is it to be believed, that he went down into Hell.]

IV. Of the Resurrection of Christ

Christ did truly rise again from death, and took again his body, with flesh, bones, and all things appertaining to the perfection of Man's nature; wherewith he ascended into Heaven, and there sitteth, until he return to judge all Men at the last day.

* The material included in brackets has been omitted in the Articles of Religion of the Methodist Church, which otherwise uses this statement of faith.

V. Of the Holy Ghost

The Holy Ghost, proceeding from the Father and the Son, is of one substance, majesty, and glory, with the Father and the Son, very and eternal God.

VI. Of the Sufficiency of the Holy Scriptures for Salvation

Holy Scripture containeth all things necessary to salvation: so that whatsoever is not read therein, nor may be proved thereby, is not to be required of any man, that it should be believed as an article of Faith, or be thought requisite or necessary to salvation. In the name of the Holy Scripture we do understand those canonical Books of the Old and New Testament, of whose authority was never any doubt in the Church.

Of the Names and Number of the Canonical Books

Genesis,
Exodus,
Leviticus,
Numbers,
Deuteronomy,
Joshua,
Judges,
Ruth,

The First Book of Samuel,
The Second Book of Samuel,
The First Book of Kings,
The Second Book of Kings,
The First Book of Chronicles,
The Second Book of Chronicles,
The First Book of Esdras,
The Second Book of Esdras,

The Book of
Esther,
The Book of Job,
The Psalms,
The Proverbs,
Ecclesiastes or
Preacher,
Cantica, or Songs
of Solomon,
Four Prophets
the greater,
Twelve Prophets
the less.

[And the other Books (as Hierome saith) the Church doth read for example of life and instruction of manners; but yet doth it not apply them to establish any doctrine; such are these following:

The Third Book of Esdras,
The Fourth Book of Esdras,
The Book of Tobias,
The Book of Judith,
The rest of the Book of Esther,

Baruch the Prophet,
The Sons of the Three Children,
The Story of Susanna,
Of Bel and the Dragon,
The Prayer of Manasses,

The Book of Wisdom,   The First Book of Maccabees,
Jesus the Son of Sirach,   The Second Book of Maccabees.]

All the Books of the New Testament, as they are commonly received, we do receive, and account them Canonical.

VII. Of the Old Testament

The Old Testament is not contrary to the New: for both in the Old and New Testament everlasting life is offered to Mankind by Christ, who is the only Mediator between God and Man, being both God and Man. Wherefore, they are not to be heard, which feign that the old Fathers did look only for transitory promises. Although the Law given from God by Moses, as touching Ceremonies and Rites, do not bind Christian men, nor the Civil precepts thereof ought of necessity to be received in any commonwealth; yet notwithstanding, no Christian man whatsoever is free from the obedience of the Commandments which are called Moral.

[VIII. Of the Creeds

The Nicene Creed, and that which is commonly called the Apostles' Creed, ought thoroughly to be received and believed: for they may be proved by most certain warrants of Holy Scripture.]

IX. Of Original or Birth-Sin

Original sin standeth not in the following of Adam, (as the Pelagians do vainly talk;) but it is the fault and corruption of the Nature of every man, that naturally is engendered of the offspring of Adam; whereby man is very far gone from original righteousness, and is of his own nature inclined to evil, [so that the flesh lusteth always contrary to the Spirit; and therefore in every person born into this world it deserveth God's wrath and damnation. And this infection of nature doth remain, yea in them that are regenerated; whereby the lust of the flesh, called in Greek, *phronema sarkos* (which some do expound the wisdom, some sensuality, some the affection, some the desire, of the flesh,) is not subject to the Law of God. And although there is no condemnation for them that believe and are baptized; yet the Apostle doth confess, that concupiscence and lust hath of itself the nature of sin.]

X. Of Free-Will

The condition of Man after the fall of Adam is such, that he cannot turn and prepare himself, by his own natural strength and good works, to faith, and calling upon God. Wherefore we have no power to do good works pleasant and acceptable to God, without the grace of God by Christ preventing us, that we may have a good will, and working with us, when we have that good will.

XI. Of the Justification of Man

We are accounted righteous before God, only for the merit of our Lord and Saviour Jesus Christ by Faith, and not for our own works or deservings. Wherefore, that we are justified by Faith only, is a most wholesome Doctrine, and very full of comfort, [as more largely is expressed in the Homily of Justification.]

XII. Of Good Works

Albeit that Good Works, which are the fruits of Faith, and follow after Justification, cannot put away our sins, and endure the severity of God's judgment; yet are they pleasing and acceptable to God in Christ, and do spring out [necessarily] of a true and lively Faith; insomuch that by them a lively Faith may be as evidently known as a tree discerned by the fruit.

[XIII. Of Works before Justification

Works done before the grace of Christ, and the Inspiration of his Spirit, are not pleasant to God, forasmuch as they spring not of faith in Jesus Christ; neither do they make men meet to receive grace, or (as the School-authors say) deserve grace of congruity: yea rather, for that they are not done as God hath willed and commanded them to be done, we doubt not but they have the nature of sin.]

XIV. Of Works of Supererogation

Voluntary Works besides, over and above, God's Commandments, which they call Works of Supererogation, cannot be taught without arrogancy and impiety: for by them men do declare, that they do not only render unto God as much as they are bound to do, but that they do more for his sake, than of bounden duty is required: whereas Christ saith plainly, When ye have done all that are commanded to you, say, We are unprofitable servants.

[*XV. Of Christ alone without Sin*

Christ in the truth of our nature was made like unto us in all things, sin only except, from which he was clearly void, both in his flesh, and in his spirit. He came to be the Lamb without spot, who, by sacrifice of himself once made, should take away the sins of the world; and sin (as Saint John saith) was not in him. But all we the rest, although baptized, and born again in Christ, yet offend in many things; and if we say we have no sin, we deceive ourselves, and the truth is not in us.]

XVI. Of Sin after Baptism

Not every [deadly] sin willingly committed after [Baptism (Justification, Meth.)] is sin against the Holy Ghost, and unpardonable. Wherefore the grant of repentance is not to be denied to such as fall into sin after [Baptism (Justification, Meth.)]. After we have received the Holy Ghost, we may depart from grace given, and fall into sin, and by the grace of God, we may arise again, and amend our lives. And therefore they are to be condemned, which say, they can no more sin as long as they live here, or deny the place of forgiveness to such as truly repent.

[*XVII. Of Predestination and Election*

Predestination to Life is the everlasting purpose of God, whereby (before the foundations of the world were laid) he hath constantly decreed by his counsel secret to us, to deliver from curse and damnation those whom he hath chosen in Christ out of mankind, and to bring them by Christ to everlasting salvation, as vessels made to honour. Wherefore, they which be endued with so excellent a benefit of God, be called according to God's purpose by his Spirit working in due season: they through Grace obey the calling: they be justified freely: they be made sons of God by adoption: they be made like the image of his only-begotten Son Jesus Christ: they walk religiously in good works, and at length, by God's mercy, they attain to everlasting felicity.

The Protestant Episcopal Church 271

As the godly consideration of Predestination, and our Election in Christ, is full of sweet, pleasant, and unspeakable comfort to godly persons, and such as feel in themselves the working of the Spirit of Christ, mortifying the works of the flesh, and their earthly members, and drawing up their mind to high and heavenly things, as well because it doth greatly establish and confirm their faith of eternal Salvation to be enjoyed through Christ, as because it doth fervently kindle their love towards God: So, for curious and carnal persons, lacking the Spirit of Christ, to have continually before their eyes the sentence of God's Predestination, is a most dangerous downfall, whereby the Devil doth thrust them either into desperation, or into wretchlessness of most unclean living, no less perilous than desperation.

Furthermore, we must conceive God's promises in such wise, as they be generally set forth to us in Holy Scripture: and, in our doings, that Will of God is to be followed, which we have expressly declared unto us in the Word of God.

XVIII. Of obtaining eternal Salvation only by the Name of Christ

They also are to be had accursed that presume to say, That every man shall be saved by the Law or Sect which he professeth, so that he be diligent to frame his life according to that Law, and the light of Nature. For Holy Scripture doth set out unto us only the Name of Jesus Christ, whereby man must be saved.]

XIX. Of the Church

The visible Church of Christ is a congregation of faithful men, in the which the pure Word of God is preached, and the Sacraments be duly ministered according to Christ's ordinance, in all those things that of necessity are requisite to the same.

[As the Church of Jerusalem, Alexandria, and Antioch, have erred; so also the Church of Rome hath erred, not only in their living and manner of Ceremonies, but also in matters of Faith.]

[XX. Of the Authority of the Church

The Church hath power to decree Rites or Ceremonies, and authority in Controversies of Faith: and yet it is not lawful for the Church to ordain any thing that is contrary to God's Word written, neither may it so expound one place of Scripture, that it be repugnant to another. Wherefore, although the Church be a witness and a keeper of Holy Writ, yet, as it ought not to decree any thing against the same, so besides the same ought it not to enforce any thing to be believed for necessity of Salvation.

XXI. Of the Authority of General Councils

(The Twenty-first of the former Articles is omitted; because it is partly of a local and civil nature, and is provided for, as to the remaining parts of it, in other Articles.)]

XXII. Of Purgatory

The Romish Doctrine concerning Purgatory, Pardons, Worshipping and Adoration, as well of Images as of Relics, and also Invocation of Saints, is a fond thing, vainly invented, and grounded upon no warranty of Scripture, but rather repugnant to the Word of God.

[XXIII. Of Ministering in the Congregation

It is not lawful for any man to take upon him the office of public preaching, or ministering the Sacraments in the Congregation, before he be lawfully called, and sent to execute the same. And those we ought to judge lawfully called and sent, which be chosen and called to this work by men who have public authority given unto them in the Congregation, to call and send Ministers into the Lord's vineyard.]

XXIV. Of Speaking in the Congregation in such a Tongue as the people understandeth

It is a thing plainly repugnant to the Word of God, and the custom of the Primitive Church, to have public Prayer in the Church, or to minister the Sacraments, in a tongue not understanded of the people.

XXV. Of the Sacraments

Sacraments ordained of Christ be not only badges or tokens of Christian men's profession, but rather they be certain sure witnesses, and effectual signs of grace, and God's good will towards us, by the which he doth work invisibly in us, and doth not only quicken, but also strengthen and confirm our Faith in him.

There are two Sacraments ordained of Christ our Lord in the Gospel, that is to say, Baptism, and the Supper of the Lord.

Those five commonly called Sacraments, that is to say, Confirmation, Penance, Orders, Matrimony, and Extreme Unction, are not to be counted for Sacraments of the Gospel, being such as have grown partly of the corrupt following of the Apostles, partly are states of life allowed in the Scriptures; but yet have not like nature of Sacraments with Baptism, and the Lord's Supper, for that they have not any visible sign or ceremony ordained of God.

The Sacraments were not ordained of Christ to be gazed upon, or to be carried about, but that we should duly use them. And in such only as worthily receive the same, they have a wholesome effect or operation; but they that receive them unworthily, purchase to themselves damnation, as Saint Paul saith.

[*XXI. Of the Unworthiness of the Ministers, which hinders not the effect of the Sacraments*

Although in the visible Church the evil be ever mingled with the good, and sometimes the evil have chief authority in the Ministration of the Word and Sacraments, yet forasmuch as they do not the same in their own name, but in Christ's, and do minister by his commission and authority, we may use their Ministry, both in hearing the Word of God, and in receiving the Sacraments. Neither is the effect of Christ's ordinance taken away by their wickedness, nor the grace of God's gifts diminished from such as by faith, and rightly, do receive the Sacraments ministered unto them; which be effectual, because of Christ's institution and promise, although they be ministered by evil men.

Nevertheless, it appertaineth to the discipline of the Church, that inquiry be made of evil Ministers, and that they be accused by those that have knowledge of their offenses; and finally, being found guilty, by just judgment be deposed.]

XXVII. Of Baptism

Baptism is not only a sign of profession, and mark of difference, whereby Christian men are discerned from others that be not christened, but it is also a sign of Regeneration or New-Birth, [whereby, as by an instrument, they that receive Baptism rightly are grafted into the Church; the promises of the forgiveness of sin, and of our adoption to be the sons of God by the Holy Ghost, are visibly signed and sealed; Faith is confirmed, and Grace increased by virtue of prayer unto God.]

The Baptism of young Children is in any wise to be retained in the Church, [as most agreeable with the institution of Christ.]

XXVIII. Of the Lord's Supper

The Supper of the Lord is not only a sign of the love that Christians ought to have among themselves one to another; but rather it is a Sacrament of our Redemption by Christ's death: insomuch as to such as rightly, worthily, and with faith, receive the same, the Bread which we break is a partaking of the Body of Christ; and likewise the Cup of Blessing is a partaking of the Blood of Christ.

Transubstantiation (or the change of the substance of Bread and Wine) in the Supper of the Lord, cannot be proved by Holy Writ; but is repugnant to the plain words of Scripture, overthrowth the nature of a Sacrament, and hath given occasion to many superstitions.

The Body of Christ is given, taken, and eaten, in the Supper, only after an heavenly and spiritual manner. And the mean whereby the Body of Christ is received and eaten in the Supper, is Faith.

The Sacrament of the Lord's Supper was not by Christ's ordinance reserved, carried about, lifted up, or worshipped.

[XXIX. Of the Wicked, which eat not the Body of Christ in the use of the Lord's Supper

The Wicked, and such as be void of a lively faith, although they do carnally and visibly press with their teeth (as Saint Augustine saith) the Sacrament of the Body and Blood of Christ; yet in no wise are they partakers of Christ; but rather, to their condemnation, do eat and drink the sign or Sacrament of so great a thing.]

XXX. Of both Kinds

The Cup of the Lord is not to be denied to the Lay-people: for both the parts of the Lord's Sacrament, by Christ's ordinance and command-ment, ought to be ministered to all Christian men alike.

XXXI. Of the one Oblation of Christ finished upon the Cross

The Offering of Christ once made is that perfect redemption, propitiation, and satisfaction, for all the sins of the whole world, both original and actual; and there is none other satisfaction for sin, but that alone. Wherefore the sacrifices of Masses, in the which it was commonly said, that the Priest did offer Christ for the quick and the dead, to have remission of pain or guilt, were blasphemous fables, and dangerous deceits.

XXXII. Of the Marriage of Priests

Bishops, Priests, and Deacons, are not commanded by God's Law, either to vow the estate of single life, or to abstain from marriage: therefore it is lawful for them, as for all other Christian men, to marry at their own discretion, as they shall judge the same to serve better to godliness.

[XXXIII. Of excommunicate Persons, how they are to be avoided

That person which by open denunciation of the Church is rightly cut off from the unity of the Church, and excommunicated, ought to be taken of the whole multitude of the faithful, as an Heathen and Publican, until he be openly reconciled by penance, and received into the Church by a Judge that hath authority thereunto.]

XXXIV. Of the Traditions of the Church

It is not necessary that Traditions and Ceremonies be in all places one, or utterly like; for at all times they have been divers, and may be changed according to the diversity of countries, times, and men's manners, so that nothing be ordained against God's Word. Whosoever, through his private judgment, willingly and purposely, doth openly break the Traditions and Ceremonies of the Church, which be not repugnant to the Word of God, and be ordained and approved by common authority, ought to be rebuked openly, (that others may fear to do the like,) as he that offendeth against the common order of the Church, [and hurteth the authority of the Magistrate,] and woundeth the consciences of the weak brethren.

Every particular [or national] Church hath authority to ordain, change, and abolish, Ceremonies or Rites [of the Church ordained only by man's authority,] so that all things be done to edifying.

[XXXV. Of the Homilies

The Second Book of Homilies, the several titles whereof we have joined under this Article, doth contain a godly and wholesome Doctrine, and necessary for these times, as doth the former Book of Homilies, which were set forth in the time of Edward the Sixth; and therefore we judge them to be read in Churches by the Ministers, diligently and distinctly, that they may be understood of the people.

Of the Names of the Homilies

1 Of the right use of the Church.
2 Against Peril of Idolatry.
3 Of repairing and keeping clean of Churches.
4 Of good Works: first of Fasting.
5 Against Gluttony and Drunkenness.
6 Against Excess of Apparel.
7 Of Prayer.
8 Of the Place and Time of Prayer.
9 That Common Prayer and Sacraments ought to be ministered in a known tongue.
10 Of the reverend Estimation of God's Word.
11 Of Alms-doing.
12 Of the Nativity of Christ.
13 Of the Passion of Christ.
14 Of the Resurrection of Christ.
15 Of the worthy receiving of the Sacrament of the Body and Blood of Christ.
16 Of the Gifts of the Holy Ghost.
17 For the Rogation-days.
18 Of the State of Matrimony.
19 Of Repentance.
20 Against Idleness.
21 Against Rebellion.

(This Article is received in this Church, so far as it declares the Books of Homilies to be an explication of Christian doctrine, and instructive in piety and morals. But all references to the constitution and laws of England are considered as inapplicable to the circumstances of this Church; which also suspends the order for the reading of said Homilies in churches, until a revision of them may be conveniently made, for the clearing of them, as well from obsolete words and phrases, as from the local references.)

XXXVI. Of Consecration of Bishops and Ministers

The Book of Consecration of Bishops, and Ordering of Priests and Deacons, as set forth by the General Convention of this Church in 1792, doth contain all things necessary to such Consecration and Ordering; neither hath it anything that, of itself, is superstitious and ungodly.

And, therefore, whosoever, are consecrated or ordered according to said Form, we decree all such to be rightly, orderly, and lawfully consecrated and ordered.

XXXVII. *Of the Power of the Civil Magistrates*

The Power of the Civil Magistrate extendeth to all men, as well Clergy as Laity, in all things temporal; but hath no authority in things purely spiritual. And we hold it to be the duty of all men who are professors of the Gospel, to pay respectful obedience to the Civil Authority, regularly and legitimately constituted.]

XXXVIII. *Of Christian Men's Goods, which are not common*

The Riches and Goods of Christians are not common, as touching the right, title, and possession of the same; as certain [Anabaptists] do falsely boast. Notwithstanding, every man ought, of such things as he possesseth, liberally to give alms to the poor, according to his ability.

XXXIX. *Of a Christian Man's Oath*

As we confess that vain and rash Swearing is forbidden Christian men by our Lord Jesus Christ, and James his Apostle, so we judge, that Christian religion doth not prohibit, but that a man may swear when the Magistrate requireth, in a cause of faith and charity, so it be done according to the Prophet's teaching, in justice, judgment, and truth.

The Book of Common Prayer, Morehouse-Gorham Co.
New York, 1938, pp. 603 ff.

THE WESTMINSTER SHORTER CATECHISM

Ques. 1. What is the chief end of man?
Ans. Man's chief end is to glorify God, and to enjoy him forever.
Ques. 2. What rule hath God given to direct us how we may glorify and enjoy him?
Ans. The Word of God, which is contained in the Scriptures of the Old and New Testaments, is the only rule to direct us how we may glorify and enjoy him.

Ques. 3. What do the Scriptures principally teach?

Ans. The Scriptures principally teach what man is to believe concerning God, and what duty God requires of man.

Ques. 4. What is GOD?

Ans. God is a Spirit, infinite, eternal, and unchangeable, in his being, wisdom, power, holiness, justice, goodness, and truth.

Ques. 5. Are there more Gods than one?

Ans. There is but one only, the living and true God.

Ques. 6. How many persons are there in the Godhead?

Ans. There are three persons in the Godhead: the Father, the Son, and the Holy Ghost; and these three are one God, the same in substance, equal in power and glory.

Ques. 7. What are the decrees of God?

Ans. The decrees of God are his eternal purpose according to the counsel of his will, whereby, for his own glory, he hath fore-ordained whatsoever comes to pass.

Ques. 8. How doth God execute his decrees?

Ans. God executeth his decrees in the works of creation and providence.

Ques. 9. What is the work of creation?

Ans. The work of creation is God's making all things of nothing, by the word of his power, in the space of six days, and all very good.

Ques. 10. How did God create man?

Ans. God created man, male and female, after his own image, in knowledge, righteousness, and holiness, with dominion over the creatures.

Ques. 11. What are God's works of providence?

Ans. God's works of providence are his most holy, wise, and powerful preserving and governing all his creatures, and all their actions.

Ques. 12. What special act of providence did God exercise towards man, in the estate wherein he was created?

Ans. When God had created man, he entered into a covenant of life with him, upon condition of perfect obedience; forbidding him to eat of the tree of knowledge of good and evil, upon pain of death.

Ques. 13. Did our first parents continue in the estate wherein they were created?

Ans. Our first parents, being left to the freedom of their own will, fell from the estate wherein they were created, by sinning against God.

Ques. 14. What is sin?

Ans. Sin is any want of conformity unto, or transgression of, the law of God.

Ques. 15. What was the sin whereby our first parents fell from the estate wherein they were created?

Ans. The sin whereby our first parents fell from the estate wherein they were created, was their eating the forbidden fruit.

Ques. 16. Did all mankind fall in Adam's first transgression?

Ans. The covenant being made with Adam, not only for himself, but for his posterity, all mankind descending from him by ordinary generation, sinned in him, and fell with him, in his first transgression.

Ques. 17. Into what estate did the fall bring mankind?

Ans. The fall brought mankind into an estate of sin and misery.

Ques. 18. Wherein consists the sinfulness of that estate whereinto man fell?

Ans. The sinfulness of that estate whereinto man fell, consists in the guilt of Adam's first sin, the want of original righteousness, and the corruption of his whole nature, which is commonly called original sin; together with all actual transgressions which proceed from it.

Ques. 19. What is the misery of that estate whereinto man fell?

Ans. All mankind by their fall lost communion with God, are under his wrath and curse, and so made liable to all the miseries in this life, to death itself, and to the pains of hell forever.

Ques. 20. Did God leave all mankind to perish in the estate of sin and misery?

Ans. God, having out of his mere good pleasure, from all eternity, elected some to everlasting life, did enter into a covenant of grace, to deliver them out of the estate of sin and misery, and to bring them into an estate of salvation by a Redeemer.

Ques. 21. Who is the Redeemer of God's elect?

Ans. The only Redeemer of God's elect is the Lord Jesus Christ, who being the eternal Son of God became man, and so was, and continueth to be, God and man, in two distinct natures, and one person forever.

Ques. 22. How did Christ, being the Son of God, become man?

Ans. Christ, the Son of God, became man, by taking to himself a true body, and a reasonable soul, being conceived by the power of the Holy Ghost, in the womb of the Virgin Mary, and born of her, yet without sin.

Ques. 23. What offices doth Christ execute as our Redeemer?

Ans. Christ, as our Redeemer, executeth the offices of a Prophet, of a Priest, and of a King, both in his estate of humiliation and exaltation.

Ques. 24. How doth Christ execute the office of a Prophet?

Ans. Christ executeth the office of a Prophet, in revealing to us by his Word and Spirit, the will of God for our salvation.

Ques. 25. How doth Christ execute the office of a Priest?

Ans. Christ executeth the office of a Priest, in his once offering up of himself a sacrifice to satisfy divine justice, and reconcile us to God, and in making continual intercession for us.

Ques. 26. How doth Christ execute the office of a King?

Ans. Christ executeth the office of a King, in subduing us to himself, in ruling and defending us, and in restraining and conquering all his and our enemies.

Ques. 27. Wherein did Christ's humiliation consist?

Ans. Christ's humiliation consisted in his being born, and that in a low condition, made under the law, undergoing the miseries of this life, the wrath of God, and the cursed death of the cross; in being buried, and continuing under the power of death for a time.

Ques. 28. Wherein consisteth Christ's exaltation?

Ans. Christ's exaltation consisteth in his rising again from the dead on the third day, in ascending up into heaven, in sitting at the right hand of God the Father, and in coming to judge the world at the last day.

Ques. 29. How are we made partakers of the redemption purchased by Christ?

Ans. We are made partakers of the redemption purchased by Christ, by the effectual application of it to us by his Holy Spirit.

Ques. 30. How doth the Spirit apply to us the redemption purchased by Christ?

Ans. The Spirit applieth to us the redemption purchased by Christ, by working faith in us, and thereby uniting us to Christ in our effectual calling.

Ques. 31. What is effectual calling?

Ans. Effectual calling is the work of God's Spirit, whereby, convincing us of our sin and misery, enlightening our minds in the knowledge of Christ, and renewing our wills, he doth persuade and enable us to embrace Jesus Christ, freely offered to us in the gospel.

Ques. 32. What benefits do they that are effectually called partake of in this life?

Ans. They that are effectually called do in this life partake of justification, adoption, sanctification, and the several benefits which, in this life, do either accompany or flow from them.

Ques. 33. What is justification?

Ans. Justification is an act of God's free grace, wherein he pardoneth all our sins, and accepteth us as righteous in his sight, only for the righteousness of Christ imputed to us, and received by faith alone.

Ques. 34. What is adoption?

Ans. Adoption is an act of God's free grace, whereby we are received into the number, and have a right to all the privileges, of the sons of God.

Ques. 35. What is sanctification?

Ans. Sanctification is the work of God's free grace, whereby we are renewed in the whole man after the image of God, and are enabled more and more to die unto sin, and live unto righteousness.

Ques. 36. What are the benefits which in this life do accompany or flow from justification, adoption, and sanctification?

Ans. The benefits which in this life do accompany or flow from justification, adoption, and sanctification, are, assurance of God's love, peace of conscience, joy in the Holy Ghost, increase of grace, and perseverance therein to the end.

Ques. 37. What benefits do believers receive from Christ at death?

Ans. The souls of believers are, at their death, made perfect in holiness, and do immediately pass into glory; and their bodies, being still united to Christ, do rest in their graves till the resurrection.

Ques. 38. What benefits do believers receive from Christ at the resurrection?

Ans. At the resurrection, believers being raised up in glory, shall be openly acknowledged and acquitted in the day of judgment, and made perfectly blessed in the full enjoying of God to all eternity.

Ques. 39. What is the duty which God requireth of man?

Ans. The duty which God requireth of man is obedience to his revealed will.

Ques. 40. What did God at first reveal to man for the rule of his obedience?

Ans. The rule which God at first revealed to man, for his obedience, was the moral law.

Ques. 41. Wherein is the moral law summarily comprehended?

Ans. The moral law is summarily comprehended in the ten commandments.

Ques. 42. What is the sum of the ten commandments?

Ans. The sum of the ten commandments is, to love the Lord our God with all our heart, with all our soul, with all our strength, and with all our mind; and our neighbor as ourselves.

Ques. 43. What is the preface to the ten commandments?

Ans. The preface to the ten commandments is in these words: I am the Lord thy God, which brought thee out of the land of Egypt, out of the house of bondage.

Ques. 44. What doth the preface to the ten commandments teach us?

Ans. The preface to the ten commandments teacheth us, that because God is the Lord, and our God and Redeemer, therefore we are bound to keep all his commandments.

Ques. 45. Which is the first commandment?

Ans. The first commandment is, Thou shalt have no other gods before me.

Ques. 46. What is required in the first commandment?

Ans. The first commandment requireth us to know and acknowledge God, to be the only true God, and our God; and to worship and glorify him accordingly.

Ques. 47. What is forbidden in the first commandment?

Ans. The first commandment forbiddeth the denying or not worshiping and glorifying the true God, as God, and our God; and the giving that worship and glory to any other which is due to him alone.

Ques. 48. What are we specially taught by these words, "before me," in the first commandment?

Ans. These words, "before me," in the first commandment, teach us that God, who seeth all things, taketh notice of, and is much displeased with, the sin of having any other God.

Ques. 49. Which is the second commandment?

Ans. The second commandment is, Thou shalt not make unto thee any graven image, or any likeness of any thing that is in heaven above, or that is in the earth beneath, or that is in the water under the earth; thou shalt not bow down thyself to them, nor serve them; for I the Lord thy God am a jealous God, visiting the iniquity of the fathers upon the children, unto the third and fourth generation of them that hate me, and showing mercy unto thousands of them that love me and keep my commandments.

Ques. 50. What is required in the second commandment?

Ans. The second commandment requireth the receiving, observing, and keeping pure and entire, all such religious worship and ordinances as God hath appointed in his Word.

Ques. 51. What is forbidden in the second commandment?

Ans. The second commandment forbiddeth the worshiping of God by images, or any other way not appointed in his Word.

Ques. 52. What are the reasons annexed to the second commandment?

Ans. The reasons annexed to the second commandment are, God's sovereignty over us, his propriety in us, and the zeal he hath to his own worship.

Ques. 53. Which is the third commandment?

Ans. The third commandment is, Thou shalt not take the name of the Lord thy God in vain: for the Lord will not hold him guiltless that taketh his name in vain.

Ques. 54. What is required in the third commandment?

Ans. The third commandment requireth the holy and reverent use of God's names, titles, attributes, ordinances, word, and works.

Ques. 55. What is forbidden in the third commandment?

Ans. The third commandment forbiddeth all profaning or abusing of any thing whereby God maketh himself known.

Ques. 56. What is the reason annexed to the third commandment?

Ans. The reason annexed to the third commandment is, that however the breakers of this commandment may escape punishment from men, yet the Lord our God will not suffer them to escape his righteous judgment.

Ques. 57. Which is the fourth commandment?

Ans. The fourth commandment is, Remember the Sabbath-day to keep it holy. Six days shalt thou labor, and do all thy work: but the seventh day is the Sabbath of the Lord thy God: in it thou shalt not do any work, thou, nor thy son, nor thy daughter, thy man-servant, nor thy maid-servant, nor thy cattle, nor thy stranger that is within thy gates; for in six days the Lord made heaven and earth, the sea, and all that in them is, and rested the seventh day: wherefore the Lord blessed the Sabbath-day and hallowed it.

Ques. 58. What is required in the fourth commandment?

Ans. The fourth commandment requireth the keeping holy to God such set times as he hath appointed in his Word; expressly one whole day in seven, to be a holy Sabbath to himself.

Ques. 59. Which day of the seven hath God appointed to be the weekly Sabbath?

Ans. From the beginning of the world to the resurrection of Christ, God appointed the seventh day of the week to be the weekly Sabbath; and the first day of the week, ever since, to continue to the end of the world, which is the Christian Sabbath.

Ques. 60. How is the Sabbath to be sanctified?

Ans. The Sabbath is to be sanctified by a holy resting all that day, even from such worldly employment and recreations as are lawful on other days; and spending the whole time in the public and private exercises of God's worship, except so much as is to be taken up in the works of necessity and mercy.

Ques. 61. What is forbidden in the fourth commandment?

Ans. The fourth commandment forbiddeth the omission, or careless performance, of the duties required, and the profaning the day by idleness, or doing that which is in itself sinful, or by unnecessary thoughts, words, or works about our worldly employments and recreations.

Ques. 62. What are the reasons annexed to the fourth commandment?

Ans. The reasons annexed to the fourth commandment are, God's allowing us six days of the week for our own employments, his challenging a special propriety in the seventh, his own example, and his blessing the Sabbath-day.

Ques. 63. Which is the fifth commandment?

Ans. The fifth commandment is, Honor thy father and thy mother: that thy days may be long upon the land which the Lord thy God giveth thee.

Ques. 64. What is required in the fifth commandment?

Ans. The fifth commandment requireth the preserving the honor of, and performing the duties belonging to, every one in their several places and relations, as superiors, inferiors, or equals.

Ques. 65. What is forbidden in the fifth commandment?

Ans. The fifth commandment forbiddeth the neglecting of, or doing any thing against, the honor and duty which belongeth to every one in their several places and relations.

Ques. 66. What is the reason annexed to the fifth commandment?

Ans. The reason annexed to the fifth commandment is, a promise of long life and prosperity (as far as it shall serve for God's glory, and their own good) to all such as keep this commandment.

Ques. 67. Which is the sixth commandment?

Ans. The sixth commandment is, Thou shalt not kill.

Ques. 68. What is required in the sixth commandment?

Ans. The sixth commandment requireth all lawful endeavors to preserve our own life, and the life of others.

Ques. 69. What is forbidden in the sixth commandment?

Ans. The sixth commandment forbiddeth the taking away of our own life, or the life of our neighbor unjustly, or whatsoever tendeth thereunto.

Ques. 70. Which is the seventh commandment?

Ans. The seventh commandment is, Thou shalt not commit adultery.

Ques. 71. What is required in the seventh commandment?

Ans. The seventh commandment requireth the preservation of our own and our neighbor's chastity, in heart, speech, and behavior.

Ques. 72. What is forbidden in the seventh commandment?

Ans. The seventh commandment forbiddeth all unchaste thoughts, words, and actions.

Ques. 73. Which is the eighth commandment?

Ans. The eighth commandment is, Thou shalt not steal.

Ques. 74. What is required in the eighth commandment?

Ans. The eighth commandment requireth the lawful procuring and furthering the wealth and outward estate of ourselves and others.

Ques. 75. What is forbidden in the eighth commandment?

Ans. The eighth commandment forbiddeth whatsoever doth, or may, unjustly hinder our own, or our neighbor's wealth or outward estate.

Ques. 76. Which is the ninth commandment?

Ans. The ninth commandment is, Thou shalt not bear false witness against thy neighbor.

Ques. 77. What is required in the ninth commandment?

Ans. The ninth commandment requireth the maintaining and promoting of truth between man and man, and of our own and our neighbor's good name, especially in witness-bearing.

Ques. 78. What is forbidden in the ninth commandment?

Ans. The ninth commandment forbiddeth whatsoever is prejudicial to truth, or injurious to our own or our neighbor's good name.

Ques. 79. Which is the tenth commandment?

Ans. The tenth commandment is, Thou shalt not covet thy neighbor's house, thou shalt not covet thy neighbor's wife, nor his manservant, nor his maid-servant, nor his ox, nor his ass, nor any thing that is thy neighbor's.

Ques. 80. What is required in the tenth commandment?

Ans. The tenth commandment requireth full contentment with our own condition, with a right and charitable frame of spirit toward our neighbor, and all that is his.

Ques. 81. What is forbidden in the tenth commandment?

Ans. The tenth commandment forbiddeth all discontentment with our own estate, envying or grieving at the good of our neighbor, and all inordinate motions or affections to any thing that is his.

Ques. 82. Is any man able perfectly to keep the commandments of God?

Ans. No mere man, since the fall, is able, in this life, perfectly to keep the commandments of God; but doth daily break them, in thought, word, and deed.

Ques. 83. Are all transgressions of the law equally heinous?

Ans. Some sins in themselves, and by reason of several aggravations, are more heinous in the sight of God than others.

Ques. 84. What doth every sin deserve?

Ans. Every sin deserveth God's wrath and curse, both in this life and that which is to come.

Ques. 85. What doth God require of us, that we may escape his wrath and curse, due to us for sin?

Ans. To escape the wrath and curse of God, due to us for sin, God requireth of us faith in Jesus Christ, repentance unto life, with the diligent use of all the outward means whereby Christ communicateth to us the benefits of redemption.

Ques. 86. What is faith in Jesus Christ?

Ans. Faith in Jesus Christ is a saving grace, whereby we receive and rest upon him alone for salvation, as he is offered to us in the gospel.

Ques. 87. What is repentance unto life?

Ans. Repentance unto life is a saving grace, whereby a sinner, out of a true sense of his sin, and apprehension of the mercy of God in Christ, doth, with grief and hatred of his sin, turn from it unto God, with full purpose of, and endeavor after, new obedience.

Ques. 88. What are the outward and ordinary means whereby Christ communicateth to us the benefits of redemption?

Ans. The outward and ordinary means whereby Christ communicateth to us the benefits of redemption, are his ordinances, especially the word, sacraments, and prayer; all which are made effectual to the elect for salvation.

Ques. 89. How is the Word made effectual to salvation?

Ans. The Spirit of God maketh the reading, but especially the preaching of the word, an effectual means of convincing and converting sinners, and of building them up in holiness and comfort through faith unto salvation.

Ques. 90. How is the Word to be read and heard, that it may become effectual to salvation?

Ans. That the Word may become effectual to salvation, we must attend thereunto with diligence, preparation, and prayer; receive it with faith and love, lay it up in our hearts, and practice it in our lives.

Ques. 91. How do the sacraments become effectual means of salvation?

Ans. The sacraments become effectual means of salvation, not from any virtue in them, or in him that doth administer them, but only by the blessing of Christ, and the working of his Spirit in them that by faith receive them.

Ques. 92. What is a sacrament?

Ans. A sacrament is a holy ordinance instituted by Christ; wherein, by sensible signs, Christ and the benefits of the new covenant are represented, sealed, and applied to believers.

Ques. 93. Which are the sacraments of the New Testament?

Ans. The sacraments of the New Testament are Baptism and the Lord's Supper.

Ques. 94. What is Baptism?

Ans. Baptism is a sacrament, wherein the washing with water, in the name of the Father, and of the Son, and of the Holy Ghost, doth signify and seal our ingrafting into Christ and partaking of the benefits of the covenant of grace, and our engagement to be the Lord's.

Ques. 95. To whom is Baptism to be administered?

Ans. Baptism is not to be administered to any that are out of the visible Church, till they profess their faith in Christ, and obedience to him; but the infants of such as are members of the visible church, are to be baptized.

Ques. 96. What is the Lord's Supper?

Ans. The Lord's Supper is a sacrament, wherein, by giving and receiving bread and wine, according to Christ's appointment, his death is showed forth, and the worthy receivers are, not after a corporal and carnal manner, but by faith, made partakers of his body and blood, with all his benefits, to their spiritual nourishment and growth in grace.

Ques. 97. What is required to the worthy receiving of the Lord's Supper?

Ans. It is required of them that would worthily partake of the Lord's Supper, that they examine themselves of their knowledge to discern the Lord's body, of their faith to feed upon him, of their repentance, love, and new obedience; lest coming unworthily, they eat and drink judgment to themselves.

Ques. 98. What is prayer?

Ans. Prayer is an offering up of our desires unto God, for things agreeable to his will, in the name of Christ, with confession of our sins, and thankful acknowledgment of his mercies.

Ques. 99. What rule hath God given for our direction in prayer?

Ans. The whole Word of God is of use to direct us in prayer, but the special rule of direction is that form of prayer which Christ taught his disciples, commonly called, The Lord's Prayer.

Ques. 100. What doth the preface of the Lord's Prayer teach us?

Ans. The preface of the Lord's Prayer, which is, 'Our Father which art in heaven,' teacheth us to draw near to God with all holy reverence and confidence, as children to a father, able and ready to help us; and that we should pray with and for others.

Ques. 101. What do we pray for in the first petition?

Ans. In the first petition, which is, 'Hallowed be thy name,' we pray that God would enable us and others to glorify him in all that whereby he maketh himself known, and that he would dispose all things to his own glory.

Ques. 102. What do we pray for in the second petition?

Ans. In the second petition, which is, 'Thy kingdom come,' we pray that Satan's kingdom may be destroyed, and that the kingdom of grace may be advanced, ourselves and others brought into it, and kept in it, and that the kingdom of glory may be hastened.

Ques. 103. What do we pray for in the third petition?

Ans. In the third petition, which is, 'Thy will be done on earth as it is in heaven,' we pray that God by his grace would make us able and willing to know, obey, and submit to his will in all things, as the angels do in heaven.

Ques. 104. What do we pray for in the fourth petition?

Ans. In the fourth petition, which is, 'Give us this day our daily bread,' we pray that of God's free gift we may receive a competent portion of the good things of this life, and enjoy his blessing with them.

Ques. 105. What do we pray for in the fifth petition?

Ans. In the fifth petition, which is, 'And forgive us our debts as we forgive our debtors,' we pray that God, for Christ's sake, would freely pardon all our sins; which we are the rather encouraged to ask, because by his grace we are enabled from the heart to forgive others.

Ques. 106. What do we pray for in the sixth petition?

Ans. In the sixth petition, which is, 'And lead us not into temptation, but deliver us from evil,' we pray that God would either keep us from being tempted to sin, or support and deliver us when we are tempted.

Ques. 107. What doth the conclusion of the Lord's Prayer teach us?

Ans. The conclusion of the Lord's Prayer, which is, 'For thine is the kingdom, and the power and the glory forever, Amen,' teacheth us to take our encouragement in prayer from God only, and in our prayers to praise him; ascribing kingdom, power, and glory to him; and in testimony of our desire and assurance to be heard, we say, Amen.

Schaff, *Creeds,* III, 676–700.

THE CONFESSION OF THE SOCIETY OF FRIENDS, COMMONLY CALLED QUAKERS

Concerning the true Foundation of Knowledge

Seeing the height of all happiness is placed in the true knowledge of God ('This is life eternal, to know thee the only true God, and Jesus Christ whom thou hast sent'), the true and right understanding of this foundation and ground of knowledge is that which is most necessary to be known and believed in the first place.

THE SECOND PROPOSITION

Concerning Immediate Revelation

Seeing 'no man knoweth the Father but the Son, and he to whom the Son revealeth him;' and seeing the revelation of the Son is in and by the Spirit; therefore the testimony of the Spirit is that alone by which the true knowledge of God hath been, is, and can be only revealed; who as, by the moving of his own Spirit, he converted the chaos of this world into that wonderful order wherein it was in the beginning, and created man a living soul, to rule and govern it, so by the revelation of the same Spirit he hath manifested himself all along unto the sons of men, both patriarchs, prophets, and apostles; which revelations of God by the Spirit, whether by outward voices and appearances, dreams, or inward objective manifestations in the heart, were of old the formal object of their faith, and remain yet so to be; since the object of the saints' faith is the same in all ages, though set forth under divers administrations. Moreover, these divine inward revelations, which we make absolutely necessary for the building up of true faith, neither do nor can ever contradict the outward testimony of the Scriptures, or right and sound reason. Yet from hence it will not follow that these divine revelations are to be subjected to the examination, either of the outward testimony of the Scriptures or of the natural reason of man, as to a more noble or certain rule or touchstone; for this divine revelation and inward illumination is that which is evident and clear of itself, forcing, by its own evidence and clearness, the well-disposed understanding to assent, irresistibly moving the same thereunto; even as the common principles of natural truths move and incline the mind to a natural assent: as, that the whole is greater than its part; that two contradictory sayings can not be both true, nor both false: which is also manifest, according to our adversaries' principle, who—supposing the possibility of inward divine revelations—will nevertheless confess with us that neither Scripture nor sound reason will contradict it: and yet it will not follow, according to them, that the Scripture or sound reason should be subjected to the examination of the divine revelations in the heart.

THE THIRD PROPOSITION

Concerning the Scriptures

From these revelations of the Spirit of God to the saints have proceeded the Scriptures of truth, which contain: 1. A faithful historical account of the actings of God's people in divers ages, with many singular and remarkable providences attending them. 2. A prophetical account of several things, whereof some are already past, and some yet to come. 3. A full and ample account of all the chief principles of the doctrine of Christ, held forth in divers precious declarations, exhortations, and sentences, which, by the moving of God's Spirit, were at several times, and upon sundry occasions, spoken and written unto some churches and their pastors: nevertheless, because they are only a declaration of the fountain, and not the fountain itself, therefore they are not to be esteemed the principal ground of all truth and knowledge, nor yet the adequate primary rule of faith and manners. Nevertheless, as that which giveth a true and faithful testimony of the first foundation, they are and may be esteemed a secondary rule, subordinate to the Spirit, from which they have all their excellency and certainty; for as by the inward testimony of the Spirit we do alone truly know them, so they testify that the Spirit is that guide by which the saints are led into all truth: therefore, according to the Scriptures, the Spirit is the first and principal Leader. And seeing we do therefore receive and believe the Scriptures, because they proceeded from the Spirit, therefore also the Spirit is more originally and principally the rule, according to that received maxim in the schools, *Propter quod unumquodque est tale, illud ipsum est magis tale.* Englished thus: 'That for which a thing is such, that thing itself is more such.'

Concerning the Condition of Man in the Fall

All Adam's posterity, or mankind, both Jews and Gentiles, as to the first Adam, or earthly man, is fallen, degenerated, and dead, deprived of the sensation or feeling of this inward testimony or seed of God, and is subject unto the power, nature, and seed of the Serpent, which he sows in men's hearts, while they abide in this natural and corrupted state; from whence it comes that not their words and deeds only, but all their imaginations are evil perpetually in the sight of God, as proceeding from this depraved and wicked seed. Man, therefore, as he is in this state, can know nothing aright; yea, his thoughts and conceptions concerning God and things spiritual, until he be disjoined from this evil seed, and united to the Divine Light, are unprofitable both to himself and others: hence are rejected the Socinian and Pelagian errors, in exalting a natural light; as also of the Papists, and most Protestants, who affirm that man, without the true grace of God, may be a true minister of the gospel. Nevertheless, this seed is not imputed to infants, until by transgression they actually join themselves therewith; for they are by nature the children of wrath, who walk according to the power of the prince of the air.

THE FIFTH AND SIXTH PROPOSITION

Concerning the Universal Redemption by Christ, and also the Saving and Spiritual Light, wherewith every man is enlightened

THE FIFTH PROPOSITION

God, out of his infinite love, who delighteth not in the death of a sinner, but that all should live and be saved, hath so loved the world that he hath given his only Son a Light, that whosoever believeth in him should be saved; who enlighteneth every man that cometh into the world, and maketh manifest all things that are reprovable, and teacheth all temperance, righteousness, and godliness: and this Light enlighteneth the hearts of all in a day, in order to salvation, if not resisted: nor is it less universal than the seed of sin, being the purchase of his death, who tasted death for every man; 'for as in Adam all die, even so in Christ shall all be made alive.'

According to which principle (or hypothesis), all the objections against the universality of Christ's death are easily solved; neither is it needful to recur to the ministry of angels, and those other miraculous means which, they say, God makes use of, to manifest the doctrine and history of Christ's passion unto such, who, living in those places of the world where the outward preaching of the gospel is unknown, have well improved the first and common grace; for hence it well follows, that as some of the old philosophers might have been saved, so also may now some—who by providence are cast into those remote parts of the world where the knowledge of the history is wanting—be made partakers of the divine mystery, if they receive and resist not that grace, 'a manifestation whereof is given to every man to profit withal.' This certain doctrine then being received, to wit, that there is an evangelical and saving light and grace in all, the universality of the love and mercy of God towards mankind—both in the death of his beloved Son, the Lord Jesus Christ, and in the manifestation of the light in the heart—is established and confirmed against all the objections of such as deny it. Therefore 'Christ hath tasted death for every man:' not only for all kinds of men, as some vainly talk, but for every one, of all kinds; the benefit of whose offering is not only extended to such, who have the distinct outward knowledge of his death and sufferings, as the same is declared in the Scriptures, but even unto those who are necessarily excluded from the benefit of this knowledge by some inevitable accident; which knowledge we willingly confess to be very profitable and comfortable, but not absolutely needful unto such, from whom God himself hath withheld it; yet they may be made partakers of the mystery of his death—though ignorant of the history—if they suffer his seed and light—enlightening their hearts—to take place; in which light communion with the Father and Son is enjoyed, so as of wicked men to become holy, and lovers of that power by whose inward and secret touches they feel themselves turned from the evil to the good, and learn to do to others as they would be done by; in which Christ himself affirms all to be included. As they then have falsely and erroneously taught who have denied Christ to have died for all men, so neither have they sufficiently taught the truth, who, affirming him to have died for all, have added the absolute necessity of the outward knowledge thereof in order to the obtaining its saving effect; among whom the Remonstrants of Holland have been chiefly wanting, and many other asserters of Universal Redemption, in that they have not placed the extent of this

salvation in that divine and evangelical principle of light and life wherewith Christ hath enlightened every man that comes into the world,
which is excellently and evidently held forth in these Scriptures: Gen.
vi.3; Deut. xxx. 14; John i. 7-9; Rom. x. 8; Titus ii. 11.

Concerning Justification

As many as resist not this light, but receive the same, in them is
produced an holy, pure, and spiritual birth, bringing forth holiness,
righteousness, purity, and all those other blessed fruits which are acceptable to God; by which holy birth, to wit, Jesus Christ formed within us,
and working his works in us, as we are sanctified, so we are justified in
the sight of God, according to the apostle's words, 'But ye are washed,
but ye are sanctified, but ye are justified, in the name of the Lord Jesus,
and by the Spirit of our God.' Therefore it is not by our works wrought
in our will, nor yet by good works, considered as of themselves, but by
Christ, who is both the gift and the giver, and the cause producing the
effects in us; who, as he hath reconciled us while we were enemies, doth
also in his wisdom save us, and justify us after this manner, as saith the
same apostle elsewhere, 'According to his mercy he saved us, by the
washing of regeneration, and the renewing of the Holy Ghost.'

THE EIGHTH PROPOSITION

Concerning Perfection

In whom this holy and pure birth is fully brought forth the body of
death and sin comes to be crucified and removed, and their hearts
united and subjected unto the truth, so as not to obey any suggestion or
temptation of the evil one, but to be free from actual sinning and
transgressing of the law of God, and in that respect perfect. Yet doth this
perfection still admit of a growth; and there remaineth a possibility of
sinning where the mind doth not most diligently and watchfully attend
unto the Lord.

294 Society of Friends

Concerning Perseverance, and the Possibility of Falling from Grace

Although this gift and inward grace of God be sufficient to work out salvation, yet in those in whom it is resisted it both may and doth become their condemnation. Moreover, in whom it hath wrought in part, to purify and sanctify them, in order to their further perfection, by disobedience such may fall from it, and turn it to wantonness, making shipwreck of faith; and 'after having tasted of the heavenly gift, and been made partakers of the Holy Ghost, again fall away.' Yet such an increase and stability in the truth may in this life be attained, from which there can not be a total apostasy.

Concerning the Ministry

As by this gift, or Light of God, all true knowledge in things spiritual is received and revealed; so by the same, as it is manifested and received in the heart, by the strength and power thereof, every true minister of the gospel is ordained, prepared, and supplied in the work of the ministry; and by the leading, moving, and drawing hereof ought every evangelist and Christian pastor to be led and ordered in his labor and work of the gospel, both as to the place where, as to the persons to whom, and as to the times when he is to minister. Moreover, those who have this authority may and ought to preach the gospel, though without human commission or literature; as, on the other hand, those who want the authority of this divine gift, however learned or authorized by the commission of men and churches, are to be esteemed but as deceivers, and not true ministers of the gospel. Also, who have received this holy and unspotted gift, as they have freely received, so are they freely to give,' without hire or bargaining, far less to use it as a trade to get money by it; yet if God hath called any from their employments or trades, by which they acquire their livelihood, it may be lawful for such, according to the liberty which they feel given them in the Lord, to receive such temporals—to wit, what may be needful to them for meat and clothing— as are freely given them by those to whom they have communicated spirituals.

Concerning Worship

All true and acceptable worship to God is offered in the inward and immediate moving and drawing of his own Spirit, which is neither limited to places, times, or persons; for though we be to worship him always, in that we are to fear before him, yet as to the outward signification thereof in prayers, praises, or preachings, we ought not to do it where and when we will, but where and when we are moved thereunto by the secret inspirations of his Spirit in our hearts, which God heareth and accepteth of, and is never wanting to move us thereunto, when need is, of which he himself is the alone proper judge. All other worship then, both praises, prayers, and preachings, which man sets about in his own will, and at his own appointment, which he can both begin and end at his pleasure, do or leave undone, as himself sees meet, whether they be a prescribed form, as a liturgy, or prayers conceived extemporarily, by the natural strength and faculty of the mind, they are all but superstitious, will-worship, and abominable idolatry in the sight of God; which are to be denied, rejected, and separated from, in this day of his spiritual arising: however it might have pleased him—who winked at the times of ignorance, with respect to the simplicity and integrity of some, and of his own innocent seed, which lay as it were buried in the hearts of men, under the mass of superstition—to blow upon the dead and dry bones, and to raise some breathings, and answer them, and that until the day should more clearly dawn and break forth.

Concerning Baptism

As there is one Lord and one faith, so there is 'one baptism; which is not the putting away the filth of the flesh, but the answer of a good conscience before God, by the resurrection of Jesus Christ.' And this baptism is a pure and spiritual thing, to wit, the baptism of the Spirit and Fire, by which we are buried with him, that, being washed and purged from our sins, we may 'walk in newness of life;' of which the baptism of John was a figure, which was commanded for a time, and not to continue forever.

As to the baptism of infants, it is a mere human tradition, for which neither precept nor practice is to be found in all the Scripture.

Concerning the Communion, or Participation of the Body and Blood of Christ

The communion of the body and blood of Christ is inward and spiritual, which is the participation of his flesh and blood, by which the inward man is daily nourished in the hearts of those in whom Christ dwells; of which things the breaking of bread by Christ with his disciples was a figure, which they even used in the Church for a time, who had received the substance, for the cause of the weak; even as 'abstaining from things strangled, and from blood;' the washing one another's feet, and the anointing of the sick with oil; all which are commanded with no less authority and solemnity than the former; yet seeing they are but the shadows of better things, they cease in such as have obtained the substance.

THE FOURTEENTH PROPOSITION

Concerning the Power of the Civil Magistrate, in matters purely religious, and pertaining to the conscience

Since God hath assumed to himself the power and dominion of the conscience, who alone can rightly instruct and govern it, therefore it is not lawful for any whatsoever, by virtue of any authority or principality they bear in the government of this world, to force the conscience of others; and therefore all killing, banishing, fining, imprisoning, and other such things, which men are afflicted with, for the alone exercise of their conscience, or difference in worship or opinion, proceedeth from the spirit of Cain, the murderer, and is contrary to the truth; provided always that no man, under the pretense of conscience, prejudice his neighbor in his life or estate, or do any thing destructive to, or inconsistent with, human society; in which case the law is for the transgressor, and justice to be administered upon all, without respect of persons.

THE FIFTEENTH PROPOSITION

Concerning Salutations and Recreations, etc.

Seeing the chief end of all religion is to redeem man from the spirit and vain conversation of this world, and to lead into inward communion with God, before whom, if we fear always, we are accounted happy, therefore all the vain customs and habits thereof, both in word and deed, are to be rejected and forsaken by those who come to this fear; such as taking off the hat to a man, the bowings and cringings of the body, and such other salutations of that kind, with all the foolish and superstitious formalities attending them; all which man has invented in his degenerate state, to feed his pride in the vain pomp and glory of this world; as also the unprofitable plays, frivolous recreations, sportings, and gamings which are invented to pass away the precious time, and divert the mind from the witness of God in the heart, and from the living sense of his fear, and from that evangelical Spirit wherewith Christians ought to be leavened, and which leads into sobriety, gravity, and godly fear; in which, as we abide, the blessing of the Lord is felt to attend us in those actions in which we are necessarily engaged, in order to the taking care for the sustenance of the outward man.

Schaff, Creeds, III, 789–798.

THE NEW HAMPSHIRE BAPTIST CONFESSION

DECLARATION OF FAITH

I. Of the Scriptures

We believe that the Holy Bible was written by men divinely inspired, and is a perfect treasure of heavenly instruction; that it has God for its author, salvation for its end, and truth without any mixture of error for its matter; that it reveals the principles by which God will judge us; and therefore is, and shall remain to the end of the world, the true centre of Christian union, and the supreme standard by which all human conduct, creeds, and opinions should be tried.

II. Of the True God

We believe that there is one, and only one, living and true God, an infinite, intelligent Spirit, whose name is *Jehovah,* the Maker and Supreme Ruler of heaven and earth; inexpressibly glorious in holiness, and worthy of all possible honor, confidence, and love; that in the unity of the Godhead there are three persons, the Father, the Son, and the

Holy Ghost; equal in every divine perfection, and executing distinct and harmonious offices in the great work of redemption.

III. Of the Fall of Man

We believe that man was created in holiness, under the law of his Maker; but by voluntary transgression fell from that holy and happy state; in consequence of which all mankind are now sinners, not by constraint, but choice; being by nature utterly void of that holiness required by the law of God, positively inclined to evil; and therefore under just condemnation to eternal ruin, without defense or excuse.

IV. Of the Way of Salvation

We believe that the salvation of sinners is wholly of grace, through the mediatorial offices of the Son of God; who by the appointment of the Father, freely took upon him our nature, yet without sin; honored the divine law by his personal obedience, and by his death made a full atonement for our sins; that having risen from the dead, he is now enthroned in heaven; and uniting in his wonderful person the tenderest sympathies with divine perfections, he is every way qualified to be a suitable, a compassionate, and an all-sufficient Saviour.

V. Of Justification

We believe that the great gospel blessing which Christ secures to such as believe in him is Justification; that Justification includes the pardon of sin, and the promise of eternal life on principles of righteousness; that it is bestowed, not in consideration of any works of righteousness which we have done, but solely through faith in the Redeemer's blood; by virtue of which faith his perfect righteousness is freely imputed to us of God; that it brings us into a state of most blessed peace and favor with God, and secures every other blessing needful for time and eternity.

VI. Of the Freeness of Salvation

We believe that the blessings of salvation are made free to all by the gospel; that it is the immediate duty of all to accept them by a cordial, penitent, and obedient faith; and that nothing prevents the salvation of the greatest sinner on earth but his own inherent depravity and voluntary rejection of the gospel; which rejection involves him in an aggravated condemnation.

VII. *Of Grace in Regeneration*

We believe that, in order to be saved, sinners must be regenerated, or born again; that regeneration consists in giving a holy disposition to the mind; that it is effected in a manner above our comprehension by the power of the Holy Spirit, in connection with divine truth, so as to secure our voluntary obedience to the gospel; and that its proper evidence appears in the holy fruits of repentance, and faith, and newness of life.

VIII. *Of Repentance and Faith*

We believe that Repentance and Faith are sacred duties, and also inseparable graces, wrought in our souls by the regenerating Spirit of God; whereby being deeply convinced of our guilt, danger, and helplessness, and of the way of salvation by Christ, we turn to God with unfeigned contrition, confession, and supplication for mercy; at the same time heartily receiving the Lord Jesus Christ as our Prophet, Priest, and King, and relying on him alone as the only and all-sufficient Saviour.

IX. *Of God's Purpose of Grace*

We believe that Election is the eternal purpose of God, according to which he graciously regenerates, sanctifies, and saves sinners; that being perfectly consistent with the free agency of man, it comprehends all the means in connection with the end; that it is a most glorious display of God's sovereign goodness, being infinitely free, wise, holy, and unchangeable; that it utterly excludes boasting, and promotes humility, love, prayer, praise, trust in God, and active imitation of his free mercy; that it encourages the use of means in the highest degree; that it may be ascertained by the effects in all who truly believe the gospel; that it is the foundation of Christian assurance; and that to ascertain it with regard to ourselves demands and deserves the utmost diligence.

X. *Of Sanctification*

We believe that Sanctification is the process by which, according to the will of God, we are made partakers of his holiness; that it is a progressive work; that it is begun in regeneration; and that it is carried on in the hearts of believers by the presence and power of the Holy Spirit, the Sealer and Comforter, in the continual use of the appointed means—especially the Word of God, self-examination, self-denial, watchfulness, and prayer.

XI. Of the Perseverance of Saints

We believe that such only are real believers as endure unto the end; that their persevering attachment to Christ is the grand mark which distinguishes them from superficial professors; that a special Providence watches over their welfare; and they are kept by the power of God through faith unto salvation.

XII. Of the Harmony of the Law and the Gospel

We believe that the Law of God is the eternal and unchangeable rule of his moral government; that it is holy, just, and good; and that the inability which the Scriptures ascribe to fallen men to fulfill its precepts arises entirely from their love of sin; to deliver them from which, and to restore them through a Mediator to unfeigned obedience to the holy Law, is one great end of the Gospel, and of the means of grace connected with the establishment of the visible Church.

XIII. Of a Gospel Church

We believe that a visible Church of Christ is a congregation of baptized believers, associated by covenant in the faith and fellowship of the gospel; observing the ordinances of Christ; governed by his laws, and exercising the gifts, rights, and privileges invested in them by his Word; that its only scriptural officers are Bishops, or Pastors, and Deacons, whose qualifications, claims, and duties are defined in the Epistles to Timothy and Titus.

XIV. Of Baptism and the Lord's Supper

We believe that Christian Baptism is the immersion in water of a believer, into the name of the Father, and Son, and Holy Ghost; to show forth, in a solemn and beautiful emblem, our faith in the crucified, buried, and risen Saviour, with its effect in our death to sin and resurrection to a new life; that it is prerequisite to the privileges of a Church relation; and to the Lord's Supper, in which the members of the Church, by the sacred use of bread and wine, are to commemorate together the dying love of Christ; preceded always by solemn self-examination.

XV. Of the Christian Sabbath

We believe that the first day of the week is the Lord's Day, or Christian Sabbath; and is to be kept sacred to religious purposes, by abstaining from all secular labor and sinful recreation; by the devout observance of all the means of grace, both private and public; and by preparation for that rest that remaineth for the people of God.

XVI. Of Civil Government

We believe that civil government is of divine appointment, for the interests and good order of human society; and that magistrates are to be prayed for, conscientiously honored and obeyed; except only in things opposed to the will of our Lord Jesus Christ, who is the only Lord of the conscience, and the Prince of the kings of the earth.

XVII. Of the Righteous and the Wicked

We believe that there is a radical and essential difference between the righteous and the wicked; that such only as through faith are justified in the name of the Lord Jesus, and sanctified by the Spirit of our God, are truly righteous in his esteem; while all such as continue in impenitence and unbelief are in his sight wicked, and under the curse; and this distinction holds among men both in and after death.

XVIII. Of the World to Come

We believe that the end of the world is approaching; that at the last day Christ will descend from heaven, and raise the dead from the grave to final retribution; that a solemn separation will then take place; that the wicked will be adjudged to endless punishment, and the righteous to endless joy; and that this judgment will fix forever the final state of men in heaven or hell, on principles of righteousness.

Schaff, *Creeds,* III, 742–748.

CONFESSION OF FAITH OF THE HURIA KRISTEN BATAK PROTESTANT

(BATAK—INDONESIA)

Preamble

1. This Confession of Faith of the H.K.B.P. is the continuation of the confessions (creeds) already existing, namely, the three confessions of faith (creeds) which were already known to our Christian forefathers and are called: (1) The Apostles' Creed; (2) The Nicene Creed; (3) The Athanasian Creed.

2. This Confession of Faith is the summary of what we believe and hope in this life and the life to come.

3. This Confession of Faith is the basis of the H.K.B.P. in preaching, in teaching and in public life.

4. This Confession of Faith is the basis of the H.K.B.P. on which to reject every false doctrine and heresy that is contrary to God's Word.

Article 1

We believe and confess: There is a God,—eternal, almighty, unchangeable, omniscient, inscrutable, righteous, gracious, all-bountiful. The earth and all that is on it, is His; He is true, all holy, full of love.

In adopting this doctrine we reject the custom of calling God grandfather ("Ompung"), and the idea that God is a gracious God only, as well as the idea that blessing may be expected from the spirits of our ancestors. We also give up striving for a good time, and reject all those who listen to fortune-tellers and read their fate in the lines of their hands.

In adopting this doctrine we also reject the heresy of considering God's power to be greater than His holiness and love.

Article 2. The Trinity of God

We believe and confess: There is one God, and at the same time He is a Trinity, namely God the Father, God the Son, and God the Holy Spirit.

Huria Kristen Batak Protestant 303

The Father has begotten His Son of His own being, for ever and ever, that is: Just as the Father is eternal, the Son also is eternal. Likewise the Holy Spirit—proceeding from the Father and the Son—is eternal.

In adopting this doctrine we reject any interpretation of the Trinity of God (Maha Esa) to the effect that the Son and the Spirit are subordinated to the Father.

We also reject the false doctrine interpreting the Trinity as God the Father, His Son, the Lord Jesus Christ, and the Mother: the Holy Spirit.

Article 3. The Special Acts of the Triune God

We believe and confess:

A. God the Father is the Maker, the Provider and the Lord of all things visible and invisible.

According to this doctrine we reject any fatalism (Takdir and the like).

B. God the Son, Who was incarnate, born of the Virgin Mary, conceived by the Holy Spirit, Who is called Jesus. Two natures are found in Him, namely, God and man at the same time in one person, which cannot be separated. Jesus Christ was very God, and at the same time He is very man. He has suffered under the judgment of Pontius Pilate, was crucified on the cross in order to deliver us from sin, from death and from the rule of the Devil. He is the abundance of all expiatory sacrifices to God because of all man's sin. He descended into hell after being buried; the third day He rose again, He ascended into heaven, sitting on the right hand of God the Father Who is glorious for ever. He is our intercessor in Heaven and Lord of all, until He will come again to judge the quick and the dead.

According to this doctrine we reject the Roman Catholic doctrines such as

1. the doctrine teaching that Mary, the mother of the Lord Jesus or, as they call her, the Glorified, may intercede for us with God;

2. the doctrine teaching that any pastor (priest) may sacrifice Christ in the Mass;

3. the false doctrine that the Roman Pope is the Vicar of Christ on earth.

Fourth, we reject the human conception teaching that the Lord Jesus is comparable to the prophets of the world.

C. God the Holy Spirit has called the Church and has taught it and preserved it in true faith and holiness in the Gospel, to the honor of God.

According to this doctrine we reject the doctrine teaching that the Holy Spirit can descend upon somebody through his own preparation, beyond the Gospel.

Furthermore, we reject the doctrine teaching that the Holy Spirit can descend only in times of ecstasy and speaking in tongues.

We also reject the doctrine teaching that all medicines are unnecessary, because physical illnesses may be properly cured only by prayer to the Holy Spirit; as well as the false prophecies made in the name of the Holy Spirit, and the dissolute life of people who say that they are established in the name of the Holy Spirit.

All these false doctrines we reject because they are a misuse of the name of the Holy Spirit.

Article 4. The Word of God (The Holy Scriptures)

We believe and confess: The words written in the Bible, in the Old and New Testaments, are certainly words of God, "For the prophecy came not in old time by the will of man." (II. Peter 1:21). "All scripture is given by inspiration of God, and is profitable for doctrine, for reproof, for correction, for instruction in righteousness: That the man of God may be perfect, thoroughly furnished unto all good works." (II. Timothy 3:16–17).

According to this doctrine we emphasize: The Holy Scripture is completely sufficient to reveal God's being and His will, and the Holy Scripture is also completely sufficient to instruct what to believe in order to gain eternal life. The Holy Scripture is the beginning and the end of all thoughts, wisdom and activity of the Church and the believers.

According to this doctrine we reject any science and wisdom of man differing from the Holy Scriptures.

Article 5

The originator of sin is the Devil, it is his will that all men become sinners and turn away from God.

Thus, although the first men (Adam and Eve) were perfect and able to act in conformity with God's will, they nevertheless infringed the commandment God had given them and turned away from God because of the seduction by the Devil. Consequently, the sin is the infringement of God's commandment.

Huria Kristen Batak Protestant 305

Article 6

We believe and confess: Since Adam and Eve had fallen into sin, sin has been passed on to all their descendants. Therefore all men are conceived in sin and are enslaved by the sin of trespassing against God's commandments. Punishment and eternal death are the result of sin.

According to this doctrine we reject the false thought that newborn children are without sin, as well as the false thought teaching that sin can only be the result of poverty, penury or distress, and that, consequently, such sin cannot be taken for sin.

We also reject the doctrine teaching that the heart of man at the time of his birth is pure like blank paper.

Article 7. Redemption from Sin

We believe and confess: No man gains redemption from sin by means of good works, or through his own power. Only the grace of God through the redemption of Jesus Christ brings us salvation. The only way to gain salvation is by faith and the working of the Holy Spirit, by which the believer receives remission of sin which is won by Jesus Christ through His death.

Such faith is also taken by God for true righteousness.

Article 8. The Church

A. We believe and confess: The Church is the communion of believers in Jesus Christ, who are called, gathered, sanctified and preserved by God through the Holy Spirit.

According to this doctrine we reject the doctrine teaching the following:

1. That the Church (communion) is established by men through their own will, and the followers of that doctrine for that reason separate from our Church, not because in our Church there is any false doctrine that does not harmonize with God's Word.

2. Likewise we reject the false thought that only the leaders and only the assemblies or the members can exert full authority over the Church; for Christ only is the Lord of the Church, and the Church has to follow only such orders that harmonize with His word. In the Church there is no democracy, but Christocracy.

3. Likewise we oppose the idea that the Church should become a

State Church, since the task of the State is different from the service of the Church.

4. We also oppose the idea that the Church should be based upon the Adat (nationalities?) and bound to it, as well as the false thought that expects organization to impart life to the Church.

B. We believe and confess: The Church is holy. The Church is holy not because its members as such are holy, but because its head, Jesus Christ, is holy.

Thus, Christ has sanctified the Church, and therefore the members, too, are considered holy by God. Because of the holiness of the Church they are also considered a holy people, a temple of the Holy Spirit and habitation of God.

According to this doctrine we reject the doctrine teaching that man can gain his holiness through his work, as well as pessimism and separation on the basis of the perception that there is still sin among the Church members.

C. We believe and confess: The Church is a congregation. The congregation is the assembly of all saints who have a share in Jesus Christ and all His gifts, namely; the Gospel, the Holy Spirit, love, and hope. They are of every country and people, every tribe and race and every language in their various ceremonies and orders.

According to this doctrine we reject the interpretation considering the Church a national Church (intended for one people), and the idea of isolating one Church from another one.

D. We believe and confess: There is one Church. The basis is Ephesians 4:4; I. Cor. 12:20. There is one body, that is the Church, and even though there are many members, there is but one body.

This unity of the Church is different from the secular unity, because it is a spiritual unity.

According to this doctrine we reject any separations of churches that are not based on differences of faith, but only on external reasons.

Features of the true Church.

We believe and confess:

1. The pure preaching of the Gospel;

2. The proper administering of the Sacraments ordered by the Lord Jesus;

3. The proper exercise of discipline in order to combat sin are the features of the true Church.

Article 9. The Servants of the Church

We believe and confess: Every Christian is called to be a witness for Christ and a worker in the Church. God has called the servants through the Church according to the services of the Church and to the three offices of Christ, namely; prophet, priest, and king.

These offices the Church has to fulfill.

The service of the Church comprehends:

1. The preaching of the Gospel to the Church members and outside of the Church.

2. The administering of the two Sacraments, namely; the Holy Baptism and the Holy Communion.

3. The pastoral care of souls.

4. The preserving of the pure doctrine, the exercise of proper discipline and the opposing of false doctrines.

5. The doing of diaconal work.

To these services God has called in the Church apostles, prophets, evangelists, pastors, and teachers.

According to this doctrine we reject the idea of denying and refusing the service of the servants on the basis of one's own opinion, unless on the basis of machinations which do not harmonize with their service.

According to this doctrine we also oppose anyone in the congregation rising to preach and to teach and to administer the Sacraments without being called to these services by the Church.

Article 10. The Holy Sacraments

We believe and confess: There are two Sacraments ordered by the Lord Jesus, namely: the Holy Baptism and the Holy Communion. The Lord Jesus Christ has ordered them for His congregation in order to grant His invisible grace, namely: remission of sin, redemption, life and glory, which are to be won by faith, through visible signs.

According to this doctrine we reject the Roman Catholic doctrine teaching that there are seven Sacraments.

A. Holy Baptism. We believe and confess: The Holy Baptism is a means of God's grace toward men, for by means of Baptism the believer is granted remission of sin, regeneration, redemption from death and Devil, and also life everlasting.

According to this doctrine we confess that also children should be baptized, since through Baptism they will be received into the com-

Huria Kristen Batak Protestant

munion of those who are saved by Christ. The Lord Jesus also accepted children.

It is not necessary that the person to be baptized be immersed.

B. Holy Communion. We believe and confess: The Holy Communion is the eating of the bread by means of which we are given the Body of our Lord Jesus Christ, and the drinking of the wine by means of which we are given the Blood of our Lord Jesus Christ, whereby we receive redemption from sin, and life, and glory.

According to this doctrine we reject the false doctrine teaching that only the bread without the wine should be given to the members of the Church. For the Lord Jesus himself, when He instituted the Lord's Supper, has spoken the words: "Drink ye all of it." And the first Church has acted in accordance with this.

Also the mass is not in accordance with the Holy Scriptures, when one says that our Lord is sacrificed again each time in the mass. Consequently, we are against this heresy.

Article 11. The Church Order

We confess: In the Church there shall be a Church order which is based upon the Holy Scriptures. For the Church order is something to give order and peace to the Church. Also in the Church the Church festivals are celebrated, namely the Birth of Jesus Christ, Good Friday, the Resurrection and Ascension of the Lord, and the pouring out of the Holy Spirit. Nevertheless everyone should remember that no one can win remission of sins by observation of all these festivals.

Article 12. The Secular Government

We confess: That the authority who has power is ordained by God. That means an authority who opposes the evil and does right in order to bring peace and certainty to the believers, as it is written in Romans 13 and I. Timothy 2:2. Nevertheless one should also remember what is written in Acts 5:29: "We ought to obey God rather than man."

According to this doctrine we confess: We ought to pray for the authority, that it may do right, and the Church shall raise its voice toward the authority.

According to this doctrine we also reject the idea that the Church should become a State Church, for the State is a State, and the Church is a Church.

Whenever it is necessary before the judge, a Christian is permitted

Huria Kristen Batak Protestant 309

to take an oath for truthfulness. The same may be done at the time of induction into an office or a responsibility.

Article 13. Sunday

We consider Sunday holy. It is the Day of the Lord, which is the first day of creation, the day of the Resurrection of the Lord, and which has been celebrated by the Church from the very beginning.

We refuse to return to the Jewish Sabbath, for we are Christians.

According to this doctrine we reject the false doctrine which declares Saturday to be the Holy Sabbath Day.

Article 14. Food

We believe and confess: Every creature of God is good, and one should not make any difference between various kinds of food, if it is received with thanksgiving and is sanctified by God's Word and by prayer.

No man can gain holiness by abstaining from certain foods, for holiness is received from God by faith. For this reason the apostles opposed the Jewish food laws. For the Gospel should not be perverted by abstaining from certain foods and by any habit or tradition.

According to this doctrine we reject any heresy teaching something different.

Article 15. Faith and Good Works

We believe and confess: Good works are the fruits of faith. Whosoever hopes to gain righteousness, life, comfort, or glory by doing good works is mistaken. The Lord Jesus Christ alone can grant remission of sins and can bring man back to God.

We have to follow the ten commandments. However, we live only by faith, not by doing good works.

The Holy Spirit moves man to do good works. (If not urged by the Spirit, good works will become sin.)

Article 16. The Funeral

We believe and confess: Men are destined to die, but after that there will be the judgment. Then they rest from their work. Jesus

Christ is the Lord of the quick and the dead. So, when conducting a funeral we think of the end of our lives, for the strengthening of our hope for the communion of the believers with God. This we do in order that we may be strengthened in our struggles in this life.

According to this doctrine we reject: The heathenish concept that the souls of the dead have influence on the living; as well as the false doctrine teaching that the soul of a dead person remains in the grave with the body. We also reject the Roman Catholic doctrine teaching that there is a purgatory which the dead must experience in order to purify their souls and to win eternal life, furthermore, that one may conduct a mass or prayers for the dead, praying to the souls of the saints and the hope that the power or the holiness of the dead may enter into their graves, their shrouds or any things or even into their bones and may be passed on in this way (relics).

Article 17. The Angels

We believe and confess: The angels are created by God to serve Him, they are ministering spirits sent by God to protect the heirs of salvation.

Article 18. The Last Judgment

We believe and confess: Our Lord Jesus Christ will come again on Judgment Day to awake the dead, and to judge men. Then He will lead the believers to everlasting life. The unbelievers, however, will go to everlasting torment.

The inheritance of the believers with God will last throughout eternity.

According to this doctrine we reject the heresy teaching that:

A. the time of Christ's coming again may be computed;

B. after death there is still a period of grace.

We confirm: that the coming again of our Lord will be unexpected. Consequently, we should be ready at any time, as He has warned us.

Missionary Research Library, 3041 Broadway,
New York 27, New York, 1957.

STATEMENT OF FAITH OF
THE UNITED CHURCH OF CHRIST

We believe in God, the Eternal Spirit, Father of our Lord Jesus Christ and our Father, and to His deeds we testify:

He calls the worlds into being, creates man in his own image and sets before him the ways of life and death.

He seeks in holy love to save all people from aimlessness and sin.

He judges men and nations by his righteous will declared through prophets and apostles.

In Jesus Christ, the man of Nazareth, our crucified and risen Lord, he has come to us and shared our common lot, conquering sin and death and reconciling the world to himself.

He bestows upon us his Holy Spirit, creating and renewing the Church of Jesus Christ, binding in covenant faithful people of all ages, tongues, and races.

He calls us into his Church to accept the cost and joy of discipleship, to be his servants in the service of men, to proclaim the gospel to all the world and resist the powers of evil, to share in Christ's baptism and eat at his table, to join him in his passion and victory.

He promises to all who trust him forgiveness of sins and fullness of grace, courage in the struggle for justice and peace, his presence in trial and rejoicing, and eternal life in his kingdom which has no end.

Blessing and honor, glory and power be unto him. Amen.

The Christian Century, Vol. LXXVI, 29
(July 22, 1959), p. 846.

Index

A

Abelard, Peter, 188–189
Adam and Eve, 139
Africa, Protestants in, 16
America, Protestants in, 16
Anglican Communion, Articles of Religion, 19, 24, 70, 267–278
Anglicans, 219, 236 (see also Episcopalians)
Anselm of Canterbury, 4, 184–186, 189
Apostle Paul, 21–22, 27, 35–36, 40–41, 53, 96, 99, 112–113, 119, 134, 168, 169, 175, 176–178, 192, 193, 200, 206, 208, 213, 215, 251
Apostles' Creed, 33, 58, 64, 174, 193, 198
  text, 253
Aquinas, Saint Thomas, 84
Aristotle, 23, 103, 106, 230, 234–235
Arminius, Jacobus, 19
Art:
  reality of, 47–48
  religious, 61–63
Articles of Religion of the Protestant Episcopal Church, 19, 24, 70, 267–278
Asia, Protestants in, 16
Athanasian Creed, 254–256
Atom bomb, 154, 155
Atonement, doctrine of, 181–189
  Christus Victor interpretation, 182–189
  moral influence interpretation, 188–189
  satisfaction interpretation, 184–187, 189
Augsburg Confession of 1530, 28–29, 210, 250
  text, 256–266

Aulén, Gustaf, 82, 99n, 107, 110

B

Bach, Johann Sebastian, 62
Baillie, D. M., 59–60
Bainton, Roland H., 224–226
Bakewell, C. M., 160n
Baptism, sacrament of, 231–233
Baptists, 219, 229
  New Hampshire Baptist Confession, 298–302
  number of, 16
Barclay, Robert, 236n
Barth, Karl, 192–193, 200
"Battle Hymn of the Republic," 211
Beach, Frank A., 39
Beauty, reality of, 47–48
Beliefs:
  definition, 3, 4
  different types of, 1–3
Believers, priesthood of all, 25–29
Bender, Harold S., 219n
Benedict, Ruth, 40
Berggrav, Eivind, 229
"Best of all possible worlds," rejected by Protestant Faith, 158–159
Bettenson, Henry S., 26n, 71n, 183n, 186n
Bible (see also Holy Scriptures)
  authority of, 24–25, 68, 71
  canon of Scriptures, 70
  carrying, 66
  Christ is the key to, 69
  Cross of Christ is the center of both the Old and New Testaments, 75–78
  inspired writings, 66–67
  of the Jewish religion, 70
  New Testament books, 70

313

Bible (*Cont.*):
Old and New Testaments, 73–78
complementary to each other, 77–78
Old Testament books, 70
proclaims God's law and Gospel, 75
Roman Catholic version, 70
as source of authority, 24–25
typology, 76
Vulgate, 71
Bishop, office of, 216–217
Boehme, Jacob, 144
Bohemia, Protestants in, 15
Bonar, Horatius, 203
Book of Daniel, 244
Book of Revelation, 243, 244, 249
Brandi, Karl, 15n
Brill, A. A., 162n
British Isles, 16
Brothers Karamazov, The (Dostoevski), 136
Buddhism, 42, 57, 64, 241
Bunyan, John, 196

C

Calhoun, Robert L., 127n–128n
Calvin, John, 19, 26, 55, 83, 101–102, 146–147, 159, 236, 238–239, 250
Calvinists, 11, 19, 222
Candide (Voltaire), 2
Capitalism, Protestantism and, 11
Catechisms, Westminster Shorter, 278–289
Charles V, Emperor, 13–15
Chesterton, G. K., 131
Children:
bringing-up, 191
need love, 103–104
Christian Century, The, 312n
Christian Existentialism, 29
Church:
apostolic, 216
both an institution and a fellowship, 204
both the proclamation of God and the people of God, 207
characteristics of, 210–211
denominations (*see* Denominations)
established or folk, 217–218
holiness of, 214

Church (*Cont.*):
Holy Spirit and the, 203–222
militant and triumphant, 210–212
ministry, 238–239
organization, 216–217
Protestant doctrine of the, 203–222
racial integration, 215–216
significance of the word and the sacraments, 222–239
unity, 212–213
universality, 214
visible and invisible, 209–210
Civil righteousness, 95–96
Classical Protestantism, 17–31
Communion, sacrament of, 233–238
Communism, 241–242
attempt to understand, 12
faith-axioms of, 12
Confession of Faith of the Huria Kristen Batak Protestant (1951), 303–311
Confession of the Society of Friends, Commonly Called Quakers, 290–298
Confucianism, 42, 57
Congregationalists, 217, 219, 229
number of, 16–17
Coué, Emile, 22
Creation, 108–116
distinction between creation and the Creator, 115
doctrine of, 114–116
Creeds, 33, 64, 253–256
Apostles, 33, 58, 64, 174, 193, 198, 253
Athanasian, 254–256
Nicene, 64, 253–254
Crime and Punishment (Dostoevski), 135–136
Cross, holiness of God's law is preserved through the, 190–192
Culture, based on Protestant Faith, 12
Cusanus, Nicolaus, 144

D

Death:

and time, 245–247
judgment after, 246
reality of, 245
result of sin, 153–155
Deism, 110, 113–114

314 Index

Teleological proof of the existence of God, 52
Temptations of Christ, 170
Ten Commandments, 41, 75, 90–92
Tersteegen Gerhard, 86
Theodicy (Leibnitz), 158
Theological use of the Law, 96
Time:
chronos, 49–52
death and, 245–247
different ways of experiencing, 49–51
eternity and, 248
in Hinduism, 57
kairos, 49–52
revelation in history and time, 58–59
Toynbee, Arnold, 49
Trinity, doctrine of, 201–203
Truth, 47

U

Unitarianism, 202
United Church of Christ, Statement of Faith, 312
United Nations, 95
United States:
Congress, 96
number of Protestants in, 16
Universalism, 251

V

Virgin Birth, doctrine of, 178–179
Visions, 33
Voltaire, 2, 96

W

Waugh, Evelyn, 153–154
Weber, Max, 11
Weil, Simone, 119, 192
Wesley, Charles, 179–180
Wesley, John, 19, 55, 159
Westminster Confession of Faith, 71
Westminster Shorter Catechism, 278–289
Will, divine, 81–82, 108–126
Williams, Tennessee, 164
Woolcombe, W. J., 76n
Word of God, significance of, 222–239
Work of Christ, 180–197
kingly, 193–196
priestly, 181–188
prophetic, 180–181
World:
creation, 108–116
expression of Divine Will, 108–126
World Council of Churches, 202, 220–221
Wycliffe, John, 213

X

Xenophanes, 159–160

Z

Zeal, religious, 44
Zinzendorf, Count von, 116
Zoroaster, 42
Zwingli, Huldreich, 26